IMAGES of America
McHenry and McCullom Lake

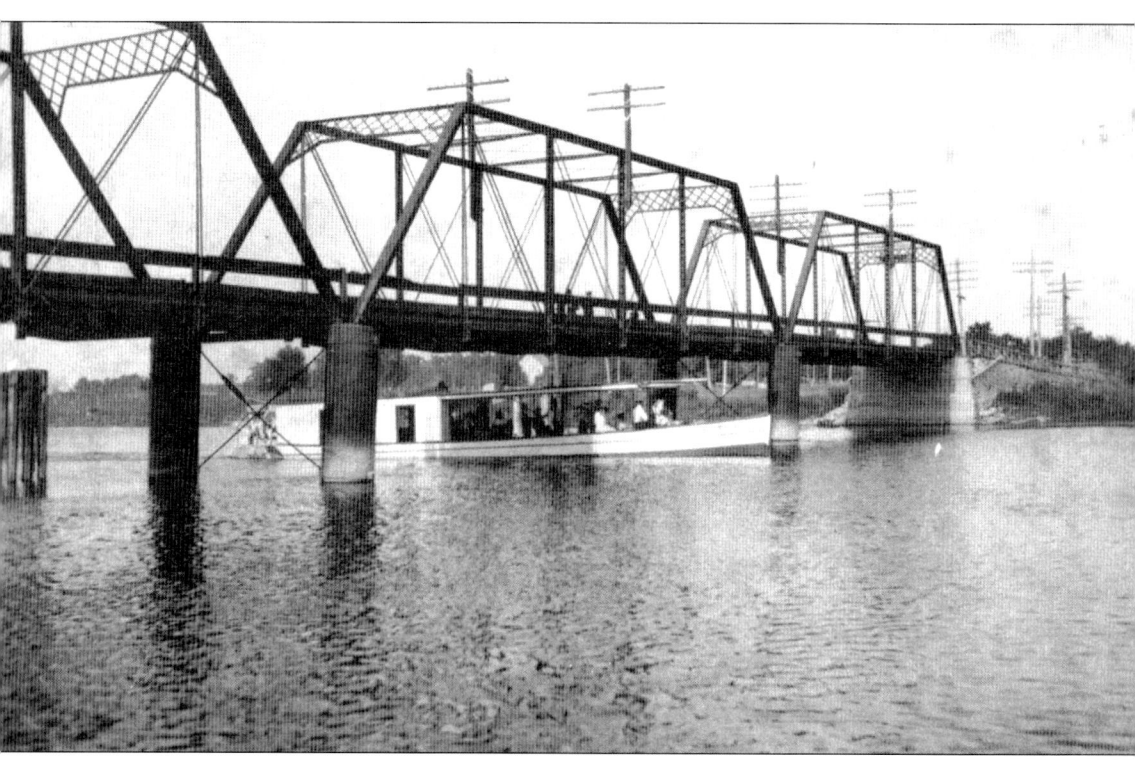

This iron bridge, which crossed the Fox River at Pearl Street, was a part of the McHenry skyline from 1880 to 1977. Originally a fording location, ferry boats were used to cross from 1837 to 1842. Various wooden bridges preceded this iron bridge. Excursion boats, such as this paddle wheel boat, were a frequent sight. (Courtesy of the McHenry County Historical Society.)

On the cover: The pull of the river often brought families to its shore to spend the day enjoying a picnic. This photograph of the Cohan family camping on the shores of the Fox River was taken on July 13, 1900. It was a day of idle leisure, yet some of these women used this time to complete their needlework as they visited with family and friends on the riverside. (Courtesy of the McHenry Public Library.)

IMAGES of America
McHenry and McCullom Lake

Sandra Landen Machaj

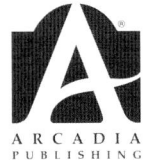

Copyright © 2007 by Sandra Landen Machaj
ISBN 978-0-7385-5060-2

Published by Arcadia Publishing
Charleston SC, Chicago IL, Portsmouth NH, San Francisco CA

Printed in the United States of America

Library of Congress Catalog Card Number: 2007925091

For all general information contact Arcadia Publishing at:
Telephone 843-853-2070
Fax 843-853-0044
E-mail sales@arcadiapublishing.com
For customer service and orders:
Toll-Free 1-888-313-2665

Visit us on the Internet at www.arcadiapublishing.com

*To Patrick: You have always encouraged me to
spread my wings and follow my dreams.
With your support I have done so. You are always in my heart.*

Contents

Acknowledgments		6
Introduction		7
1.	In the Beginning	9
2.	Faces and Places	29
3.	Life on the Fox River	45
4.	Serving the People	61
5.	Building Business	73
6.	Churches, Schools, the Hospital, and Sports	91
7.	Life at McCullom Lake	103
8.	A Small Village Grows	115
9.	McHenry Today and Tomorrow	123

Acknowledgments

Compiling a history is never the work of only one person. Without the many memories and photographs that so many of you shared, this book would not have been completed. From everyone I have spoken with, whether it was the mayor or the citizens of McHenry, it was obvious that they had one thing in common, they all loved McHenry and were knowledgeable about its past and willing to share their knowledge.

The wealth of information about the history of McHenry is unbelievable. When searching through the files at the McHenry County Historical Society or those of the McHenry Public Library, there was always more information than I could digest.

Nancy Fike your knowledge of McHenry's history is unbelievable and I appreciate the time you spent sharing it with me. Pat Schafer your never-ending list of names and telephone numbers was most appreciated.

To Jim Althoff, Wayne Amore, John Baumgarner, Henry Buch, Mike Clark, Marya Dixon, Don and Rosalie Doherty, Katherine Edstrom, David Gelwicks, Kathleen Giambalva, Barb Gilpin, Debra Gust, Mark Justen, John Haley, Bill Hobson, Jeanne Hansen, Mark Justen Kit Karstens, Shirley Klapperich, Susan Low, Pete Merkel, John Henry Miller, Bill and Amy Moeschbaecher, Bob Novak, Thomas O'Meara, Larry Phalin, Gerhard Rosenberg, Susan Rutherford, Sandy Speciale, Don Wattles, Ilene Wiedemann, Nancy Williams, and Pat, Chris, and Joan Wirtz, thank you for sharing your memories and allowing me to use your photographs.

To the staff of the McHenry Public Library, especially Henry Kenyon who was always willing to search for more information, thank you.

Thanks to Jeff Ruetsche, my editor, for guiding me through this process.

To anyone that I have inadvertently forgotten to list, thank you.

And finally, I would like to thank my friend, Priscilla Rutter, for not only helping research this work, and accompanying me on many fact finding missions, but also for turning her home into my personal bed and breakfast.

Introduction

Why a book about McHenry? Why not? What is there not to like about McHenry? Located on the banks of the Fox River, about 50 miles from Chicago in northwest Illinois, McHenry has much to offer. It blends the flavor of a small town community, the openness of country living, with the convenience of easy access to the city.

While McHenry is a river town, it is unlike many of the other towns that have sprouted along the Fox River. McHenry is known for having three downtown business centers that grew independently. It was the first county seat of the newly formed McHenry County. Known for farming and dairy, it was a center for processing and shipping milk products to northern Illinois and Chicago. It was a self-sufficient town that attracted manufacturing business and tourists.

The area that is known today as McHenry was once a vast prairie covered with native grasses that grew both tall and deep. The lakes and rivers of the area made it a popular hunting and fishing area for local Native Americans. The Potawatomi Indian tribes, known for being peaceful hunters, populated the area.

In 1836, change occurred. The legislature separated what are now Lake and McHenry Counties from Cook County, and by the end of their legislative session in 1837, created the new McHenry County. The town of McHenry, which was near the county's geographical center, was designated as the county seat. McHenry itself was just being settled at the time it became the county seat and in fact had not even been incorporated as a village.

The name McHenry was chosen by the legislature as a tribute to Maj. William McHenry, known for his service during the War of 1812. In 1832, he volunteered to fight against the Sac and Fox Indians, led by Black Hawk. McHenry was elected to the state legislature seven times serving part of this time with Abraham Lincoln.

McHenry did not remain the county seat for long. The 1838–1839 legislature again looked at McHenry County and decided it should be broken into two separate counties, Lake and McHenry. The city of McHenry was now on the very eastern edge of the county. A movement was started to move the county seat to a more central location. The legislature of 1842–1843 passed an act allowing the people of McHenry County to vote on a new location. Centerville, which is now known as Woodstock, was selected to replace McHenry as the county seat.

Dr. Christy Wheeler is recognized as the first white settler of McHenry. He arrived in early 1836 with his wife and two children. He is considered to be the first medical doctor in McHenry in spite of not being formally trained in medicine. In McHenry, he opened a small store and was the first postmaster. Wheeler, William Way, and John McLean were the first appointed judges.

Many early settlers played important parts in the development of McHenry. John McOmber built an early log cabin, and Benjamin B. Brown built the famous two-room log cabin that was known as the Log Cabin Tavern on the river. Rev. Joel Wheeler, brother to Christy Wheeler, built the first frame house in McHenry and in 1838, opened the first boarding school in his home. Names such as Henry McLean, William and John Boone, and John and William McCullom also played a significant role in the growth of McHenry.

Early settlers of McHenry came westward from the East Coast particularly the New England states. Irish immigrants escaping the potato famine made their way here and settled in the southern part of McHenry, which became known as the Irish prairie. Johnsburg, the town located north of McHenry, was a German settlement. With growth, the German immigrants began to drift down toward McHenry.

Generally towns along the river grew first on the riverfront then gradually spread from there, maintaining the river center as the town hub. McHenry did not quite follow that plan, due in large part to George Gage. Gage purchased a large tract of land west of the city and began to develop it. Gage became the first senator from McHenry and was instrumental in securing the railroad for McHenry. In 1854, the railroad arrived and of course the railroad station was located in Gagetown, which later became known as West McHenry.

While two distinct business centers would be unique enough, McHenry developed one more. Located between Riverside Drive and Main Street in West McHenry, the Green Street or Centerville district began to grow. Daniel Owen began operating a gristmill and a sawmill along Boone Creek, creating a 60-acre mill pond that physically separated at least two of the business districts.

Each center of McHenry grew. Grocery stores, pharmacies, restaurants, and hardware stores were duplicated on each of the three main streets. McHenry citizens were loyal to their section of the town supporting the businesses that were located in their town center.

Farming was a major component of the McHenry economy. In addition to crops, McHenry became known for its dairy products and soon became a part of the milk shed for northern Illinois, in particular for the growing city of Chicago. Numerous small dairies prospered and Borden Milk built a large milk processing plant in West McHenry along the railroad line. Milk was processed and transported to other areas in Illinois and Wisconsin.

The soil around McHenry was known for its high clay and gravel content. Gravel pits provided materials for the building of roads and the clay from the clay pits was used in the production of bricks. Boat building companies, such as Hunter and Switzer, built their products along the river. In the winter, ice was harvested from the Fox River, McCullom Lake, and Boone Creek. The ice was used both locally and transported to Chicago.

By the end of the 19th century, McHenry had become known as a recreational destination. Easy access to McHenry by train encouraged visitors to escape the heat and dusty air of the city. Hotels provided lodging and entertainment. Boats along the Fox River carried passengers for recreational rides or transportation up to Pistakee Bay. Health resorts grew along the Fox, along with vacation homes, from small basic cabins to large estates.

Today as McHenry moves along in the 21st century, it is a growing vibrant city of over 24,000 citizens. It is still a working city that attracts both businesses and families. Boats cruising along the Fox River and stopping to eat at one of the restaurants along the shores, continue to be a welcome sight. The proposed riverwalk will attract more visitors. The true measure of the greatness of McHenry is seen when one looks at the names on many businesses and peruse the phone books. The descendants of many of the early settlers are still proud to call McHenry home.

So come join us as we follow McHenry through time.

One
IN THE BEGINNING

McHenry is a river town. It began with its first log cabins built along the waterfront. On what was first called Water Street, later to be changed to Riverside Drive, it came to life. It was in the year 1837 when a Chicago surveyor, A. S. Burnham, laid out the village. It had already been designated as the county seat of the new McHenry County, even though it had not yet been incorporated. As such, it brought visitors, people doing business with the county government. The river provided easy access to the village and was also a convenient route for shipping in the merchandise that the local business owners would sell to their customers.

The riverfront would not remain the only business center in McHenry. With the arrival of the railroad in 1854, new businesses developed along Main Street in the area that became known as West McHenry. Competition grew between the centers as hotels, restaurants, and grocery stores developed in each district. Visitors would arrive by train in West McHenry, and then be transported to the riverfront to enjoy its recreational activities.

To get from West McHenry to Riverside Drive, it was necessary to travel down Main Street to Green Street and cross Boone Creek. And here was the third of the McHenry city centers. The Green Street area was originally called Centerville, and it too developed as a separate business district, located between the other two major centers.

Many services were duplicated in each of the three business districts, yet each continued to grow and prosper during the early days of McHenry.

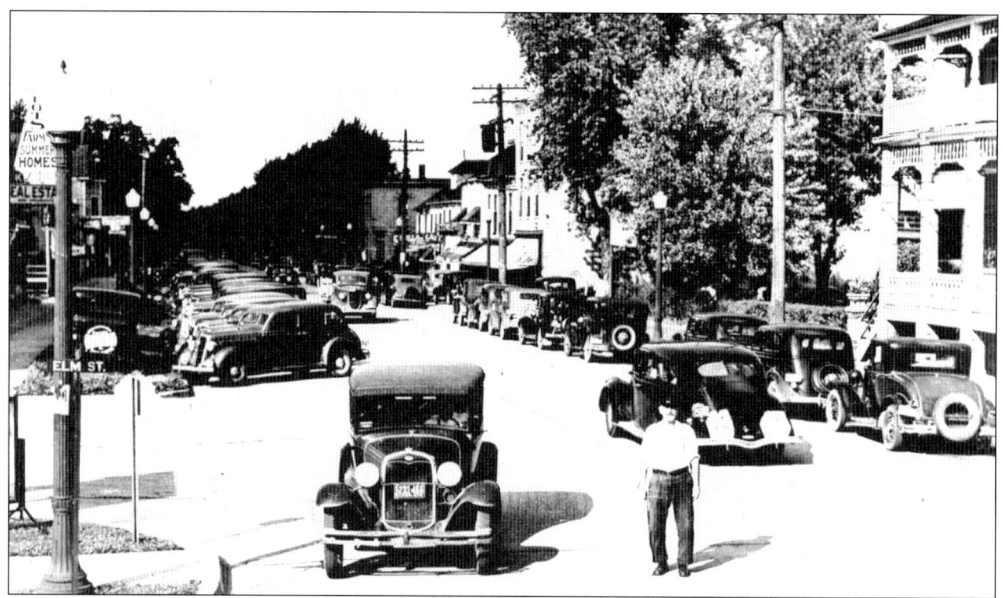

Riverside Drive was a bustling street on this day in the early 1900s. Automobiles were parked on both sides of the street as their occupants were enjoying the activities along the river or sharing a meal at one of the local restaurants. Even this early traffic control was necessary. (Courtesy of the McHenry Public Library.)

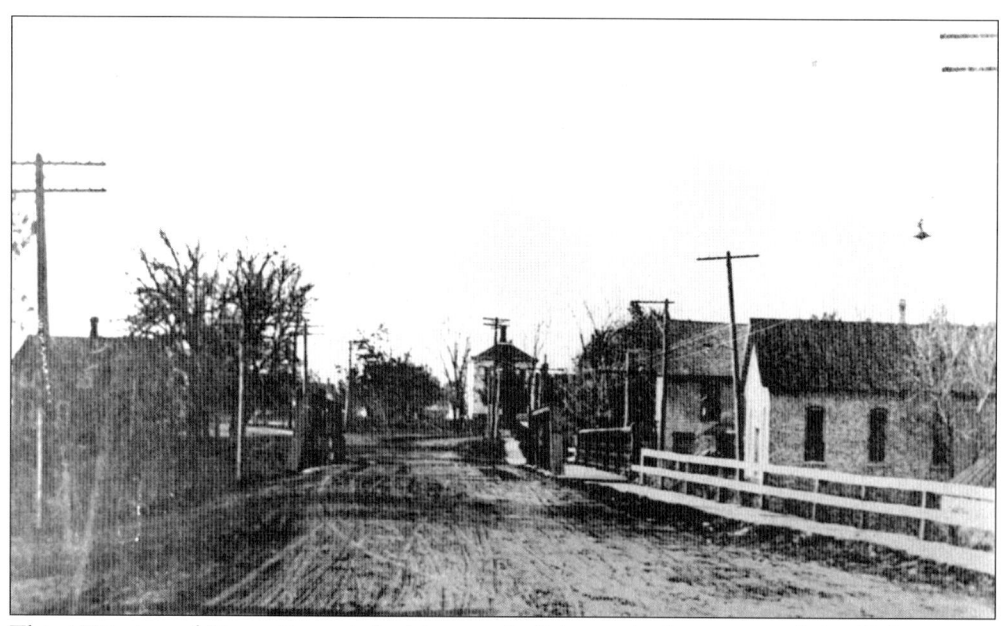

This 1894 view of Green Street is looking south. Prior to the beginning of the 20th century, roads were unpaved. William Bonslett's house can be seen at the end of the street. L. Schoewer had a blacksmith shop at the corner of Green Street and Waukegan Road. (Courtesy of the McHenry Public Library.)

George Gage was born in New York and came west in 1835 at 22 years old. Originally he lived in a cabin on the south side of what today is named Gage's Lake. Gage purchased a large tract of property west of McHenry. It became known as Gagetown as it developed. Gage was instrumental in bringing the railroad to McHenry in 1854. (Courtesy of the McHenry Landmark Commission.)

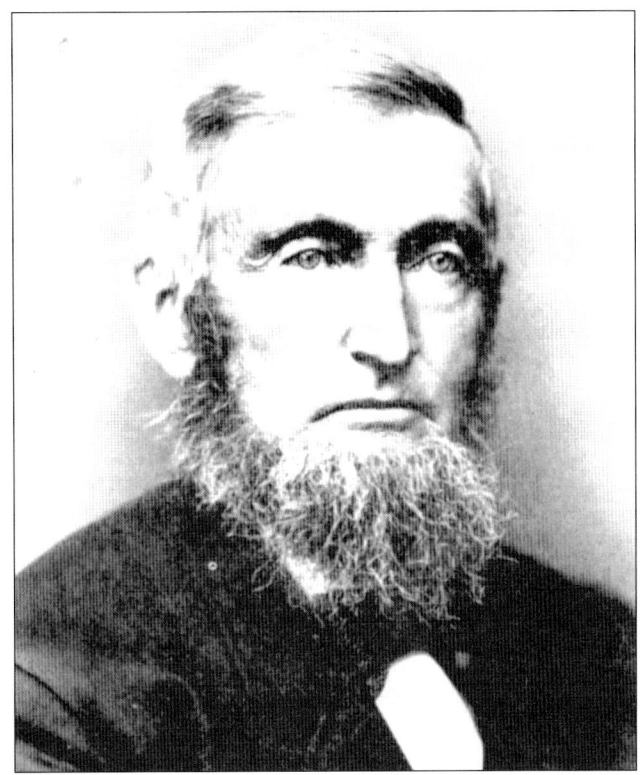

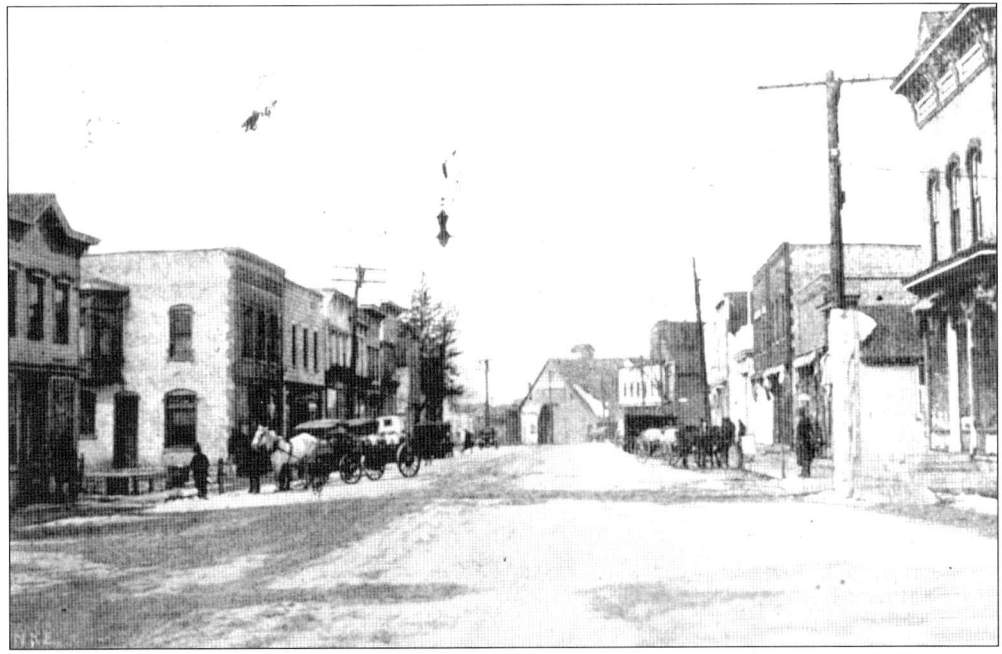

Main Street was a busy street with the coming of the railroad in 1854. This scene is looking west down Main Street towards the railroad station. Horse-drawn wagons were the most common means of transportation to get to the other side of McHenry. (Courtesy of the McHenry Public Library.)

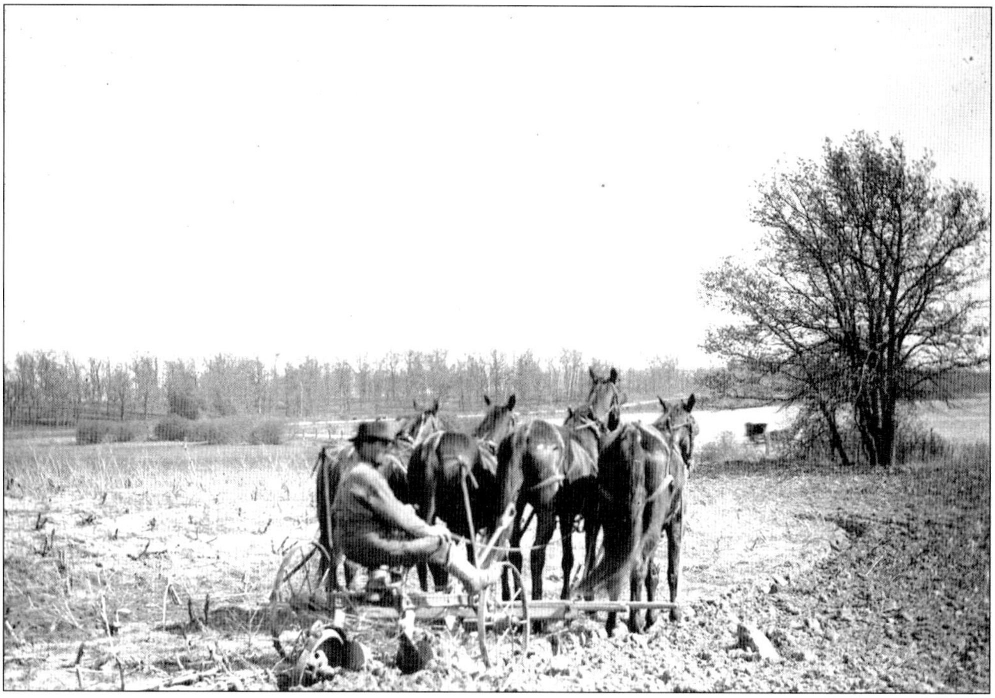

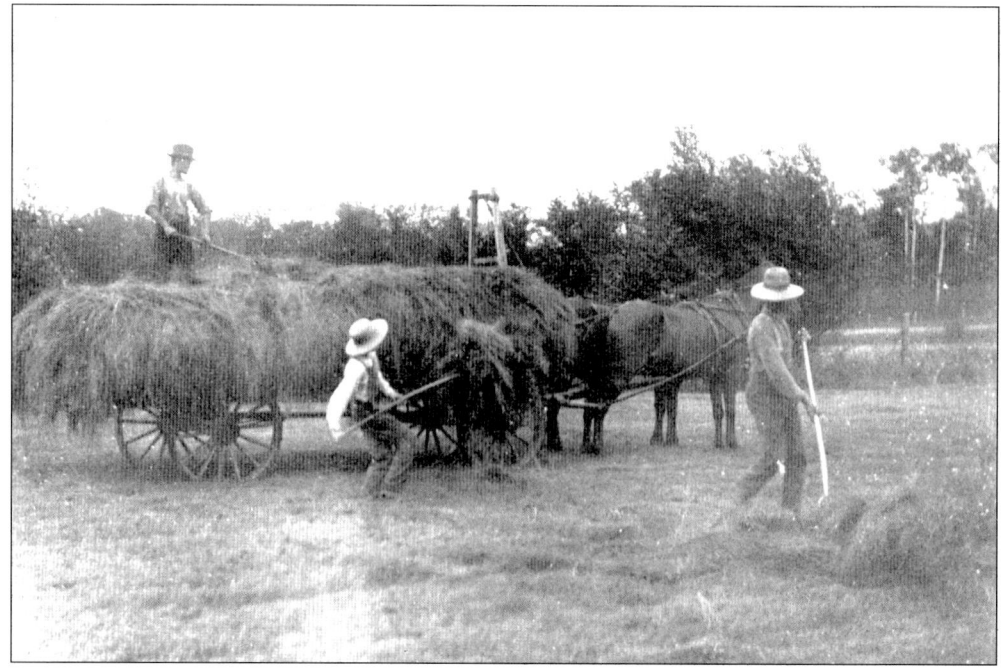

Many of the early settlers to the McHenry area made their living by farming the land. This farmer spent his days in the company of his four horses, tilling the land to prepare it for the spring planting. (Courtesy of the McHenry Public Library.)

Harvesting the crops was a long and arduous job that had to be completed in a short period of time. Loading hay onto the horse-driven wagon from left to right are Collier Young, Chester Schaefer, and John Schaefer. (Courtesy of the McHenry Public Library.)

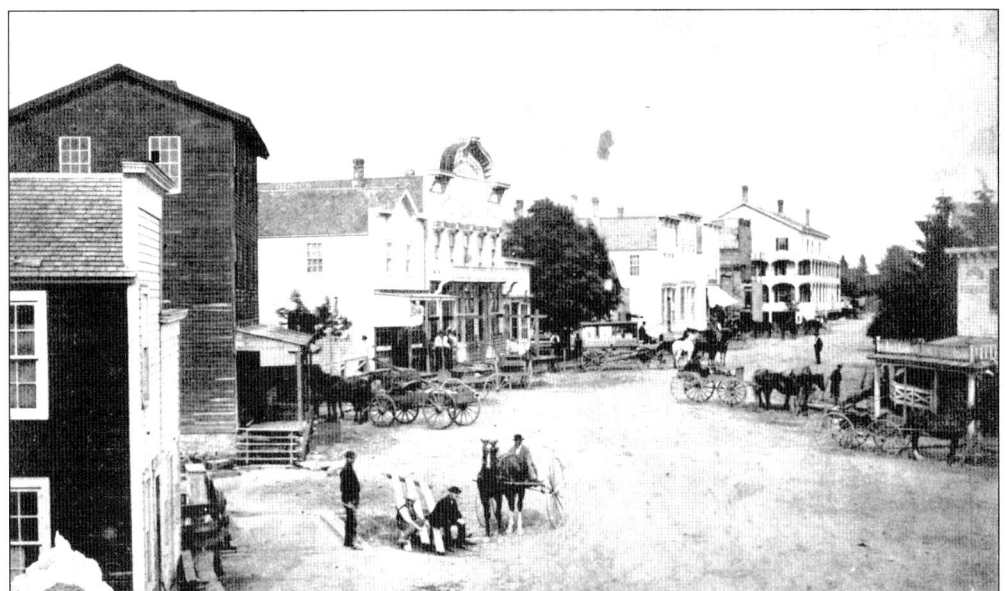

Main Street in West McHenry was unpaved in 1883. The arrival of the railroad in 1854 increased the number of visitors to the area. Sitting on the broken gate are C. H. Granger (left) and Shell Collier. The man in the cart is Fayette Huson. (Courtesy of the McHenry Landmark Commission.)

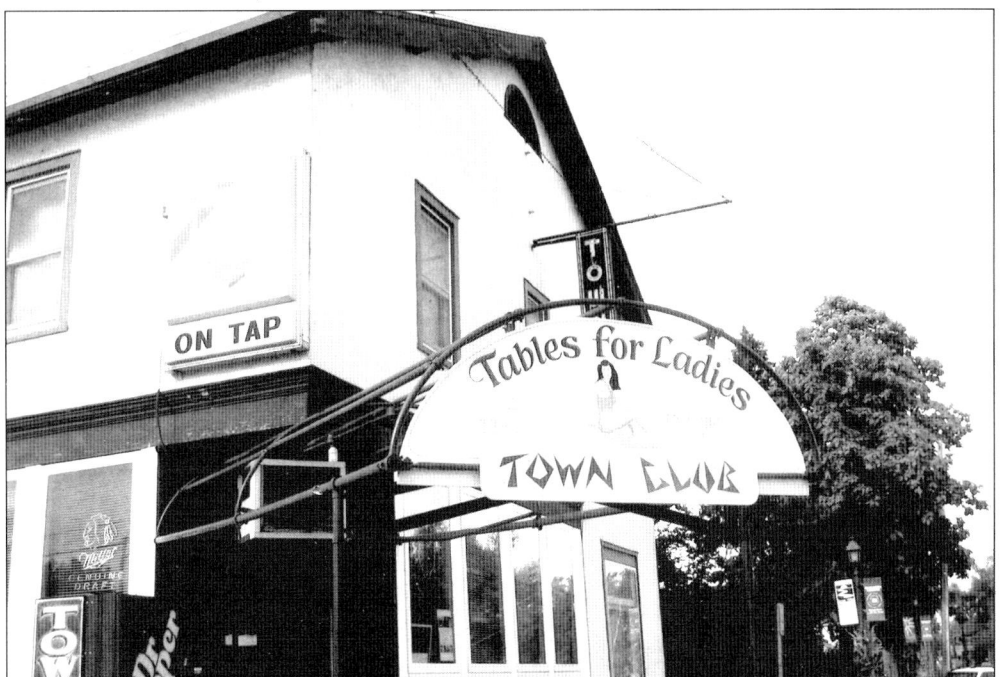

The original portion of this building was built on the Court Street side of the public square, which today is Veteran's Memorial Park. In 1840, it became the first county courthouse of McHenry County. Its use as the courthouse was short lived as the county seat was moved to Woodstock. In 1844, the structure was sold to Horace Long, who moved the building to Riverside Drive and Pearl Street. In December 2006, a plaque commemorating its original use was dedicated.

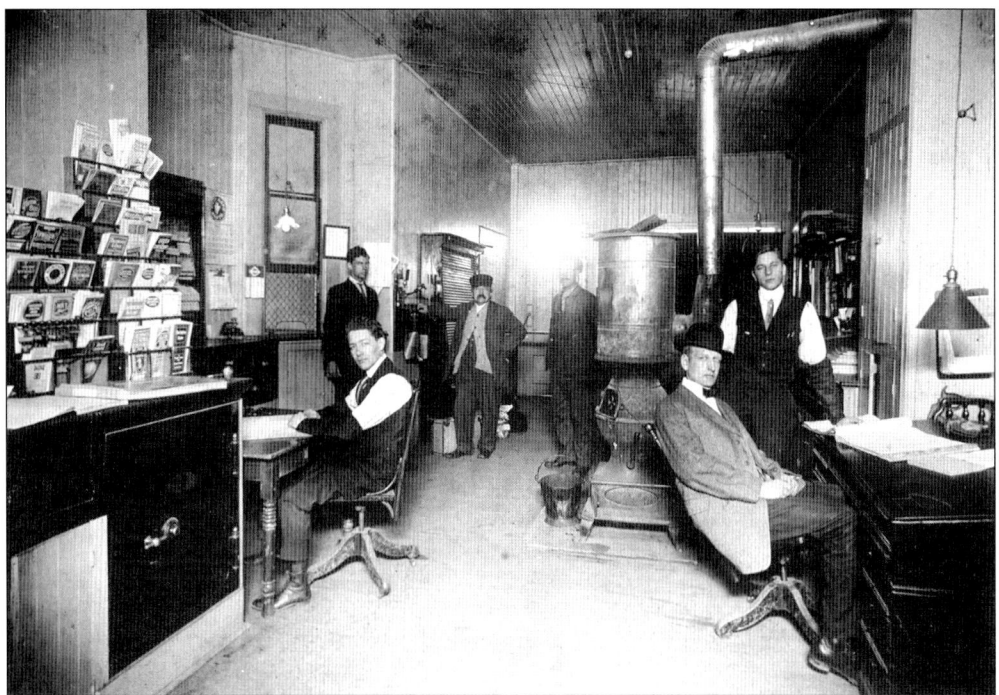

The inside of the train depot was a good place to stay warm while waiting for the train to pull into the station. Note the wood-burning stove in the center that provided heat. Tickets were purchased here and the proceeds placed in the safe on the left. There were no credit cards in those days. (Courtesy of Christopher Wirtz.)

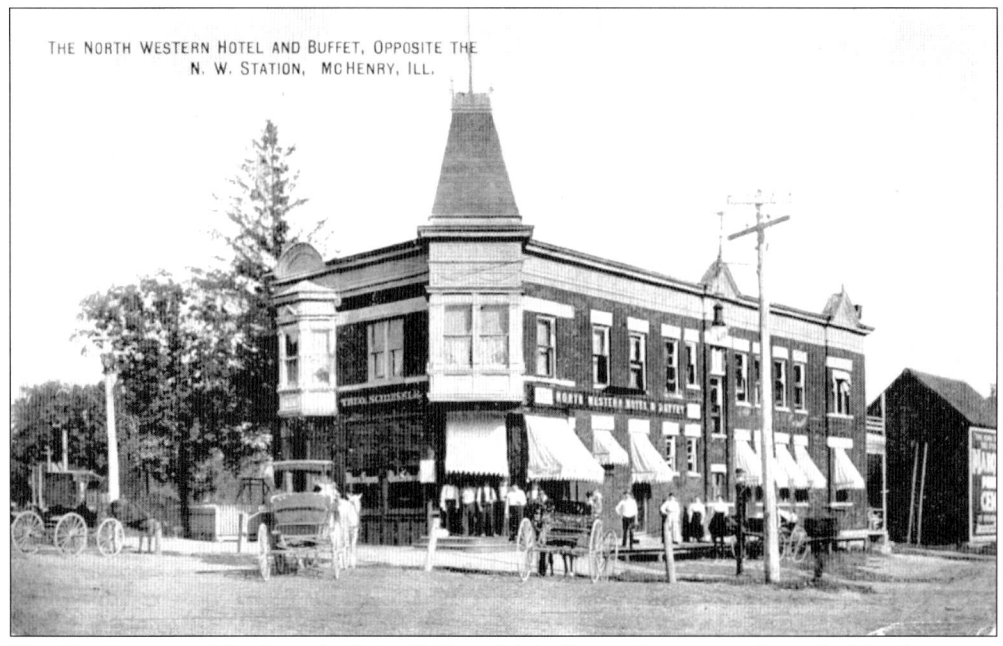

The Northwestern Hotel was built in 1901 on Main Street, just across from the Northwestern Railroad Depot in West McHenry. It was built by Stephen H. Freund for Robert Schiessle. Visitors arriving by train found the location convenient. (Courtesy of Patricia Schafer.)

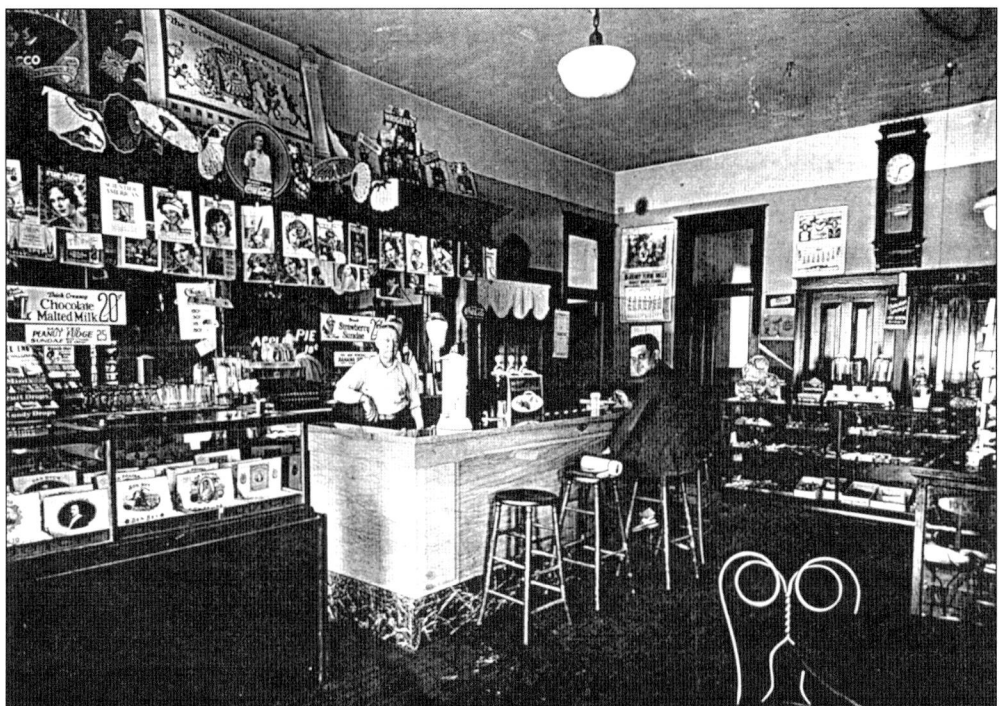

Local residents as well as visitors found the ice-cream parlor in the hotel a great destination for a cold treat. Strangely, in addition to ice cream, it was also the place to pick up a fine cigar. Note the display case on the left. (Courtesy of Shirley Klapperich.)

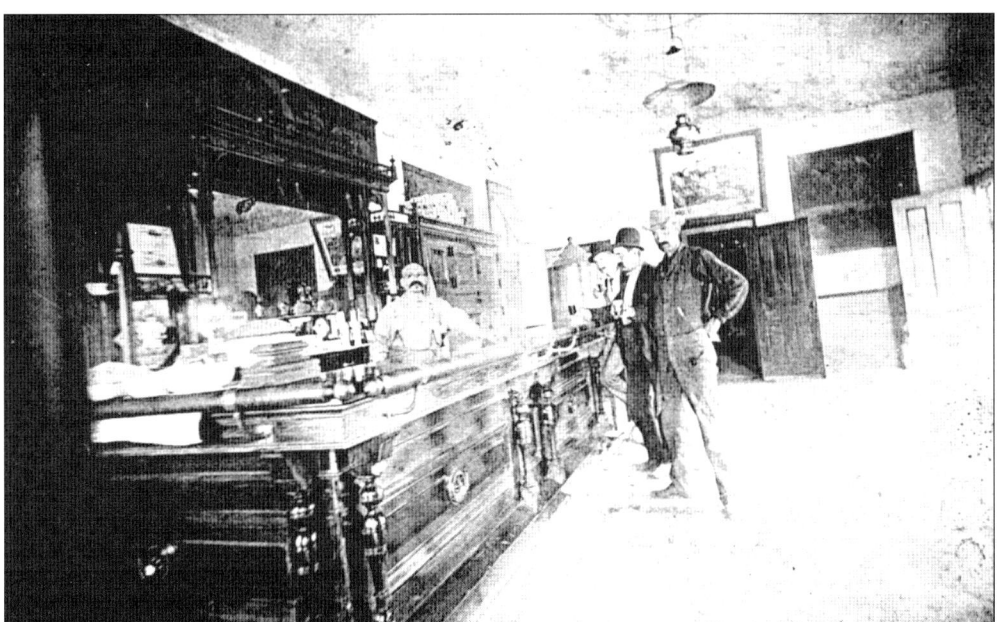

The Northwestern Hotel was also known for its large, polished-wood bar. Shown in the early 1900s, bartender and owner Robert Schiessle serves his customers. It was the closest place to stop for a drink after arriving on the train. (Courtesy of Shirley Klapperich.)

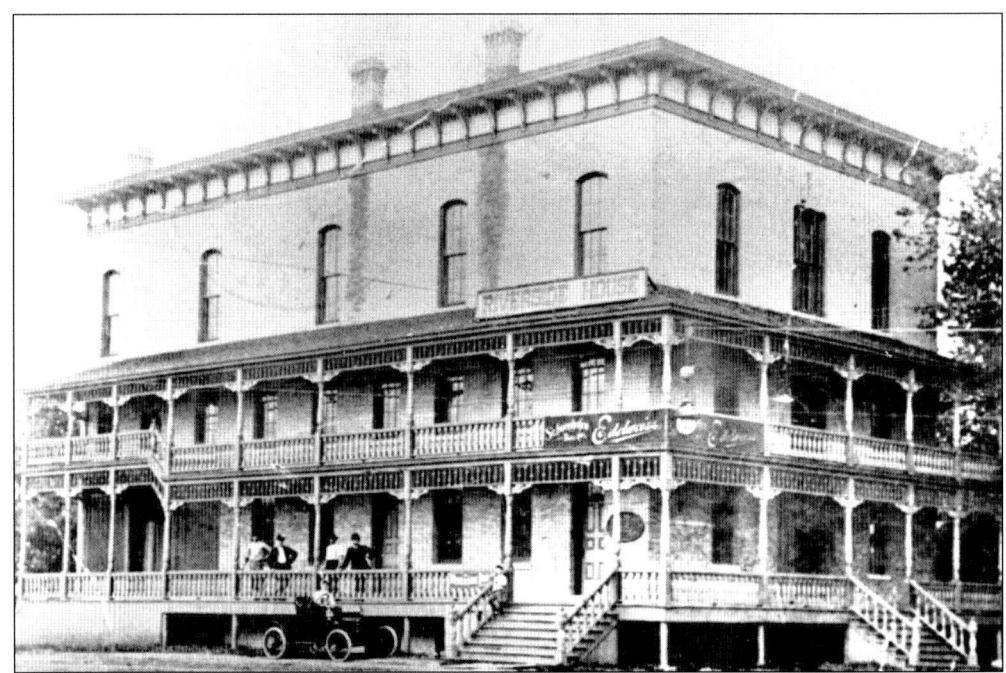

The Riverside Hotel dates back to 1869. Located on the northeast corner of Riverside Drive and Elm Street, it was built near the site of B. B. Brown's Log Cabin Tavern (built 1836) and just east of the site of the first log cabin in the village. The hotel, built by John Wire Smith and D. S. Smith, still stands but has a different look as the pillars of McHenry artificial stone, used to support the building's awnings until 1940, were removed for the widening of the road. This is the look of the hotel in the 1920s. (Courtesy of the McHenry Public Library.)

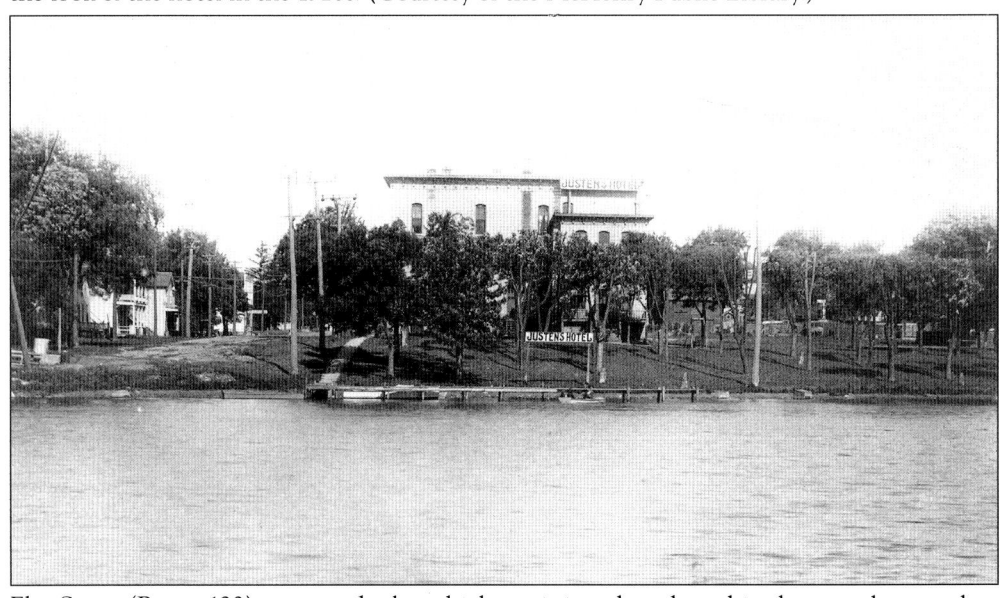

Elm Street (Route 120) was not the busy highway it is today when this photograph was taken in the early 1900s. The unpaved road ended at the river. The three-story building behind the trees is the above Riverside Hotel, but at this time, it was known as Justen's Hotel. (Courtesy of Ilene Wiedemann.)

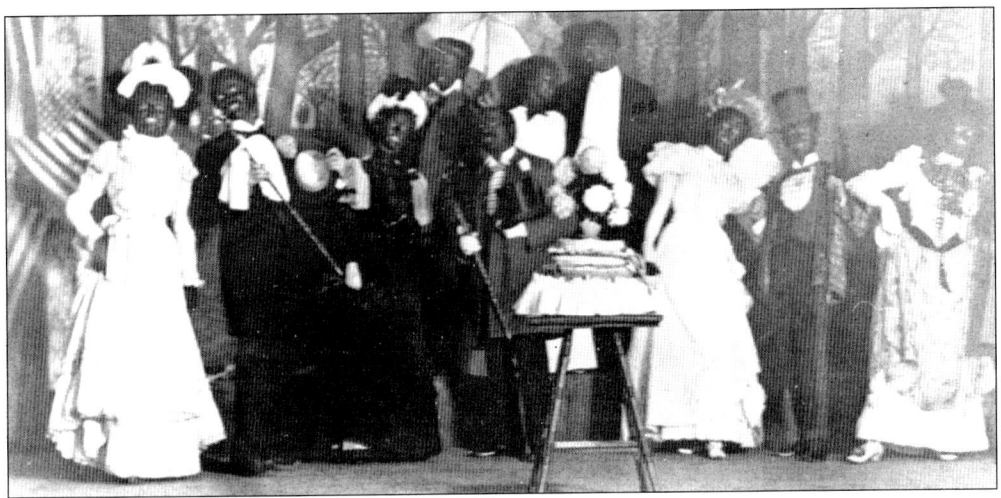

Entertainment brought crowds to the Riverside Hotel. Various types of entertainment from bands to minstrels were brought to McHenry beginning in the late 1800s. This minstrel show played on December 3, 1898. (Courtesy of the McHenry Public Library.)

Riverside House

F. O. GANS, Proprietor

AMERICAN PLAN   RATES: $2.00 and $2.50 Per Day; $10.00 to $12.00 Per Week

The Rate of This Room, Each Person, is $_____

RULES AND REGULATIONS

1. Persons engaging rooms will be charged from the time they are placed at their disposal, whether they are occupied or not.
2. The management will not be responsible for jewelry or other valuables left in rooms.
3. Guests without baggage are requested to pay in advance.
4. All bills payable weekly.
5. Meals served in room 25 cents extra.

FIRE NOTICE

Fire escapes are situated at end of hallways and are indicated by signs and red lights.

MEAL HOURS

Breakfast, 7:00 to 8:30;   Dinner, 12:00 to 2:00;   Supper, 6:00 to 7:30
SUNDAYS: Breakfast, 7:00 to 8:30;   Dinner, 12:00 to 2:00;   Supper, 6:00 to 7:30

THE LAW TO REGULATE THE LIABILITY OF HOTEL KEEPERS
SECTION I.

ACT. 5.—Whenever the proprietor of any hotel shall post in a conspicuous manner about the room occupied by any guest, a notice requiring each guest to bolt the door, on retiring, or on leaving to lock the door and leave the key at the office, and to deposit his money, jewels and ornaments in the office, and if any such guest shall fail to do so, the proprietor of such hotel shall not be liable for anything lost or stolen from said room.

In 1911, the Gans family purchased the Riverside Hotel. Prices for the American plan included three meals per day for $2 or $2.50. For a real splurge, room service could be obtained for an additional 25¢ per meal. (Courtesy of James Althoff.)

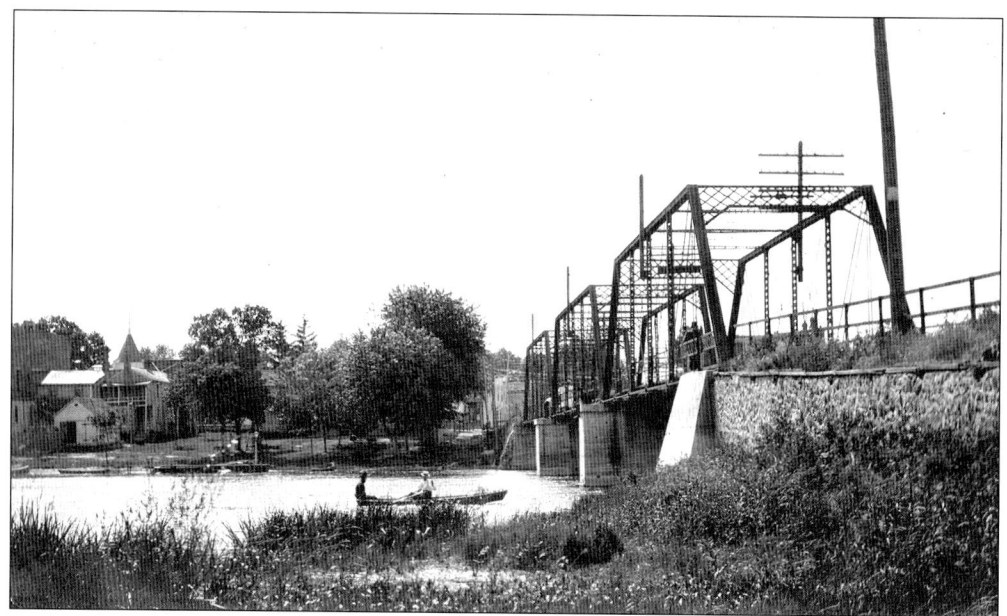

Prior to 1880, crossing the Fox River in McHenry was accomplished by small ferry boats, or by stepping on stones placed in the water. There were no bridges in McHenry that crossed the Fox River. That changed in 1880 when the Pearl Street bridge was built by the Milwaukee Iron Works Company. A three-span truss bridge of iron, it stood 16 feet high and was 285 feet long. When the bridge was first built, the road width of 15 feet and 11 inches seemed more than adequate for the horse-drawn wagons. With the advent of the automobile, and especially the large automobiles of the 1950s and 1960s, crossing the bridge with oncoming traffic was a challenge. The bridge was dismantled in 1977 and replaced with a concrete bridge. (Above, courtesy of Patricia Schafer; below, courtesy of the McHenry County Historical Society.)

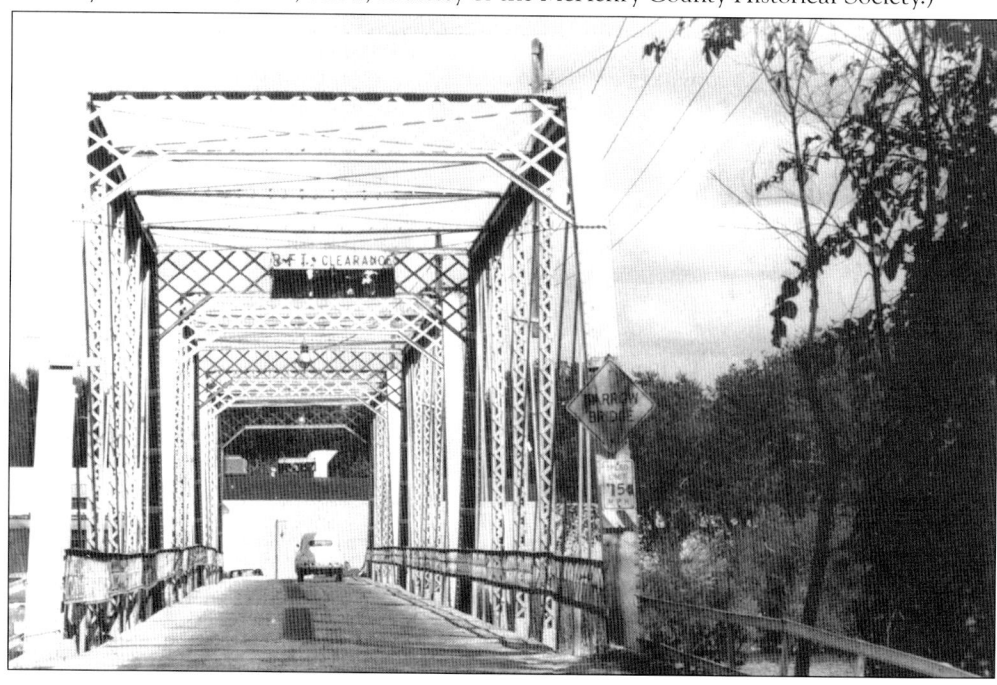

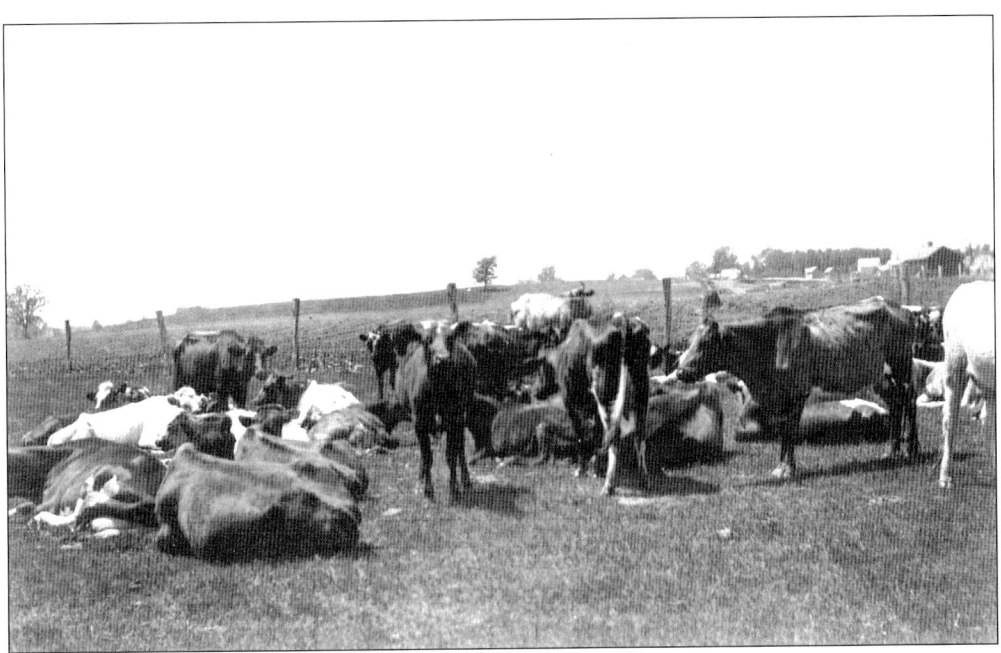
This photograph of Collier Young's pasture was taken on March 18, 1901. Cows were found on most McHenry farms as milk production was one of the leading products of McHenry County. Milk products were collected by dairies for processing. (Courtesy of the McHenry Public Library.)

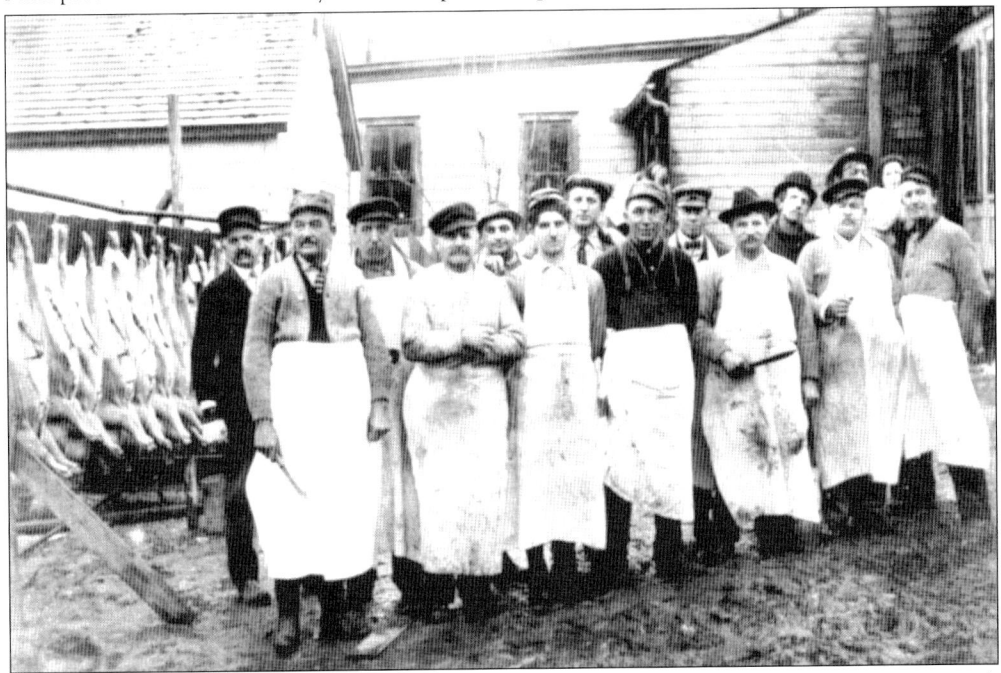
Farming was not just a job but a lifestyle requiring many hours of work daily. Often it took the farm family, their extended family, and friends to accomplish tasks. Butchering was one of these jobs. In 1911, while wearing aprons to protect their clothing, this group of farmers joined together to butcher hogs. This farm was located on Riverside Drive. (Courtesy of the McHenry Public Library.)

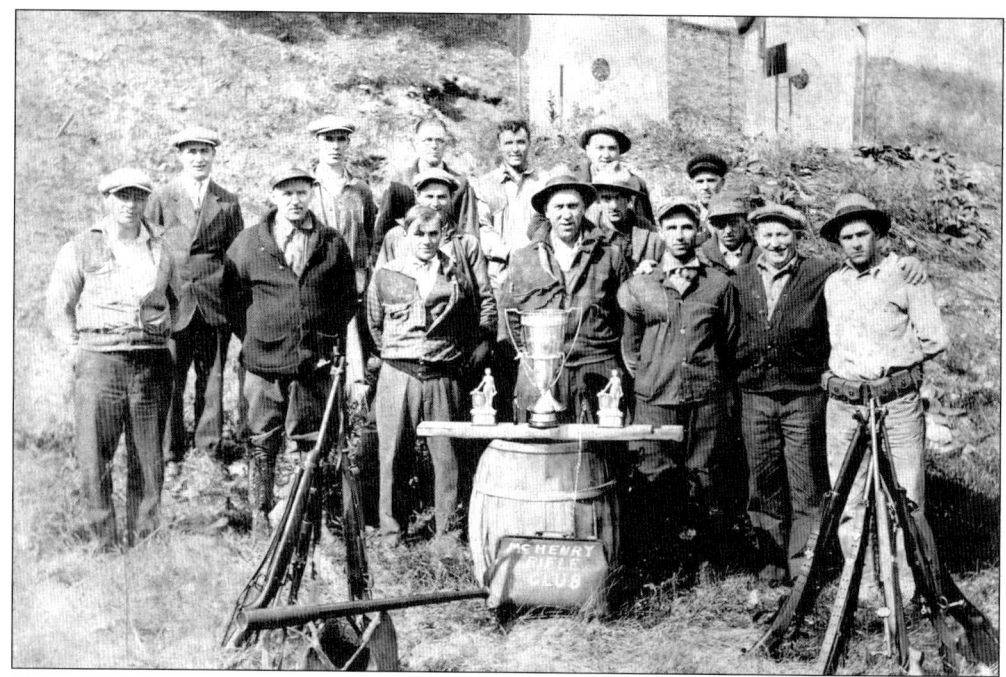

Henry H. Freund founded the McHenry Rifle Club in 1927. He and fellow hunters began meeting at the gravel pits in Lily Lake to shoot at decoys. As the population increased in the area, they built a tin structure on Riverside Drive in McHenry. Membership continued to grow. The local police department often used the club as a place for target practice. Today the club has a membership of approximately 35 members. (Courtesy of Barbara Gilpin.)

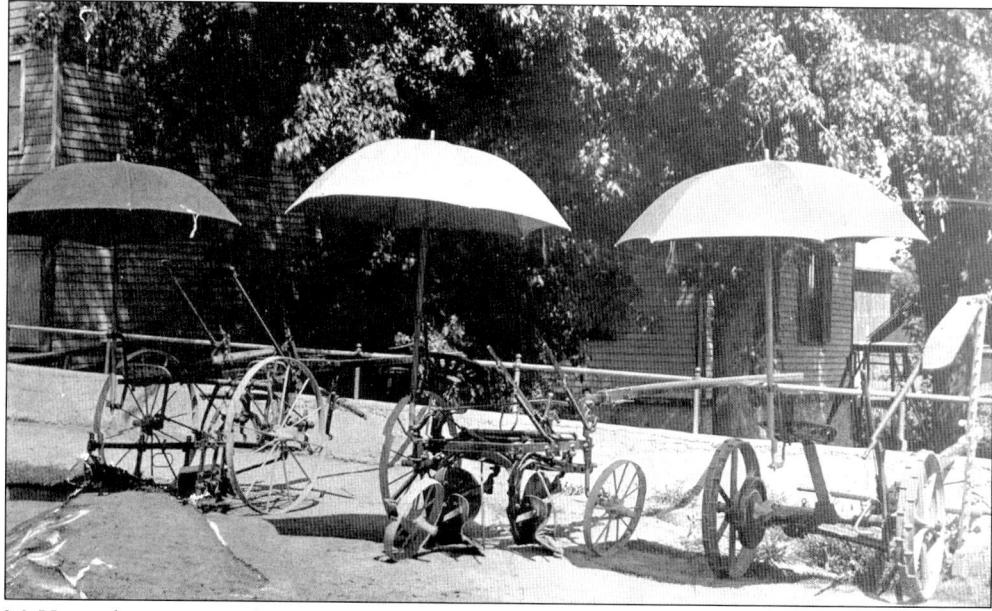

McHenry farmers were always interested in the newest and best farming equipment, even though finances did not always permit their purchase. A walk down Green Street, passing the William Stoffel Implement Company, was a good way to view the plows and tillers on display. (Courtesy of the McHenry Public Library.)

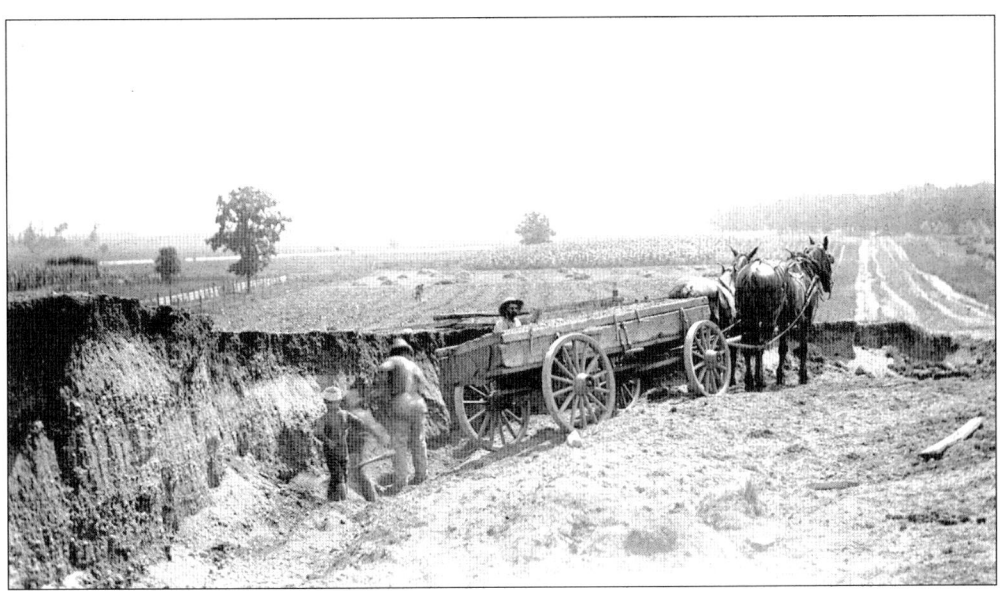

The gravel pits provided stone for roads and buildings. In 1900, this crew was hard at work digging out the gravel and loading it into the wagon. The horse-drawn wagon would then deliver the gravel to the purchasers. (Courtesy of the McHenry Public Library.)

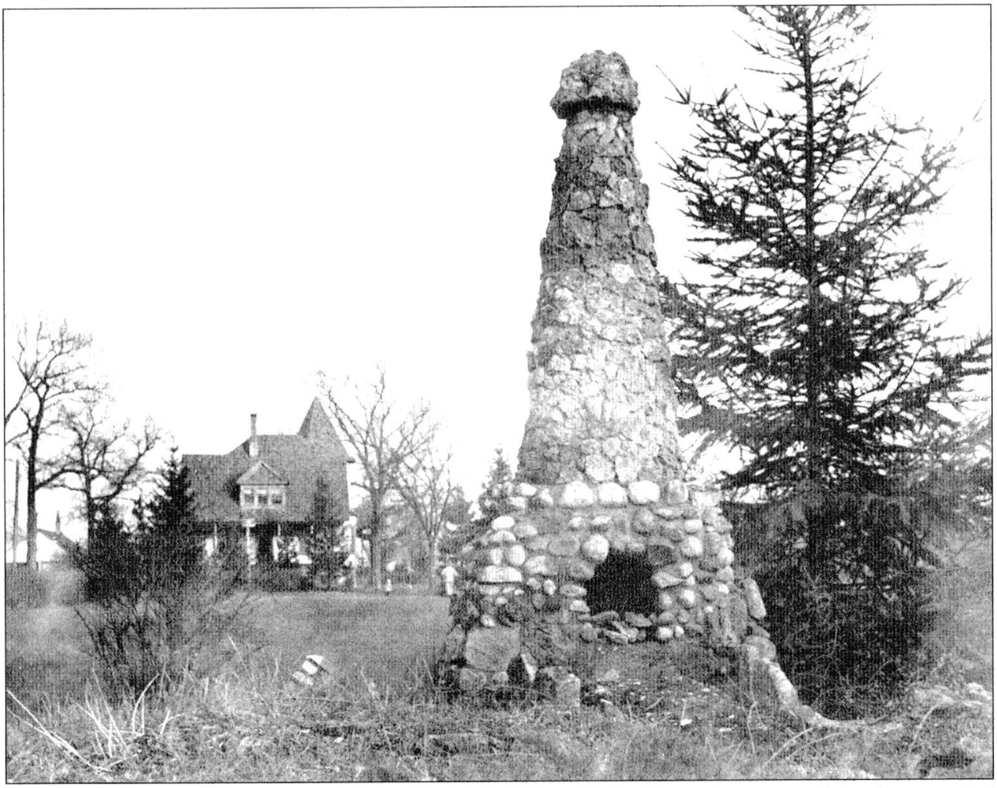

The high rock and gravel content of the ground in the McHenry area encouraged residents to find unique ways to use the stones. Decorative grottos and rock gardens decorated many of the properties in the area. This tall grotto was located at the Rosedale Resort. (Courtesy of Debra Gust.)

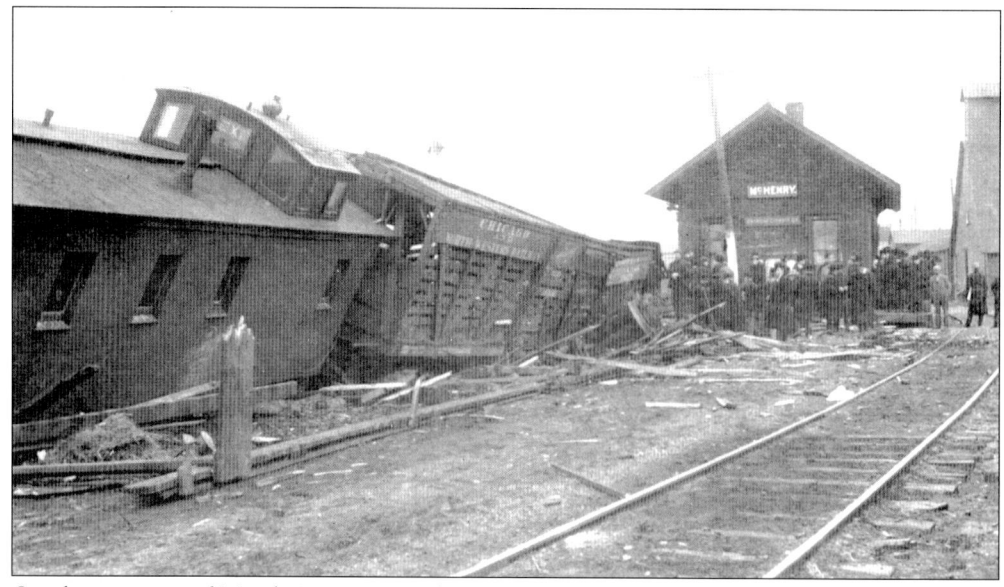

On the morning of March 30, 1908, a Chicago and Northwestern Railroad train transporting 24 head of cattle and 6 calves from Crystal Lake to Ringwood crashed into the McHenry depot. It was the worst wreck this line had ever experienced. Engineer Jewell escaped death by jumping out the cab window. Fireman Ernest Auler was killed by the scalding steam. Cattle owner S. W. Smith, along with the conductor, escaped injury in the way car (caboose). The 24 head of cattle also escaped injury, but one calf was killed. (Courtesy of the McHenry Public Library.)

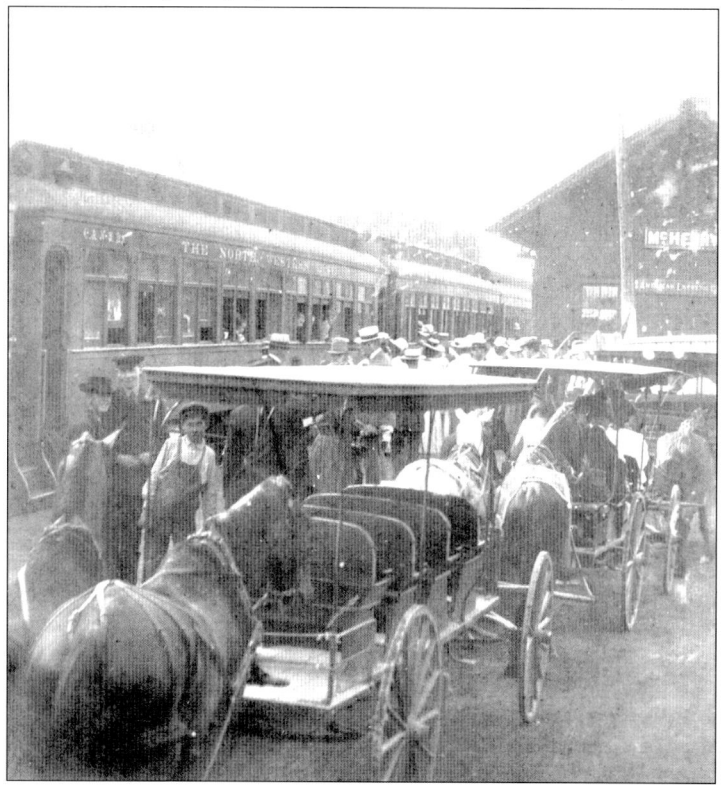

The train station was a busy place when the train arrived from Chicago. Local residents waiting to meet their friends and family crowded on the station platforms. The livery provided these horse-drawn carriages to transport visitors to the river. (Courtesy of Patricia Schafer.)

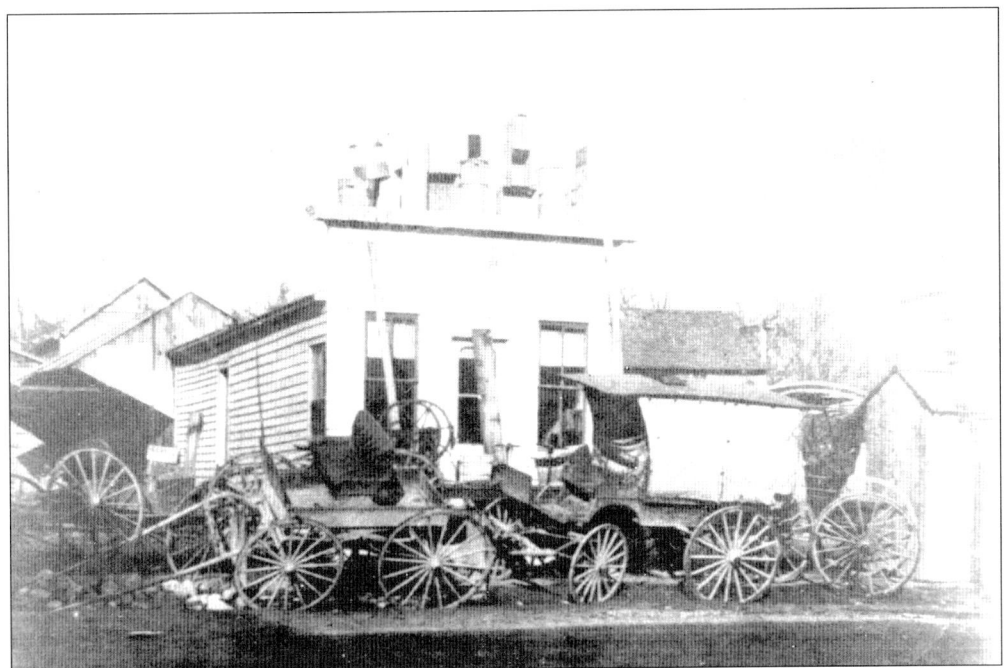

Even in 1911, Halloween pranks were common. Imagine the reaction of the owners of Bishop's Barber Shop when they were faced with this display in front of their business on November first. Wagons were piled in front of the entrance to their shop making it impossible for customers to enter. (Courtesy of John Baumgartner.)

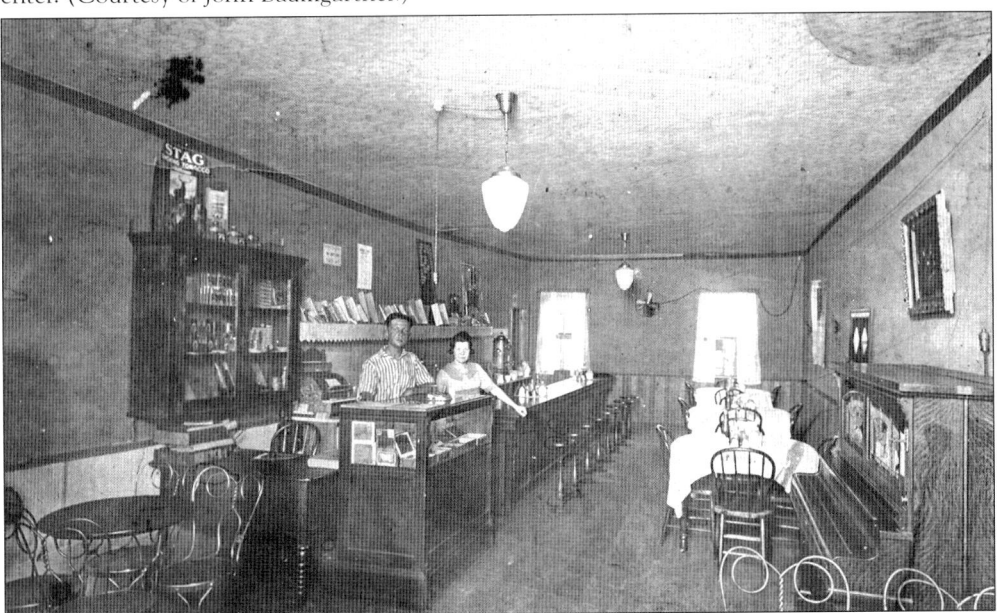

Restaurants were always popular in McHenry, whether they were full service or small coffee shops. Pictured here is the Busy Bee Restaurant, which was located in the rear portion of the building on the southeast corner of Main and Front Streets. The entrance to the restaurant faced Front Street. Pictured here are owners Matt Laures and his sister Rose waiting for customers. (Courtesy of Christopher Wirtz.)

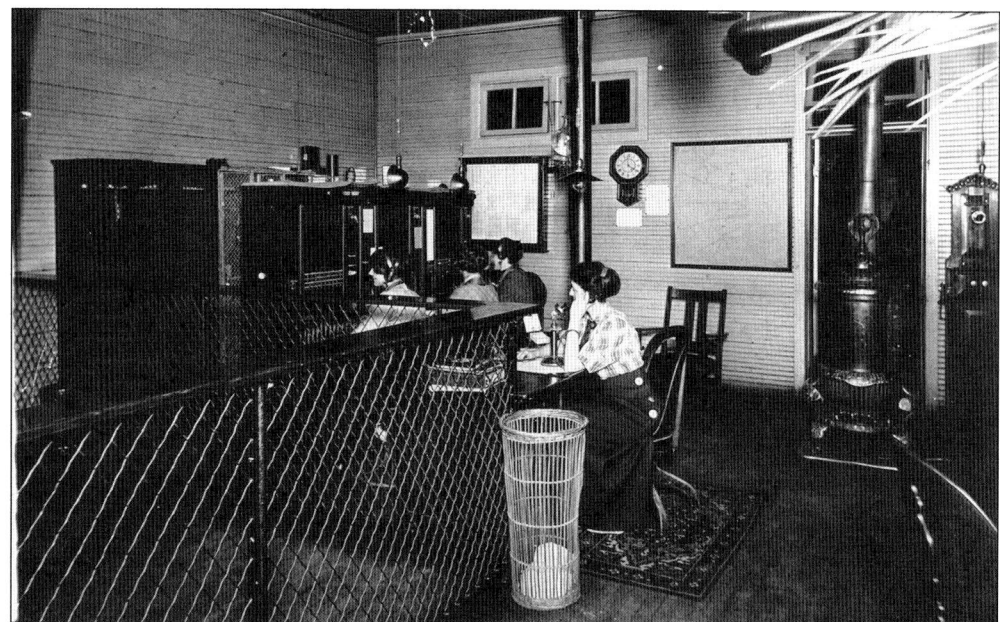

Telephone service first came to McHenry in 1897. At first telephone companies were small and independent. In the early 1900s, the Chicago Telephone Company consolidated many of the smaller companies. The first telephone exchange in McHenry was located in the Stoffel building. Until the middle of the 20th century, telephone calls were connected by operators after receiving the number from the caller. The familiar sound of "number please" instead of a dial tone was heard when initiating a telephone call. The photograph above was taken on April 16, 1912. Operators sitting at the switchboard are, from left to right, Agnes Tuech Bienapfl, Bertha Wolf Mertes, and Alice Simes. The other operator is not identified. The photograph below is also from 1900. Note the large ornate stove used to heat the office. (Courtesy of the McHenry Landmark Commission.)

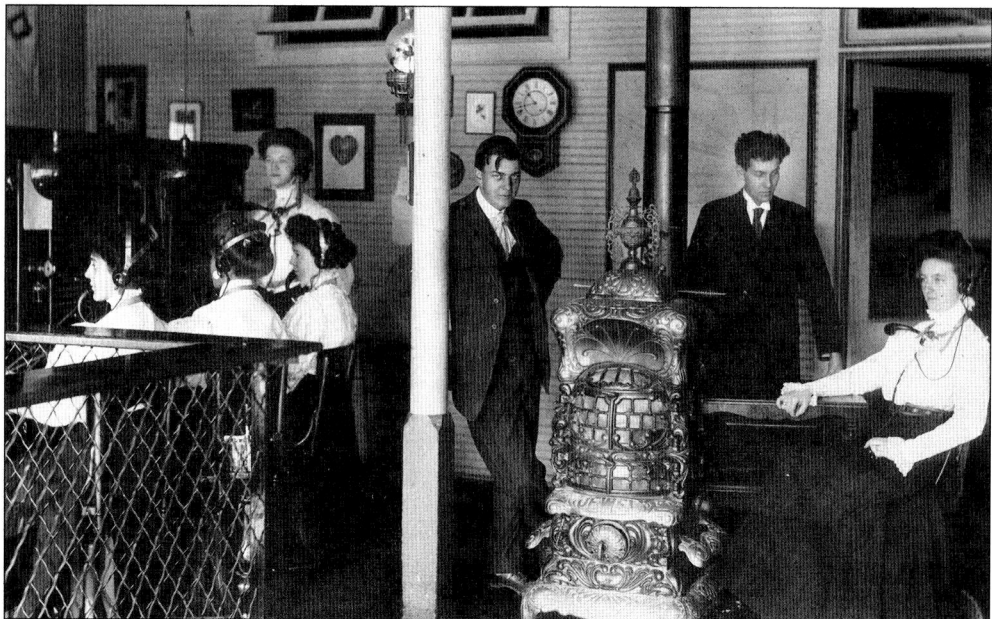

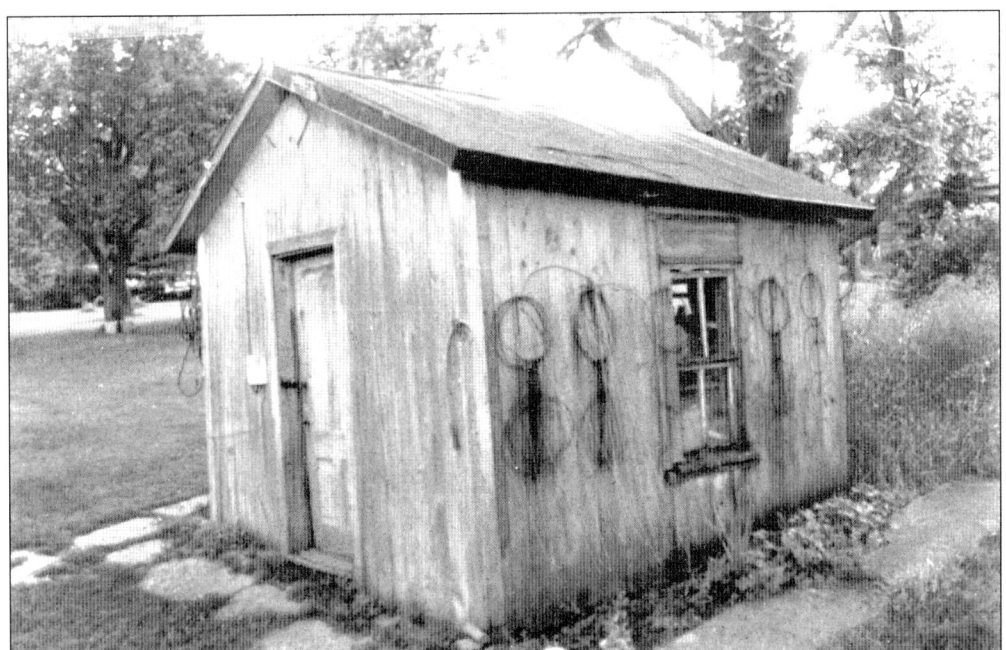

While the history of this small wooden building is not known for certain, it is believed to have served as the office of the brick factory in McHenry. The brick factory produced the bricks that were used to build many McHenry homes and business buildings. (Courtesy of the McHenry County Historical Society.)

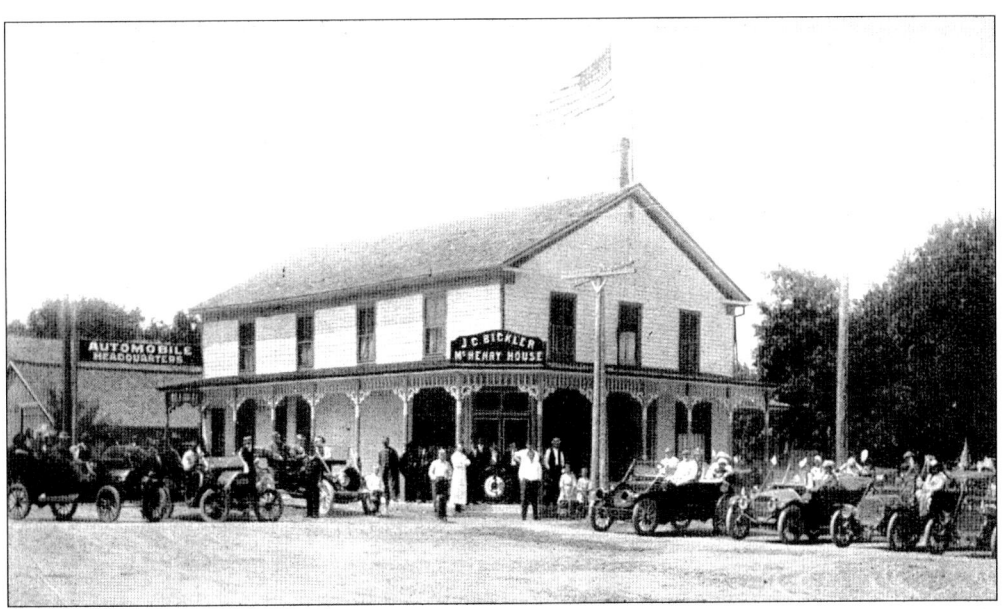

Pictured is the J C Bickler McHenry House restaurant in 1911, located on the corner of Riverside Drive and Pearl Street. It was the second hotel in the city, the first being the log cabin built by B. B. Brown in 1836. It was also known as "Automobile Headquarters." (Courtesy of Michael Clark.)

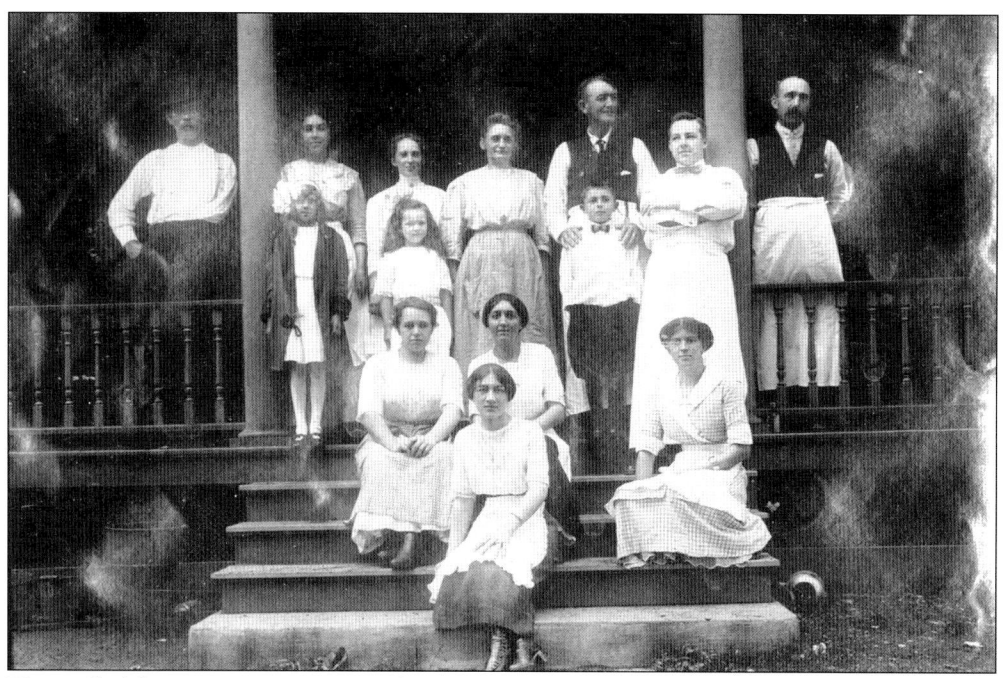

The staff of this restaurant on Riverside Drive gathers on the back porch in the 1890s. Standing in the back row, second from right is owner John J. Buch with his hands on the shoulders of his son Henry Buch. Seated in the front on the steps is Katherine (last name unknown), who worked as a waitress and also played the organ. Today the Little Chef Restaurant is located at this site. (Courtesy of Henry Buch.)

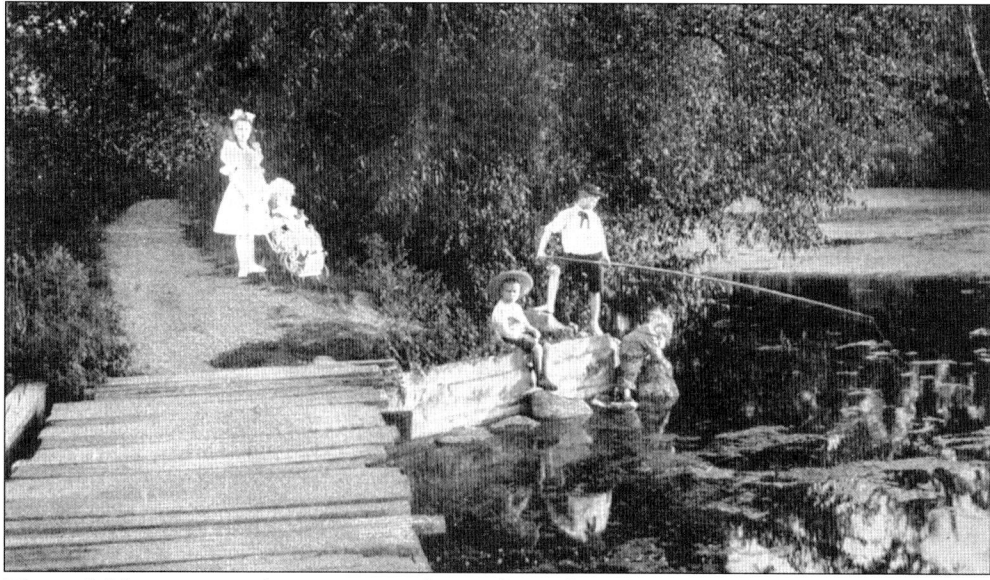

These children seem to be enjoying a day at the millpond. While the pond was a place for fishing in the summer and ice-skating in the winter, it was not always the safe, tranquil place it appears to be in this photograph. In 1897, eight-year-old Lillie Buss and seven-year-old Bernie Buss drowned here. In 1912, 10-year-old Willie Worts was also reported to have drowned in the icy waters of the pond. (Courtesy of Patricia Schafer.)

After the draining of the millpond, Route 120 became a through street allowing traffic to move from West McHenry to Riverside without having to go over the Green Street bridge. This corner of Route 31 and 120 looks much the same as it does today. (Courtesy of Patricia Shafer.)

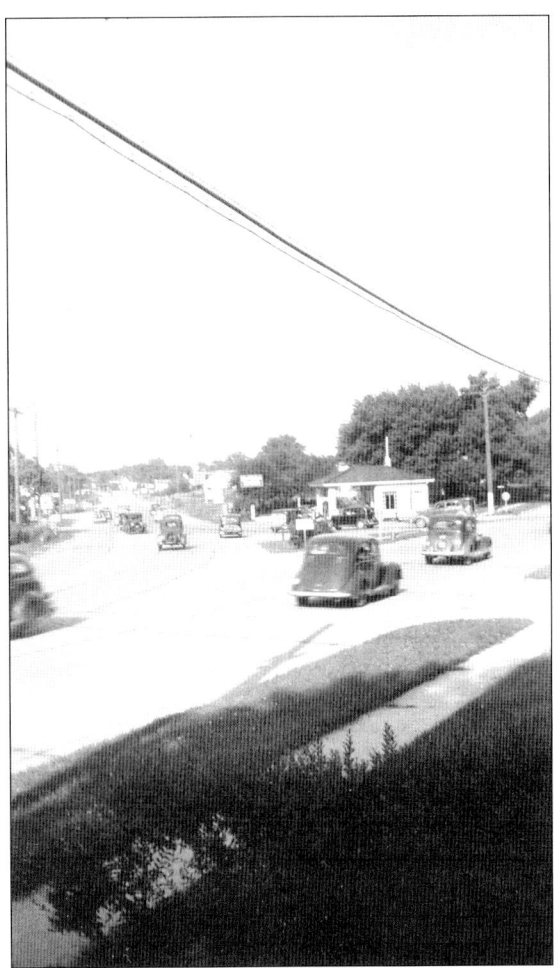

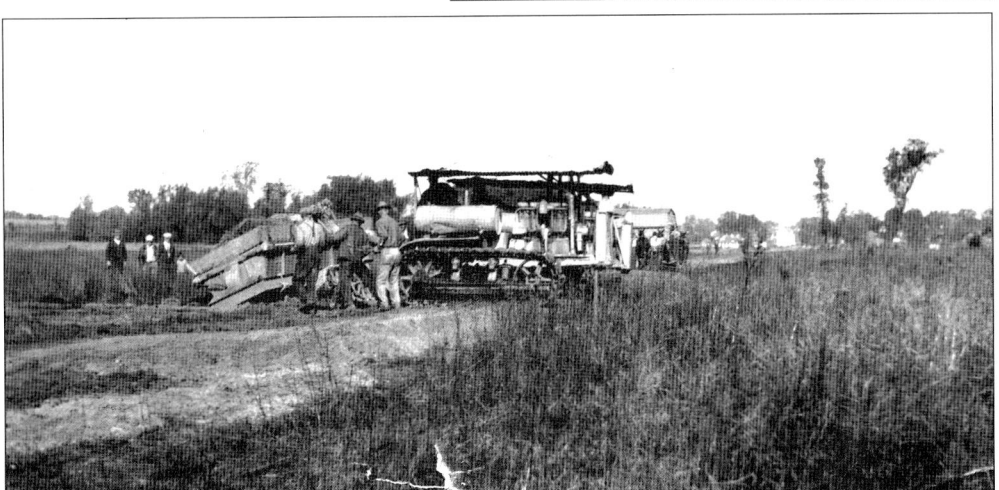

Building a new road took much man power and machinery. These workmen are building Route 31, just south of John Street. This photograph was taken in 1933. (Courtesy of the McHenry Public Library.)

27

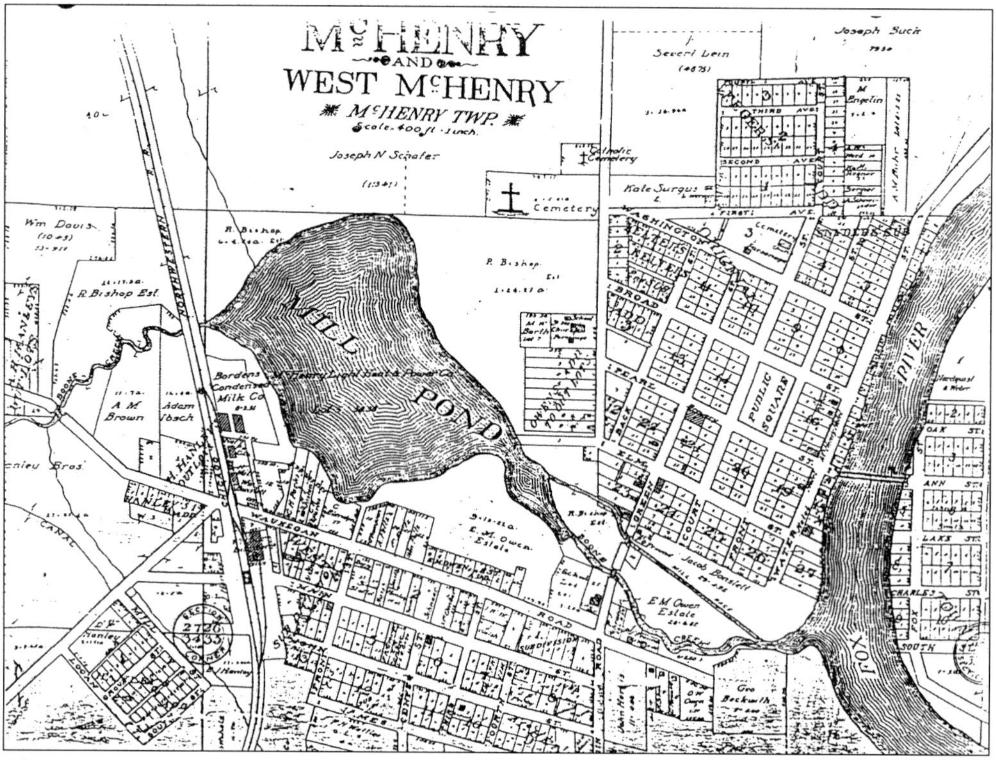

This map of the city of McHenry depicts the city as it looked in the early 1900s. The millpond can be seen covering much of what today is dry land. Route 120 was not present as it is known today because of the pond. (Courtesy of John Baumgartner.)

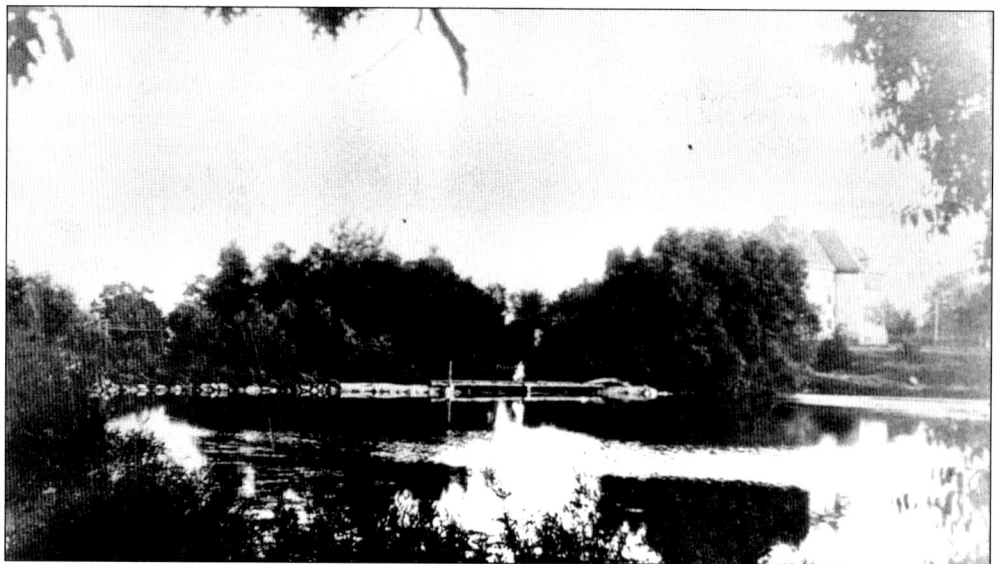

The damming of Boone Creek created the millpond. The pond was used by the residents of McHenry for boating, swimming, and fishing in the summer. Ice was cut from the pond in the winter to provide refrigeration. The dam was removed in the late 1920s. Landmark School can be seen in the background. (Courtesy of John Baumgartner.)

Two

FACES AND PLACES

The character of any city is determined in large part by that of the people who inhabit the area. Many of the early settlers to McHenry were from the East Coast who traveled either by land through Chicago or who used the waterways of the Great Lakes to arrive in the Midwest. By following Native American trails, they eventually made their way to the shores of the Fox River.

Most of the early settlers were good people who were looking for a place to establish roots, build a home, and support their families, building a respectable community. As with any group of people there was also a minority who were only interested in living off others and wreaking havoc on the area. That group did not thrive in McHenry.

The Irish immigrants, for the most part, settled along the southern edges of McHenry in an area that became known as the Irish Prairie. Through hard work, they transformed the virgin prairie into workable farmland and turned the area into a family-oriented community.

To the north of McHenry, the large German population in Johnsburg encouraged extended family members to join them. These families often settled on the northern and western edges of McHenry with much the same result as the Irish immigrants. Farms, business, churches, and schools flourished.

These early families gathered together sharing chores that were not possible to complete alone. Yearly jobs such as harvesting crops and butchering livestock were often completed as a group activity. Families remained close and gathered together to share their joys and their sorrows.

Working together, these early families made McHenry the city it is today.

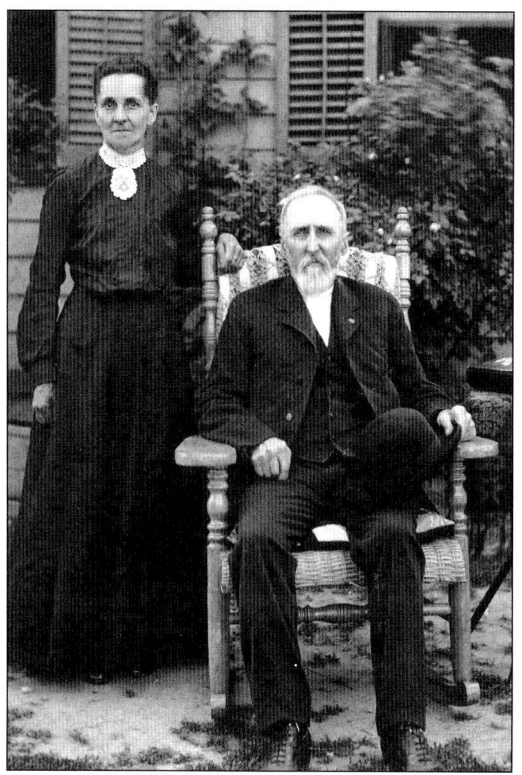

In 1882, Page Colby purchased 80 acres of land around McCullom Lake for $130. He later purchased an additional 800 acres. From this land the multi-generational Colby-Petersen farm was developed. This photograph of Page Colby and Mehitabel (Smith) Colby was taken in the late 1800s. (Courtesy of the McHenry Landmark Commission.)

This photograph of Kenneth and Beatrice (Wilson) Petersen was taken in the mid-1900s. The Petersens and their son, Robert, were the last of the Petersen line. The farm was purchased by the City of McHenry and is to be preserved. (Courtesy of the McHenry Landmark Commission.)

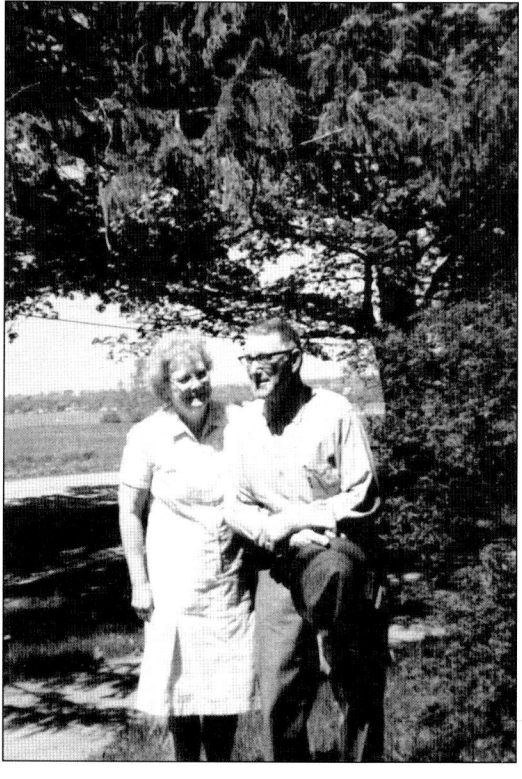

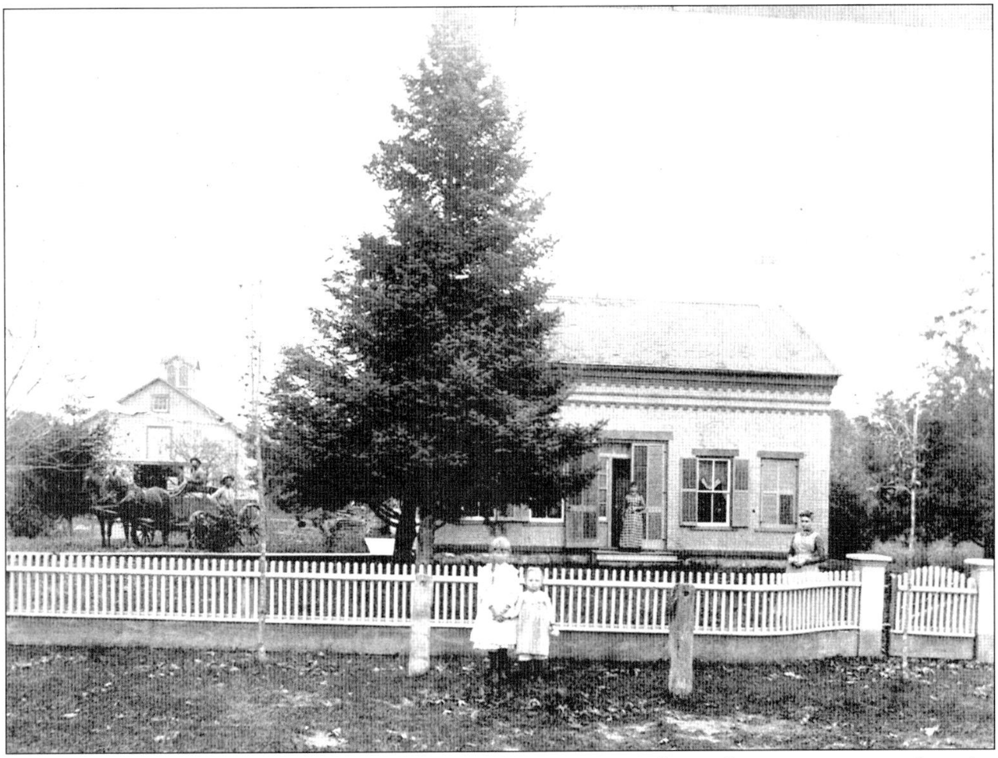

The Colby-Petersen farmhouse with its white-picket fence is shown here as it appeared in the 1800s. The brick farmhouse was the home of five generations of the Colby-Petersen family. The names of the people in front of the residence are unknown. (Courtesy of the McHenry Landmark Commission.)

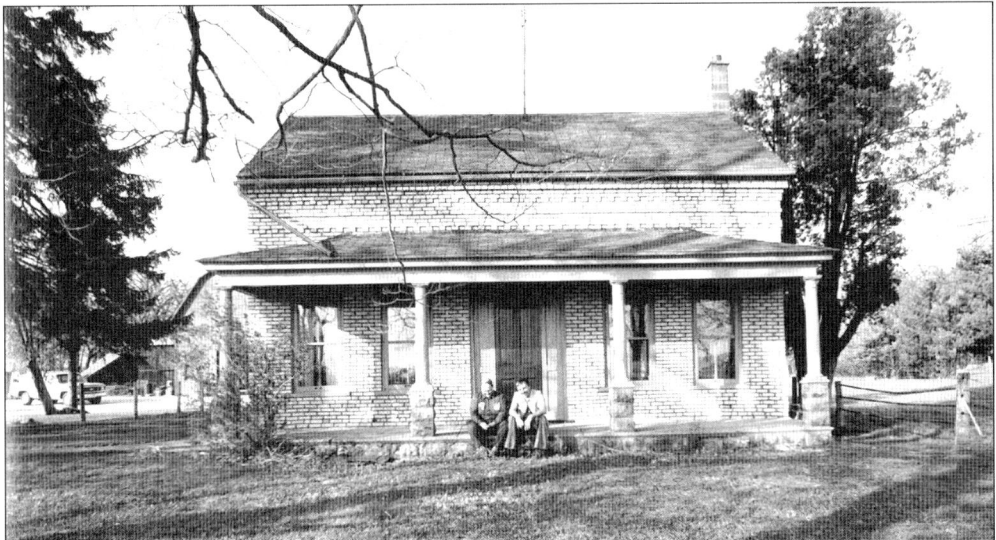

After Caroline Colby married Peter Petersen in 1901, they continued to farm the family farm, which then began to be known as the Petersen farm. This photograph of the farmhouse was taken in the mid-1900s. Note the addition of the covered porch. (Courtesy of the McHenry Landmark Commission.)

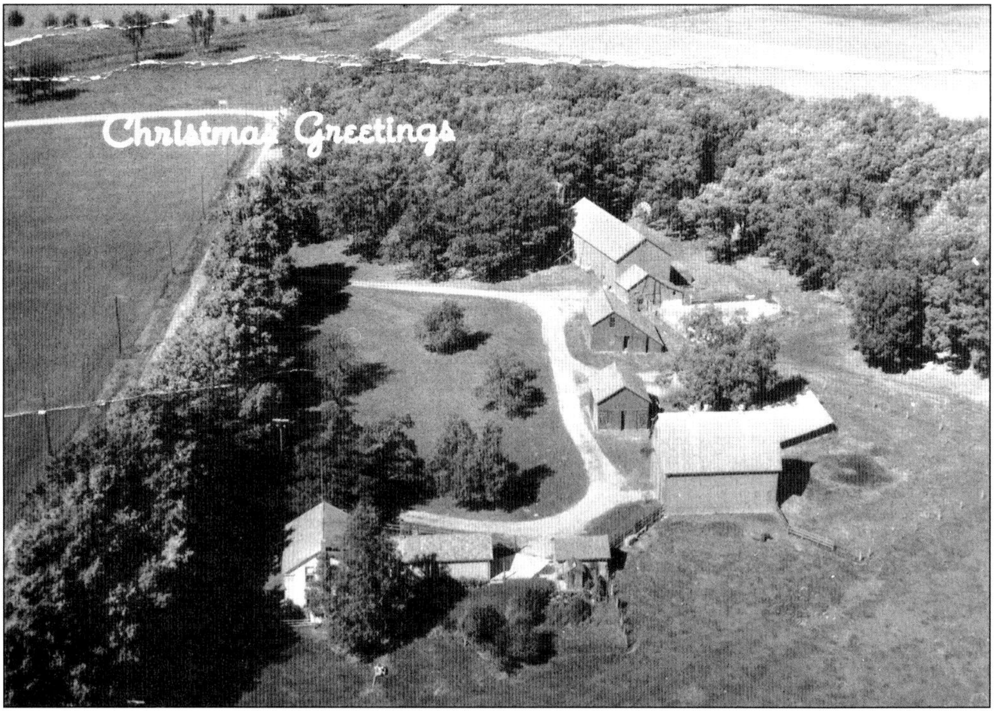

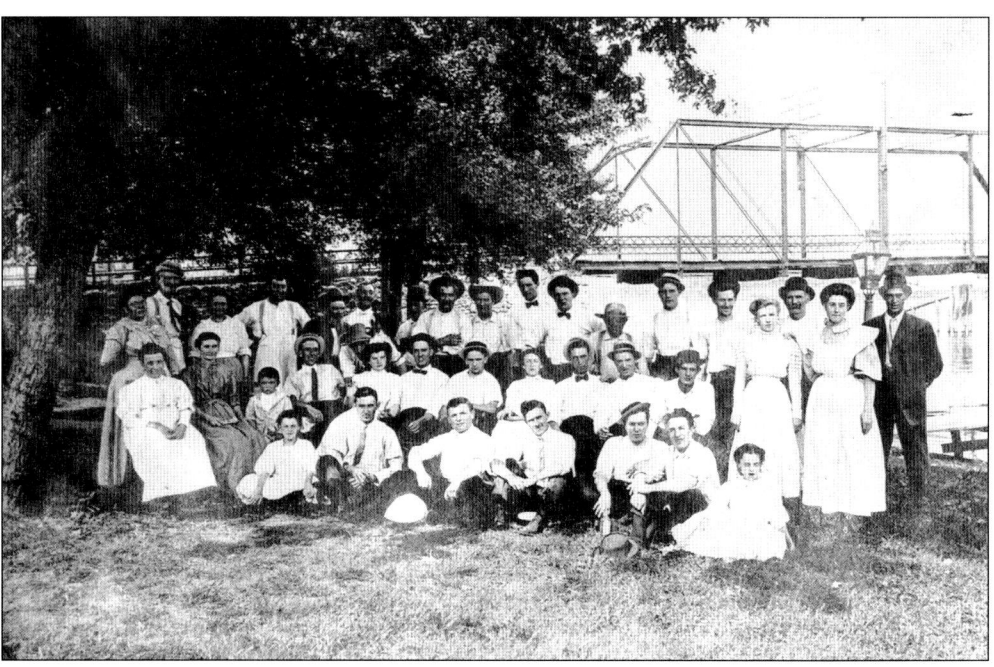

The Petersen family extended Christmas greetings to their friends and neighbors with this aerial view of the farm in 1955. (Courtesy of John P. Haley.)

On a warm, sunny day in the 1890s, the Buch family gathered on the shore of the Fox River for a family portrait. Everyone is dressed in their Sunday finery. This location, with the old iron bridge in the background, was a favorite place for photographers. (Courtesy of Henry Buch.)

Ellen Frisby Phalin was an Irish immigrant who came to McHenry in 1848 with her father, George Frisby, and sister, Catherine. They made their way to the Irish Prairie in McHenry where many other Irish farmers had settled after fleeing the famine in Ireland. Ellen married Tom Frisby (not a known relative) soon after her arrival in McHenry. When Tom was killed in a dispute with a friend, Ellen was left a widow with 40 acres of land and three children. (Courtesy of Larry Phalin.)

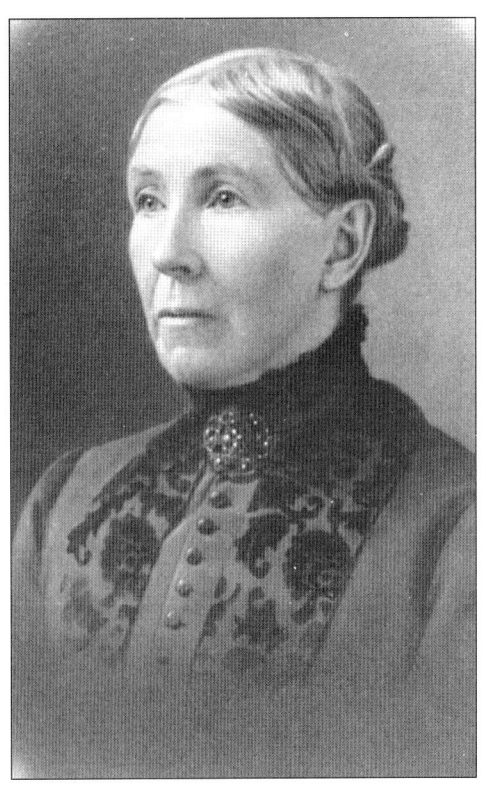

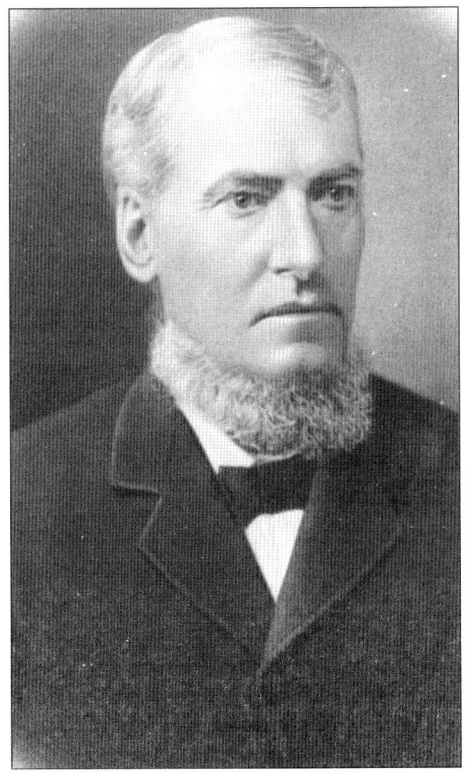

Thomas Phalin also arrived in McHenry after fleeing the poverty of Ireland. A young man of about 20 years of age, he was introduced to the widow Ellen Frisby by the pastor of St. Patrick's Church. Despite being 13 years her junior, they were married in St. Patrick's Church, one of the first marriages recorded there. (Courtesy of Larry Phalin.)

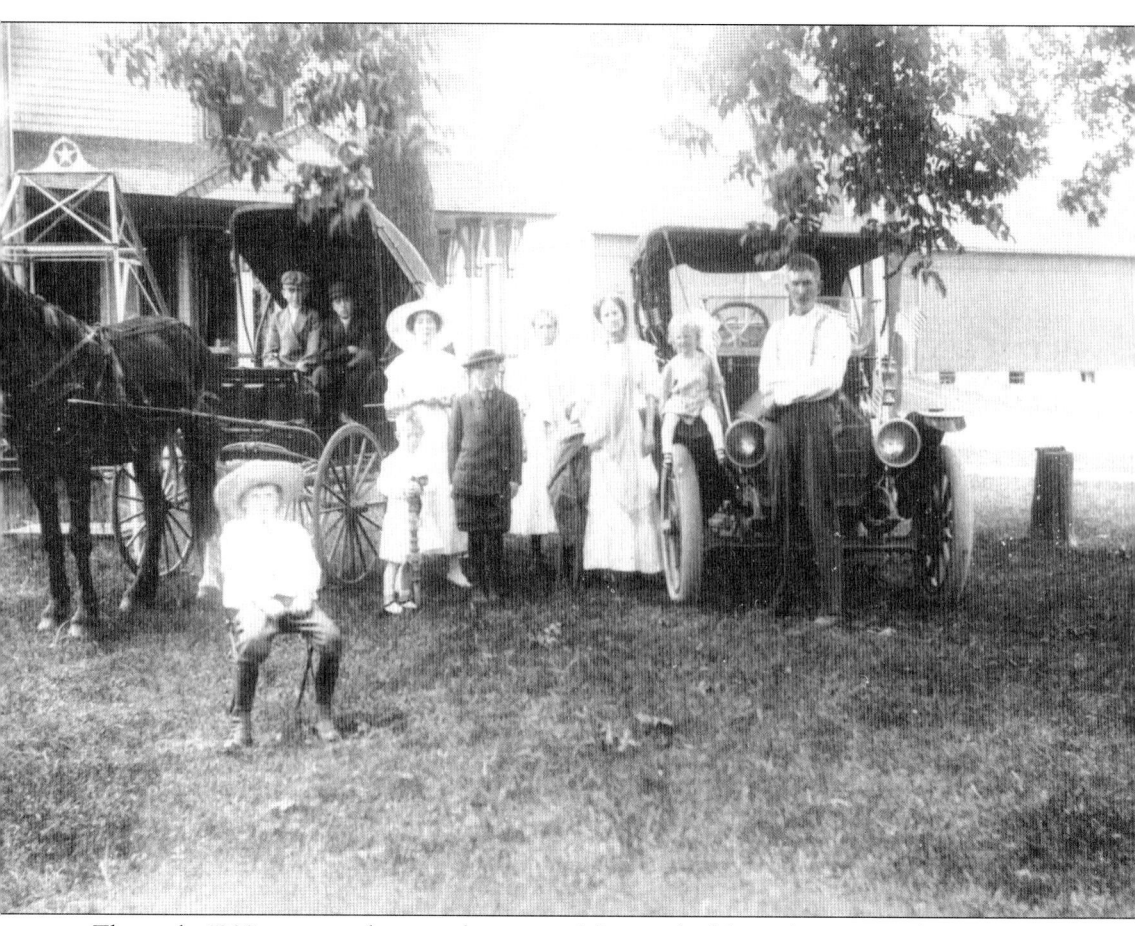

The early 1900s presented many changes in life as it had been known on the prairie. The dichotomy of the past and the present is seen here. The Phalin family stands in front of the family farm in their Sunday dress, flanked between the past and the present. On the left, the family's horse, Major, is shown hitched to the wagon. This horse and wagon had been their method of transportation. The far right, with Tom Phalin standing in front, is the family's new 1913 Velie automobile. Seated in the chair is Howard Phalin, who in later years donated the organ to St. Patrick's Church. (Courtesy of Larry Phalin.)

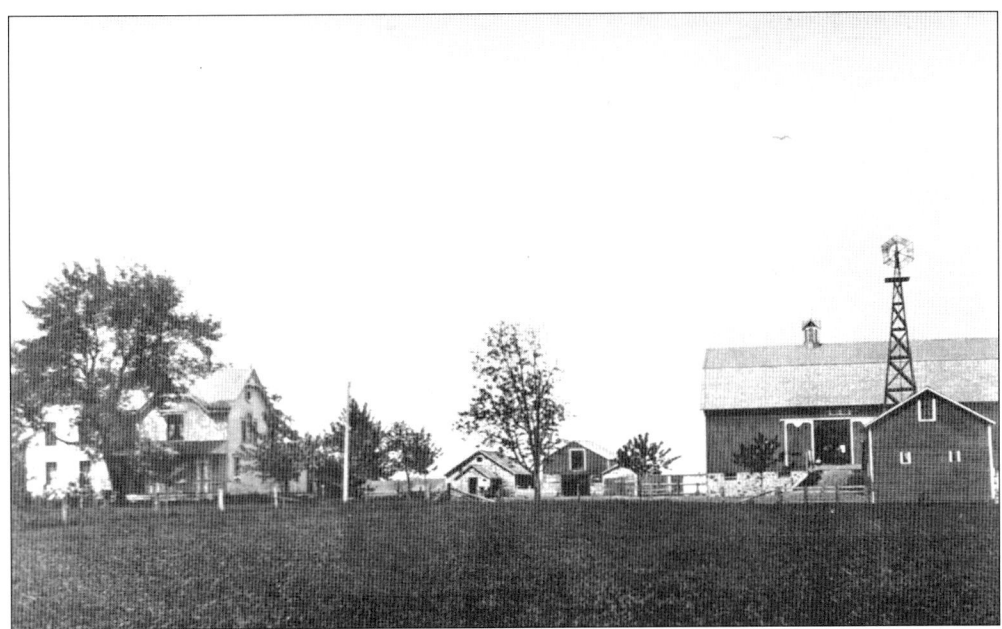

In the late 1800s, farms such as this one located on Route 31 in West McHenry dotted the countryside. Immigrants, particularly those from Ireland and Germany, found their way to the fertile northern Illinois region where crops such as wheat, hay, and corn grew well. Dairy farming provided milk products that were processed in local dairies and distributed throughout the Chicago area. (Courtesy of Larry Phalin.)

Auction notices such as these were seen frequently on farms in the late 1920s and early 1930s. Along with the financial setbacks caused by the stock market crash, farmers were faced with herds of cattle being destroyed because of tuberculosis. Remaining livestock were often sold to meet mortgage payments or to purchase seeds for spring planting. (Courtesy of Larry Phalin.)

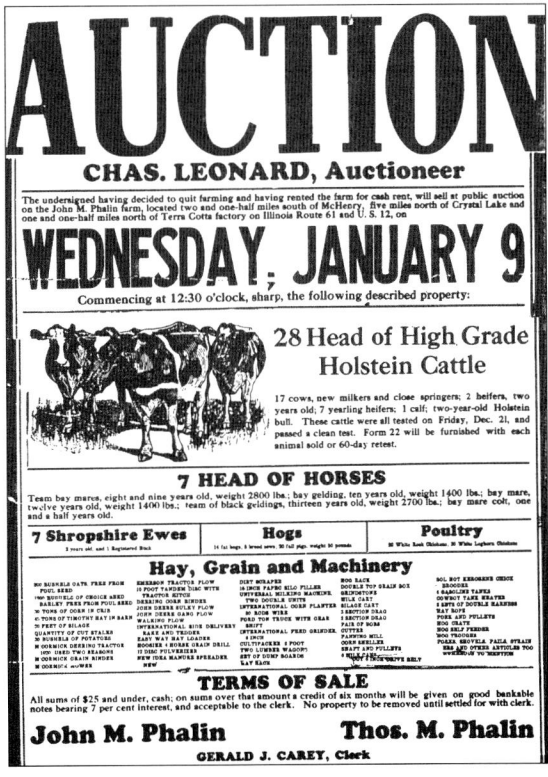

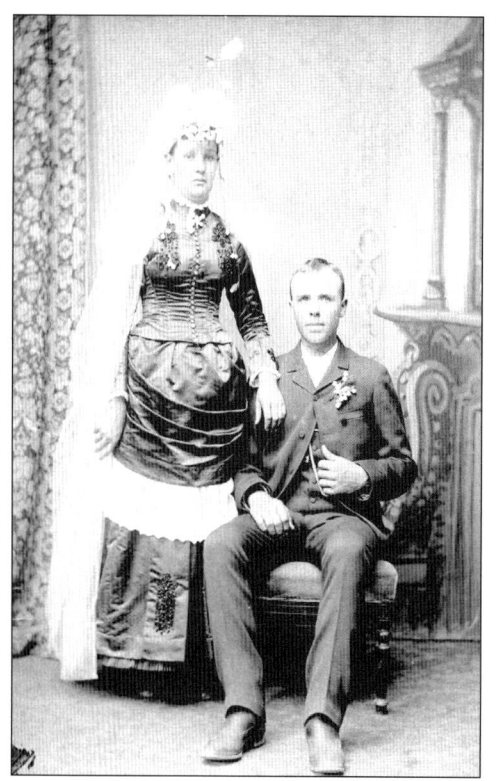

In the 1880s, weddings were very formal affairs. While bridal gowns had a much different style and color than those of the current era, they were still opulent with embroidery and lace decorating the gown. The traditional long white veil is seen in both these formal wedding pictures. In 1888, Stephen Freund married Katherine Klapperich (above) while his sister Mary Freund was married to Katherine's brother Henry Klapperich in a double ceremony. (Courtesy of Barbara Freund Gilpin)

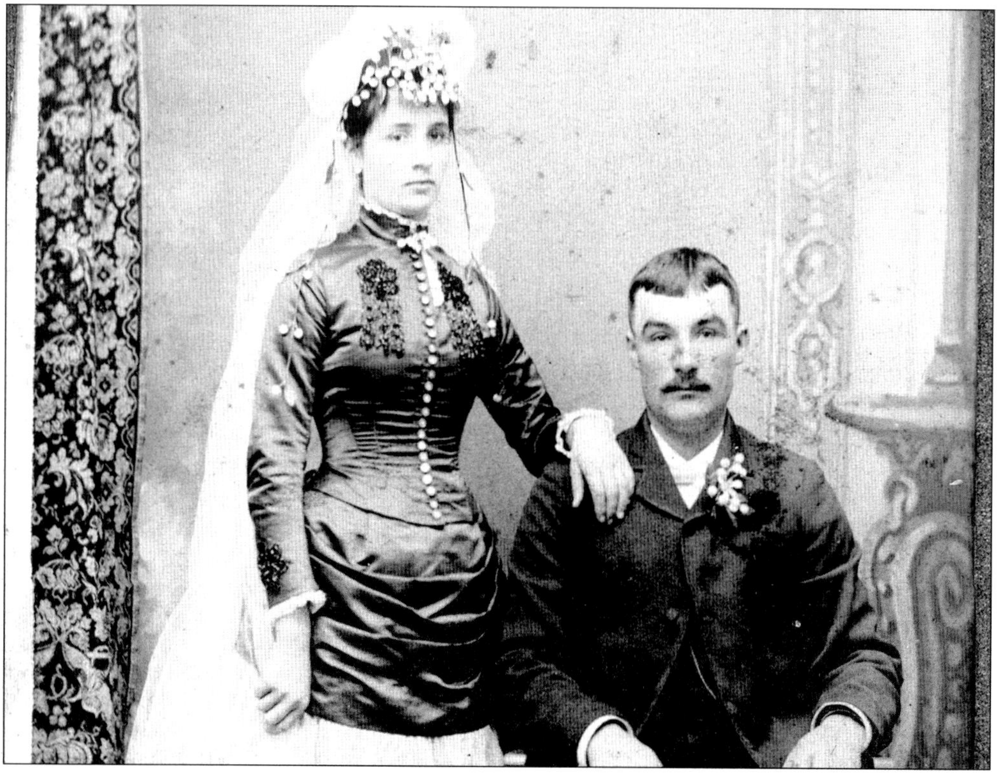

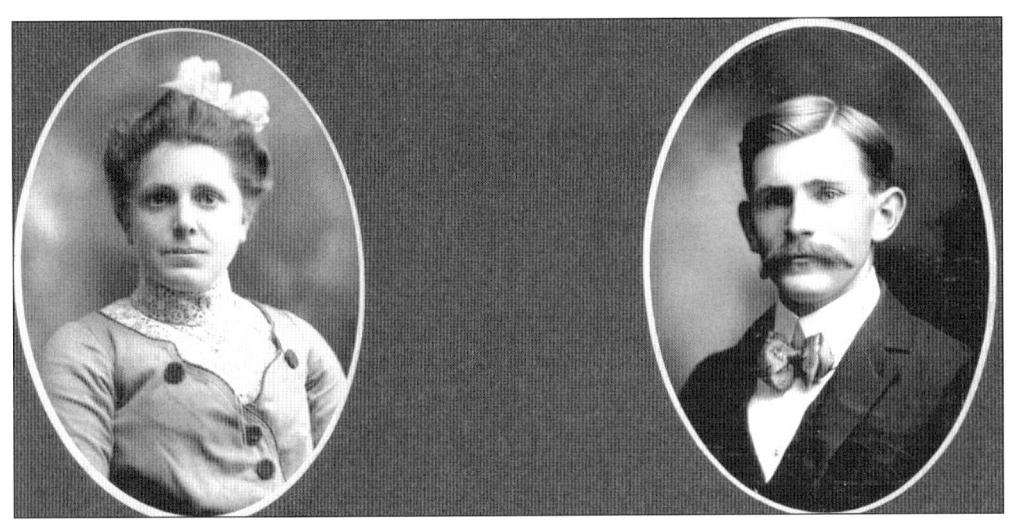

Eber Bassett, one of the early West McHenry postmasters, is shown with Cara Martin on their wedding day, December 18, 1897. The bride has chosen a less traditional look and she has forgone the wearing of a veil. They chose individual vignettes rather than a formal posed wedding picture. (Courtesy of Ilene Wiedemann.)

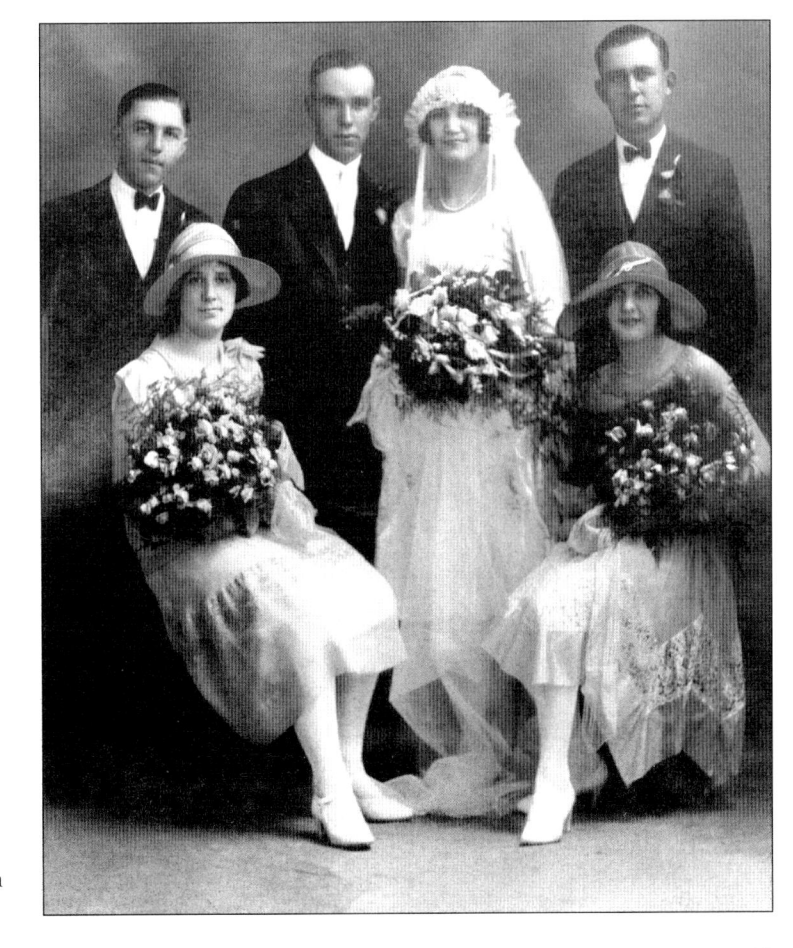

By the 1900s weddings had a different look. The bride wears a long white dress with a cloche headpiece and a shorter veil. Attendants wear the look of the 1920s, brimmed hats and shorter length dresses. All carry large bouquets. This formal photograph of the wedding of Herbert H. Freund and Hildagard Weber includes, from left to right, (first row) Bertilla Freund and Amelia Weber; (second row) Henry Weber, groom Herbert, bride Hildegard, and Martin Weber. (Courtesy of Barbara Freund Gilpin.)

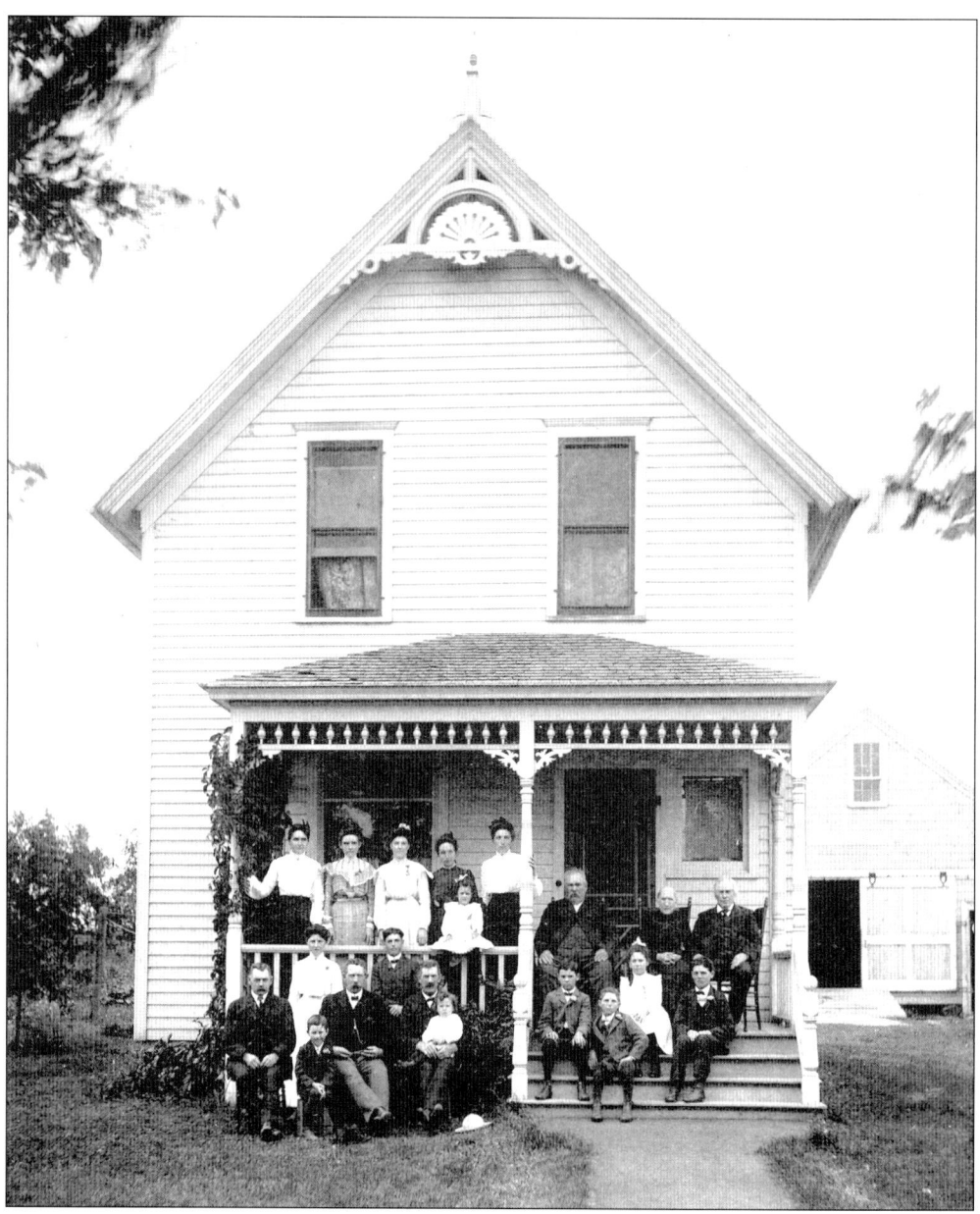

Sunday breakfast was a tradition in the Doherty family. Relatives came into McHenry from their farms to attend mass at St. Patrick's Church. After mass they would join James and Johanna McDonald, who immigrated from Ireland in 1850, at the family home on Green Street. It was a tradition that was continued by their daughters. This photograph taken in 1903 shows, from left to right, (first row) William Doherty, O'Neill Doherty, Peter Doherty, James J. Doherty, and Frank Doherty (in his father's lap); (second row) Grace Doherty Bolger and James Doherty; (children seated on steps) Paul J. Doherty, William Doherty, Vera Doherty, and Thomas Doherty; (adults in chairs) Michael Doherty, Johanna Doherty, and James Doherty; (adults standing on porch) Bridget Doherty, Mary (Welch) Doherty, Mabel (Doherty) Powers, Anna (Knox) Doherty (holding daughter Nellie), and Mary Ann Doherty. (Courtesy of Kathleen Giambalvo and Donald Doherty.)

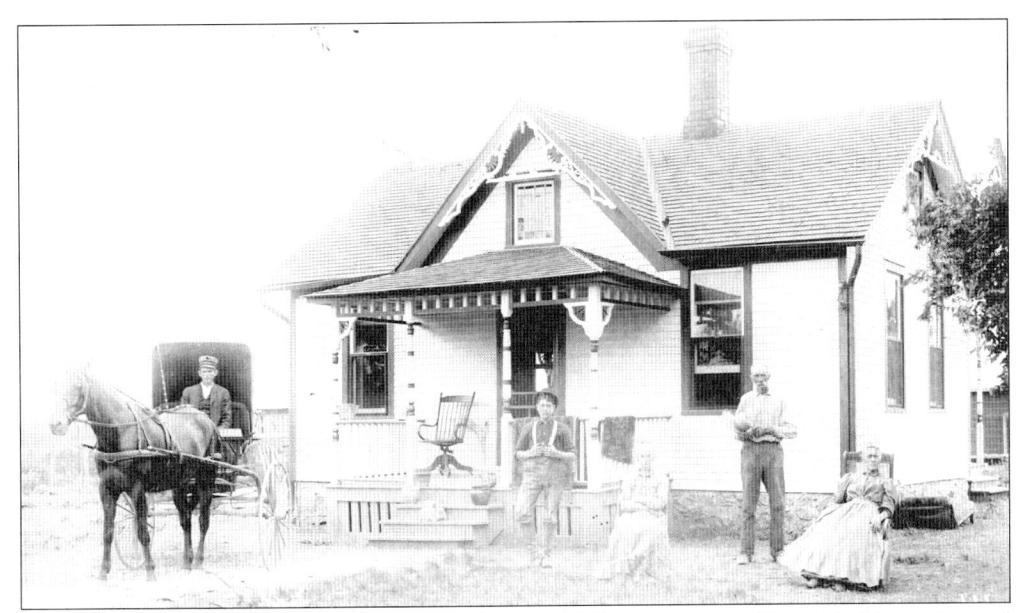

This small farmhouse on Elm Street was the home of Wilbur Bassett and his wife, Mary, pictured on the far right. On the left is their son, Eber, in his horse and buggy, which he used to deliver the mail from 1904 to 1914. Wilbur moved from the farm into the city of McHenry in 1912. The farm later became known as the Benwell farm. (Courtesy of Ilene Wiedemann.)

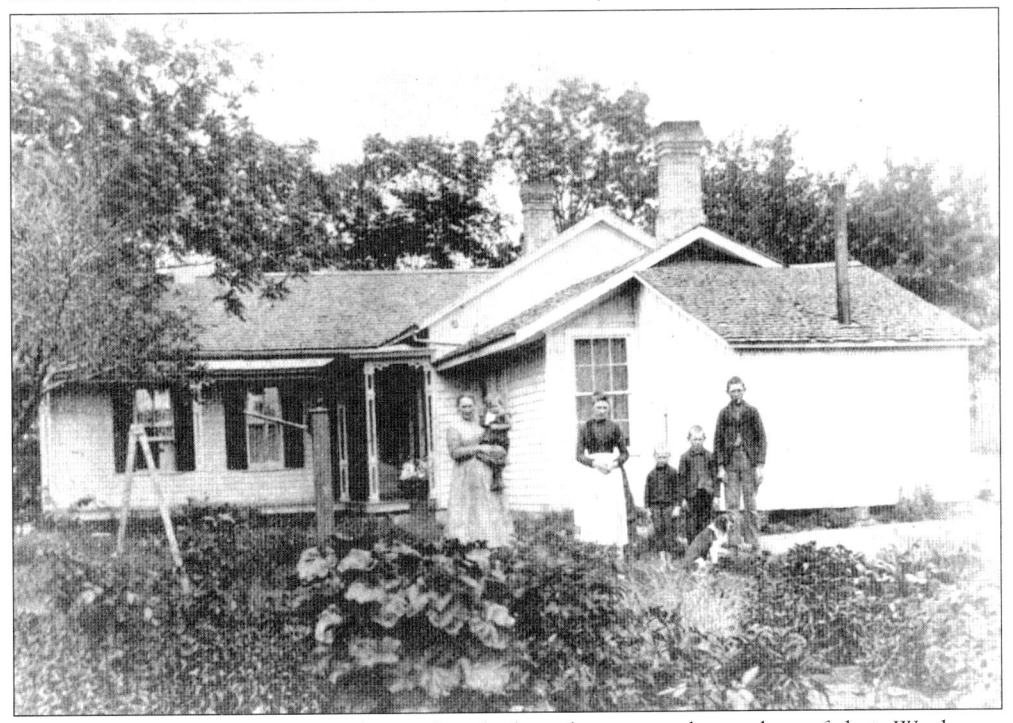

This early McHenry family stands posed with their dog out in the gardens of their Waukegan Road home. The house was built in 1859. The smokehouse, seen on the right, is attached to the kitchen for easy access. Smokehouses were used to preserve meat prior to refrigeration. (Courtesy of David Gelwicks.)

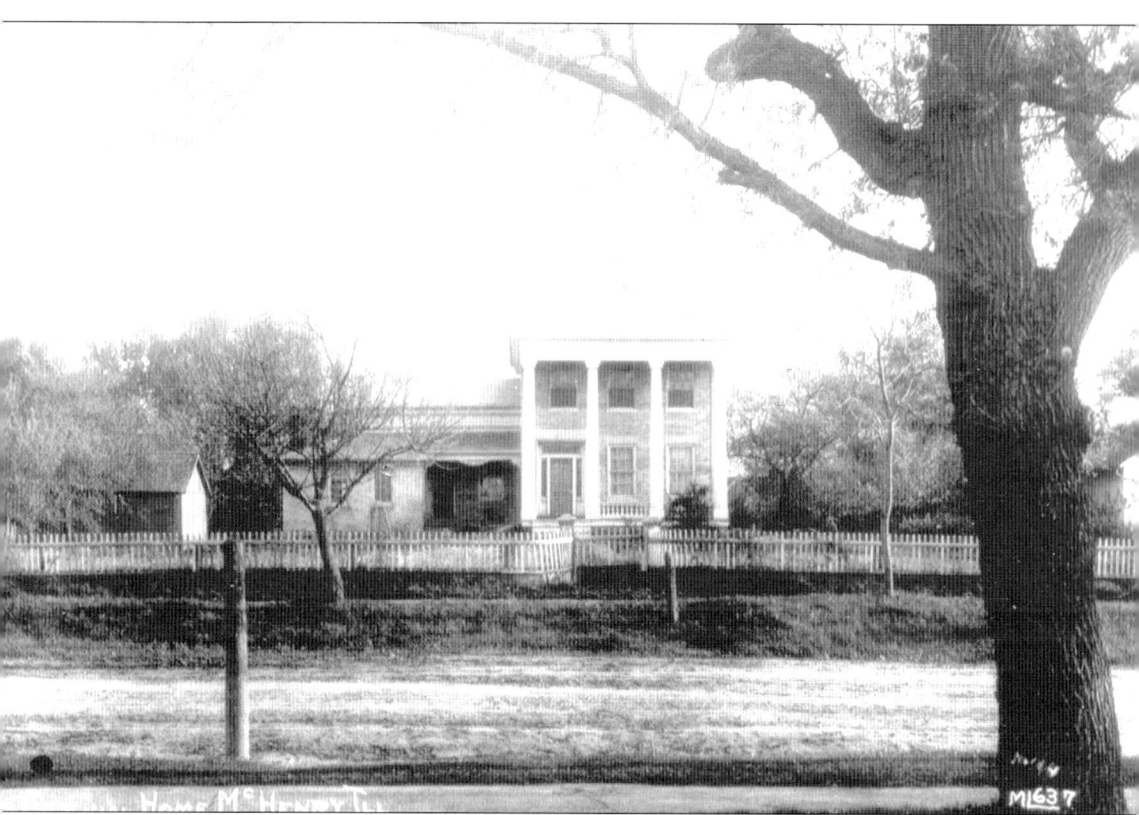

This stately Greek Revival–style house sits high on the hill commanding an outstanding view of the city. Originally built around 1860, it had two main facades, one facing Main Street, the other facing Waukegan Road. Today its official address is 3803 Waukegan Road. In its early days, the Main Street entrance was considered the front. There are several unique architectural features of this house. The six-foot double-hung windows grace the Waukegan side of the house. This house known as the Count's House was placed on the National Register of Historic Places on June 3, 1982, because of its architectural significance. It is the only building in McHenry listed in the National Register of Historic Places. (Courtesy of Marya Dixon.)

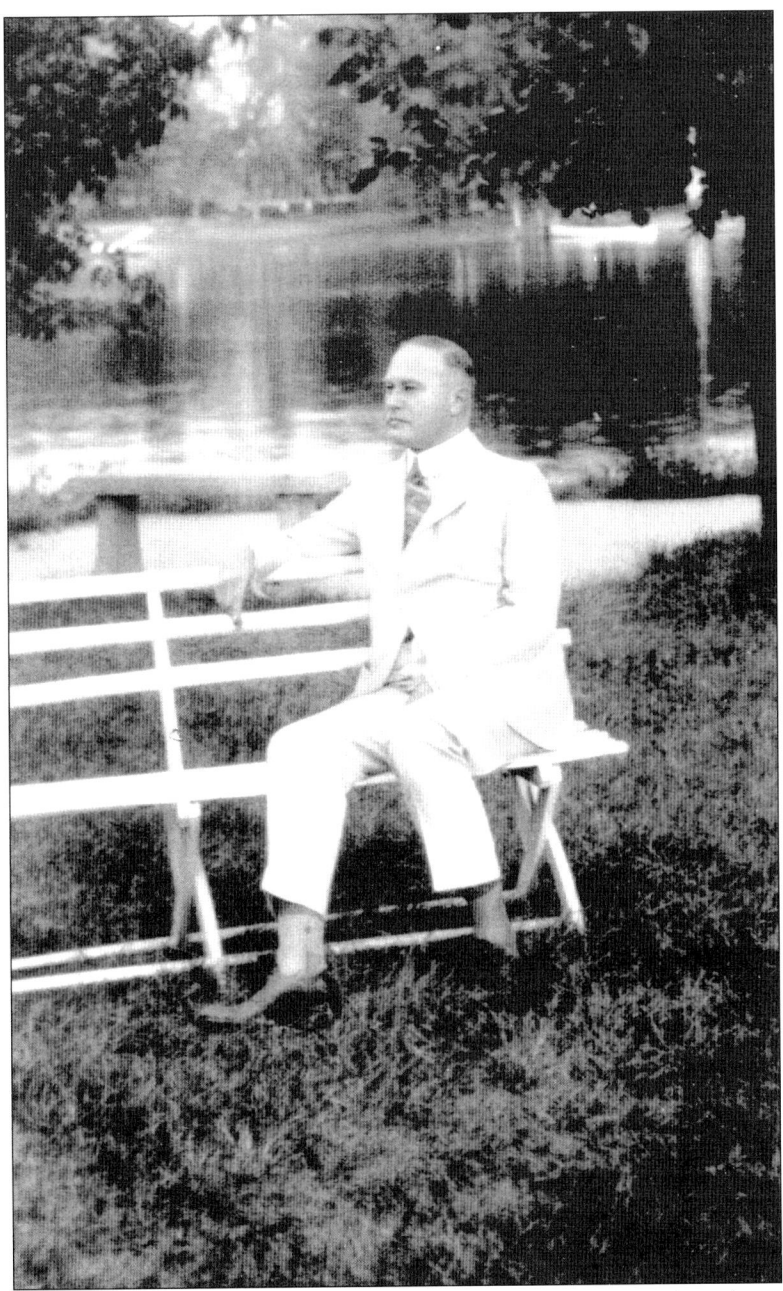

Count Oskar Bopp von Oberstand, shown here in 1918, was rumored to have been a German spy and had been imprisoned in England. After the end of World War I, he was released but not allowed to return to Germany. He, along with his American-born wife Elizabeth Schoenhoefen, came to America and settled in McHenry. It is believed that he came here to learn more about American beer production as his wife's family were well-known brewers. He purchased the pre–Civil War house on Waukegan Road where he lived with his family during his stay in McHenry. Thereafter the home was known as the Count's House. The title of count was given to him by the pope. He donated a bell to St. Patrick's Church, which has his seal engraved on it. It continues to hang in the sacristy bell tower. (Courtesy of Marya Dixon.)

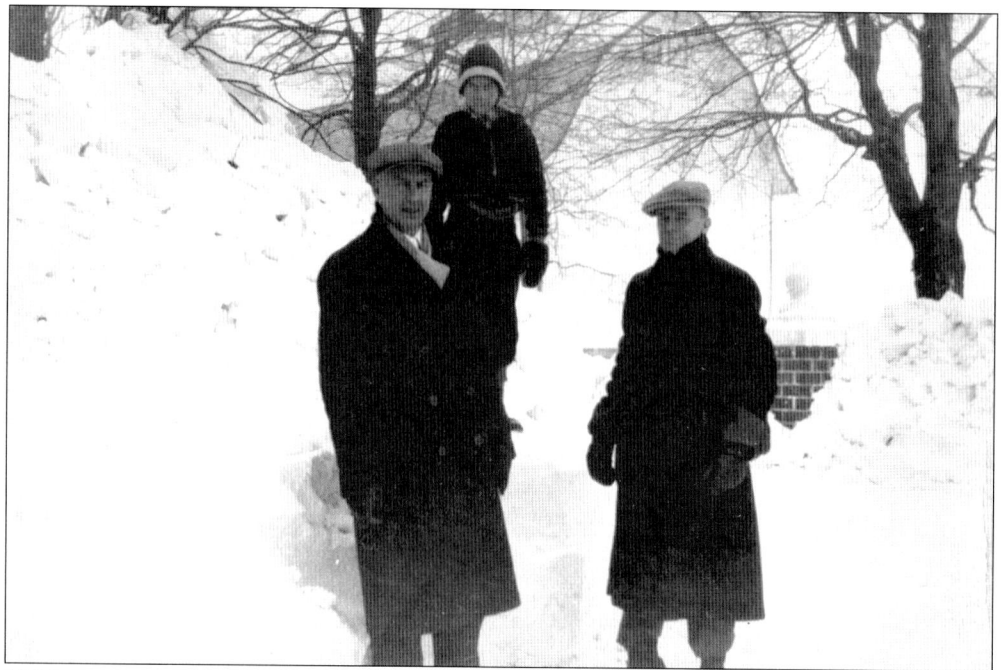

McHenry has suffered from many cold and snowy winters. The year 1936 has been described as one of the coldest with temperatures reported as low as in the 30s, that is below zero. Snow closed the roads. The rural ones remained closed for weeks at a time. In an effort to open them, a call went out for volunteers to shovel the snow for 50¢ per hour. For those who survived working a full day under these cold and snowy conditions, two meals were included. Pictured here after the snowstorm are Henry John Miller (left) and Harry Durland. The child in the rear is John Henry Miller. This photograph was taken at the corner of Elm Street and Greenwood Road. (Courtesy of John Henry Miller.)

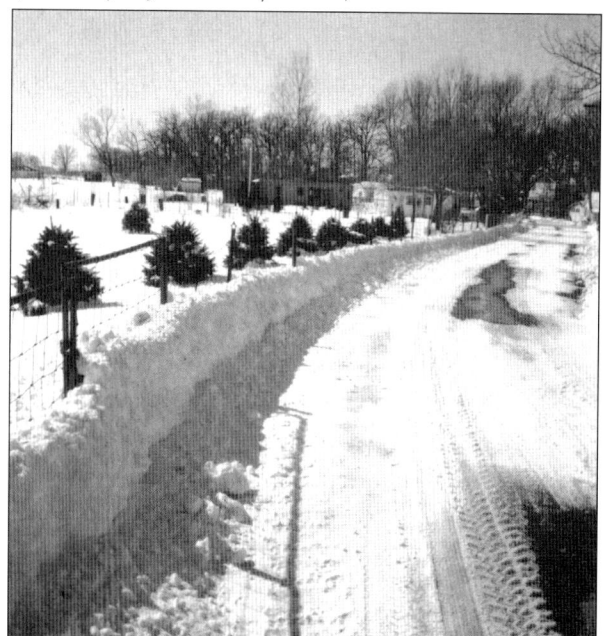

Lakewood Road along McCullom Lake did not escape the snow as this photograph from the 1930s shows. The snow would keep residents in their homes until the roads could be cleaned. Once the roads were cleared, the wall of snow along the side acted as a fence. (Courtesy of John P. Haley.)

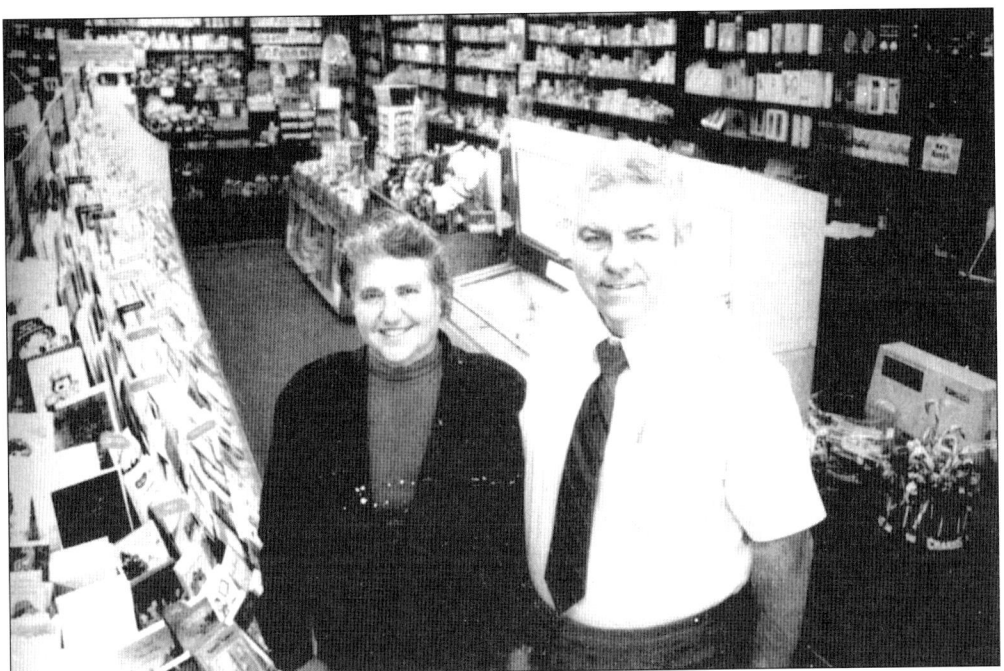

Family-owned drugstores were the rule rather than the exception until the 1970s. Bolger Drugs on Green Street opened for business in 1925 with Thomas P. Bolger as the owner/pharmacist. After Bolger's death in 1961, Donald Doherty, his nephew, took ownership of the drug store and operated it until 1989. Shown are Doherty and his wife Rosalie inside the store prior to the closing. Donald served as mayor of McHenry from 1961 to 1973. (Courtesy Donald and Rosalie Doherty.)

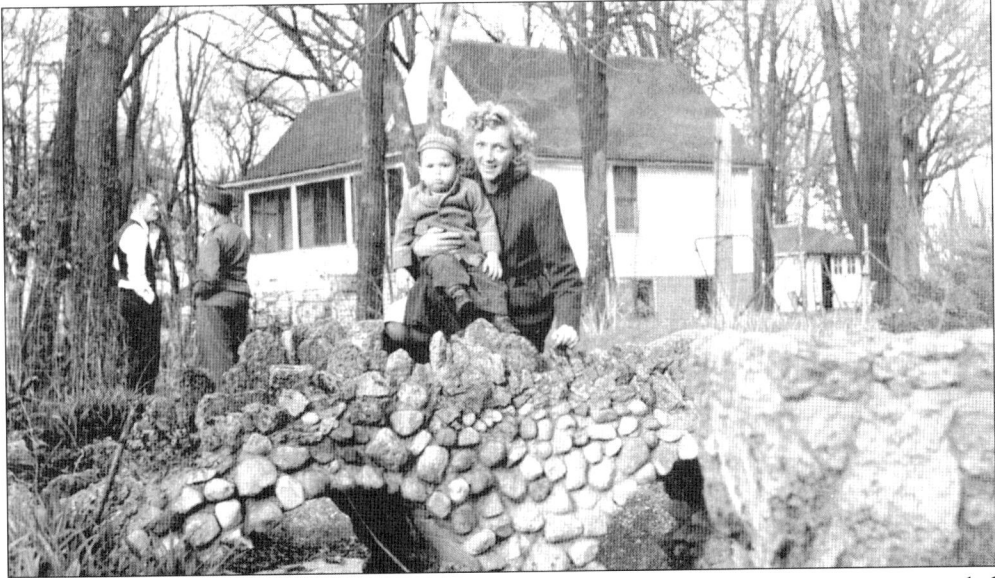

This stone and cement structure, made from the many stones found on the property, provided a decorative touch along with serving as a small bridge. It was the perfect place for Evelyn Varese to pose for a photograph with nephew Billy Marquart, while husband Ralph speaks to the unidentified man on the left. (Courtesy of Debra Gust.)

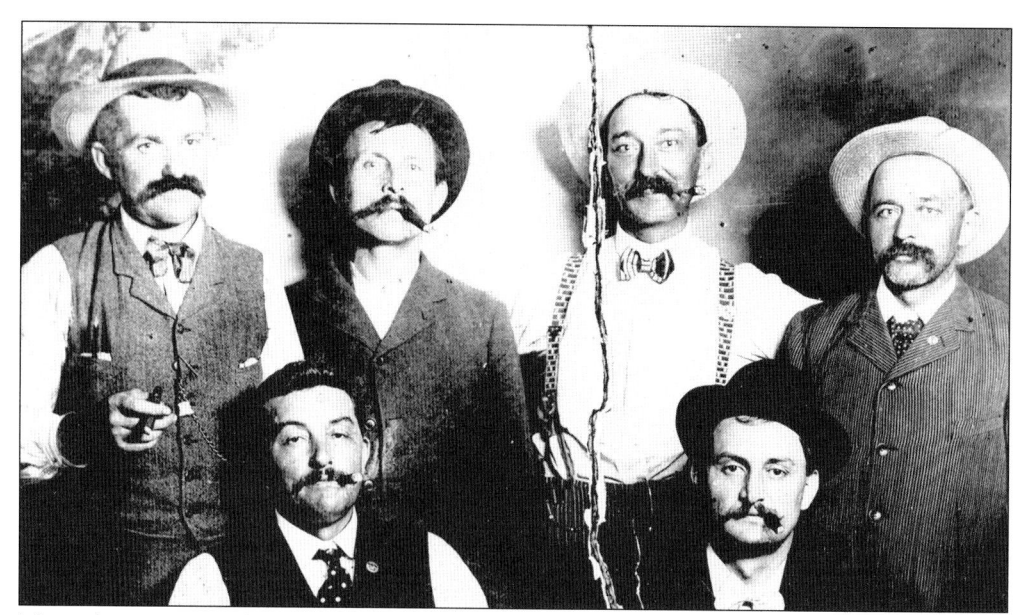

Mustaches were popular in the late 1800s and early 1900s as seen in this photograph of local businessmen. Seen here from left to right are (first row) John Heimer and Henry Heimer; (second row) John Miller, Ben Laurie, Joe Troth, and George Meyers. (Courtesy of the McHenry Public Library.)

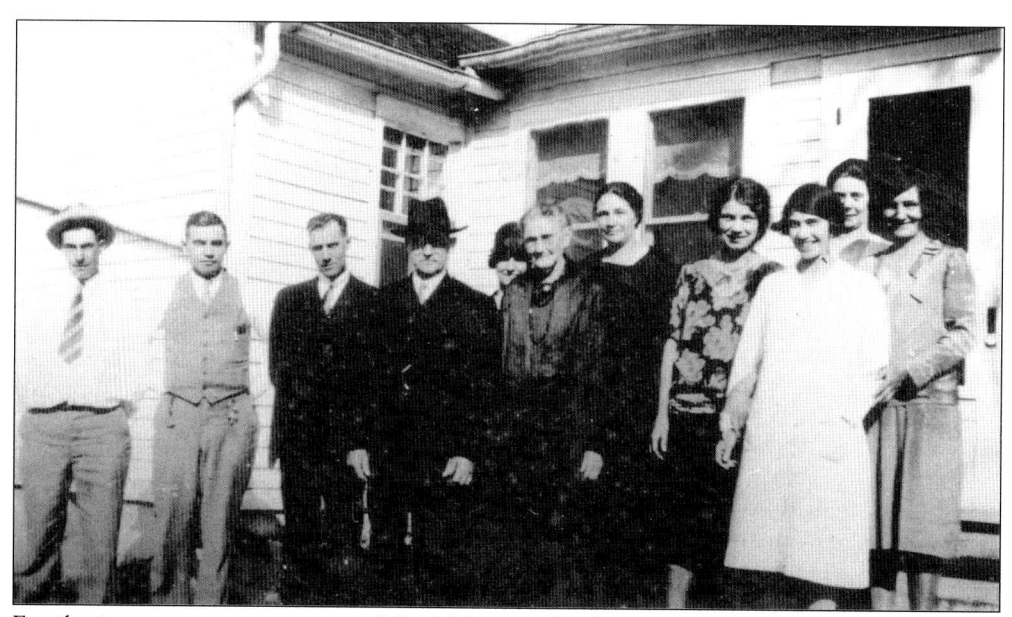

Family ties were strong in many of the McHenry families. Here the extended Althoff family stands posed in front of a family home in 1925. (Courtesy of James Althoff.)

Three
Life on the Fox River

As early as the late 1800s, visitors came to McHenry for recreational activities. Swimming, boating, and fishing drew many visitors. For some, other recreational activities enticed them. Having a beer in a local tavern (according to legend, even during prohibition), playing the slot machines found in many businesses, or visiting the local book maker to place your bets brought others. Card games could be found in many back rooms. In the evening, music from local taverns or from the dance pavilion located on the east side of the Fox River permeated the air.

Along the river, boats were plentiful transporting visitors up to Pistakee Bay, the lotus beds in Grass Lake, or just taking a leisurely ride. Even mail was delivered by boat to houses and resorts along the river. Along the shore, swimmers, or bathers as they were called at that time, frolicked in the water. Fishermen cast their lines from the shores or fished from their boats.

Houses were built up along the banks of the river, some large and lavish, others small little weekend cottages. Resorts varying from one or two cottages to large health resorts or sanatoriums provided a place to stay and enjoy the country air for the many Chicagoans who made their way by automobile or train. Hotels and other local business thrived as visitors partied and shopped.

But nothing stays the same. Eventually the lotus beds died out. Transportation to the other lakes became easier as better roads and trains made their way. McHenry was no longer a primary recreation destination.

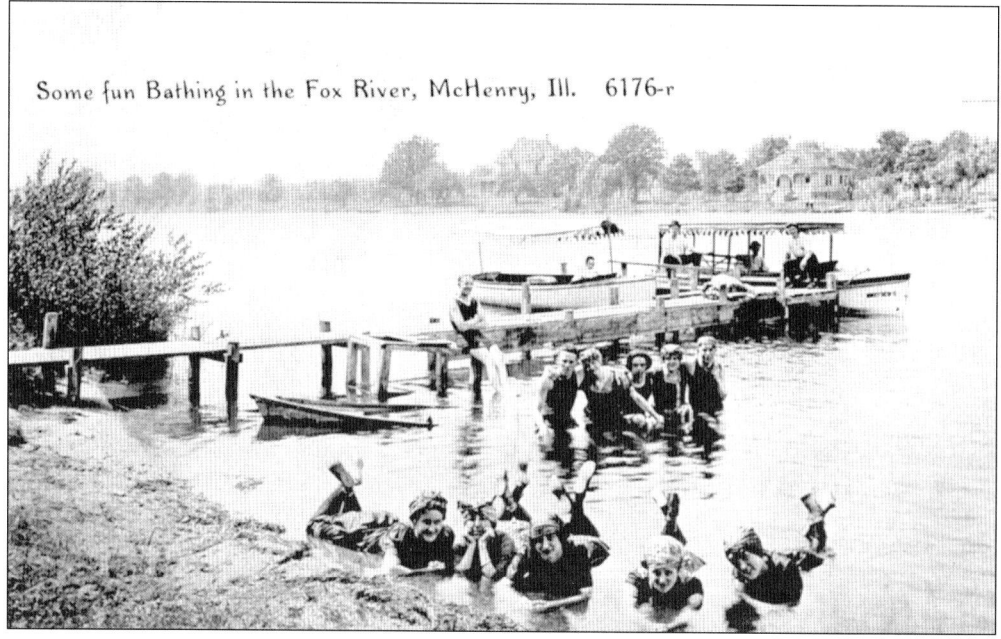

Some fun Bathing in the Fox River, McHenry, Ill. 6176-r

For many Chicagoans, a trip to McHenry in the summer was a vacation. It was a time to get away from the heat and grime of the city and enjoy an afternoon in the country. Here a group of people are enjoying swimming in the Fox River. (Courtesy of Patricia Schafer.)

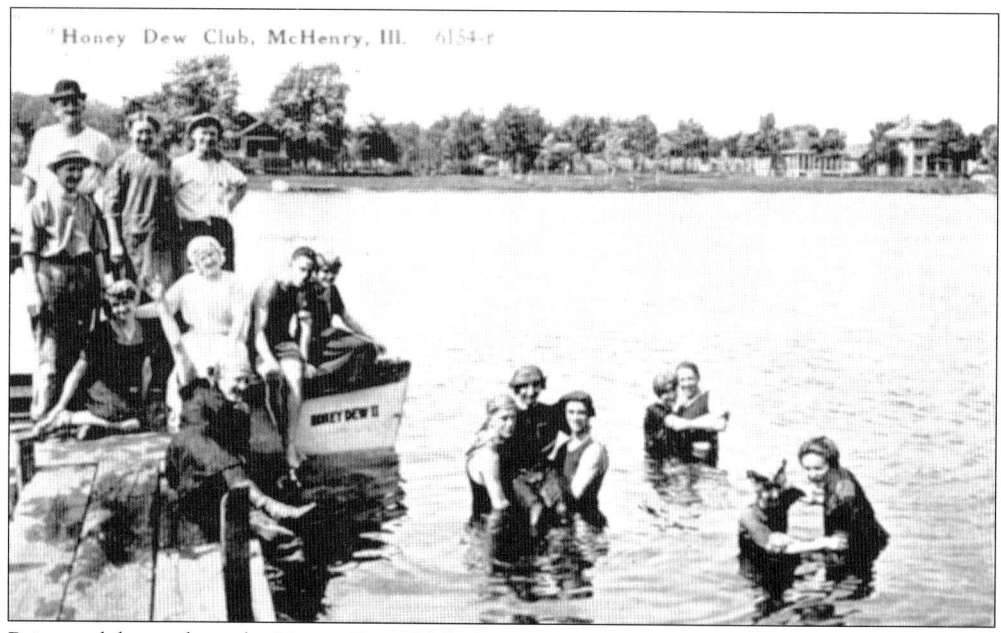

Honey Dew Club, McHenry, Ill. 6154-r

Private clubs, such as the Honey Dew Club shown here, could be found along the river. Often these were individual houses, purchased by a family or group of friends from the city who shared the cost and use of the property. Often on summer weekends, the entire extended family would meet out at the river. (Courtesy of Michael Clark.)

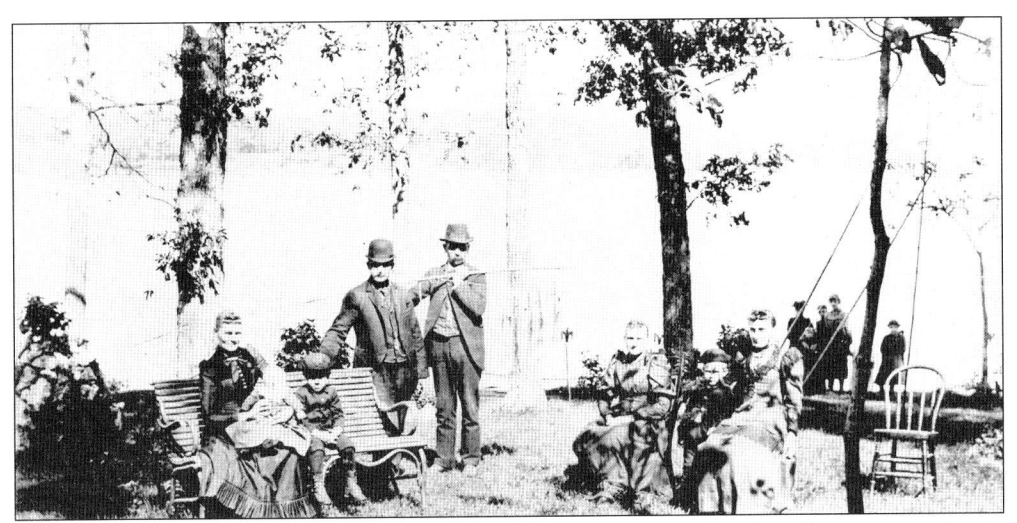

In this late 1800s photograph, local families spend an afternoon at Pistakee Bay enjoying the air and the scenery. Swimming is not on their agenda as they are dressed in their Sunday clothing. Pictured are Mrs. Michael Freund holding infant daughter Rose, and son John. Michael Freund stands leaning against the bench while Michael Justen balances a long pole. Could it be a fishing pole? Seated on the right are Kathryn Justen, Henry Freund, and Barbara Regner. (Courtesy of the McHenry Public Library.)

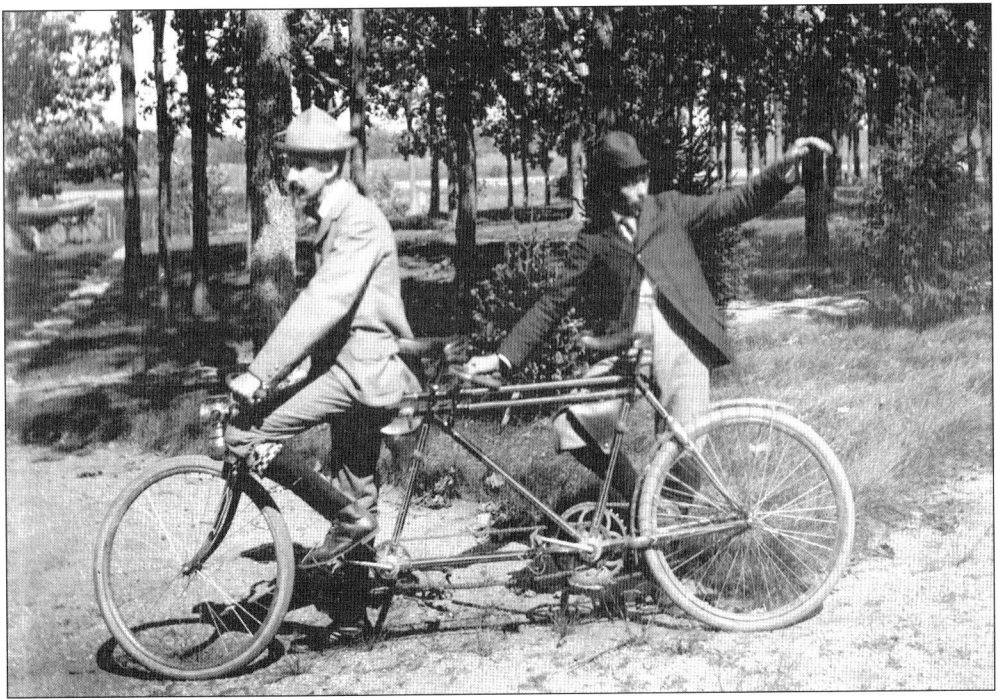

These two unidentified gentlemen are spending a leisurely day biking along the Fox River dressed in suit, tie, and hat. Often visitors spent their free time enjoying the outdoor scenery. (Courtesy of the McHenry Public Library.)

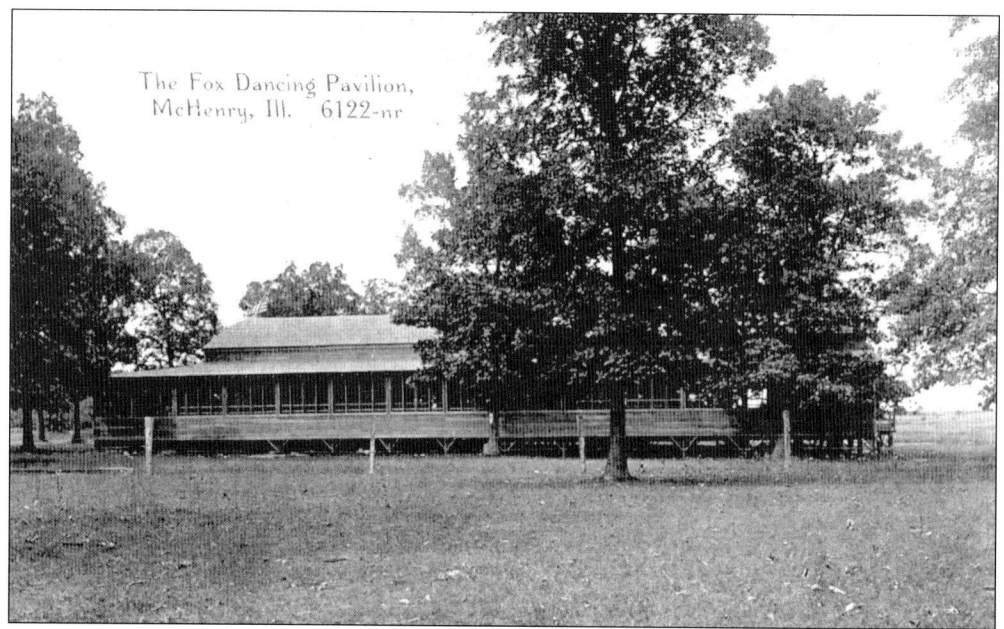

On warm summer evenings in the Roaring Twenties, men and women headed for the Fox Dance Pavilion, on the east side of the Fox River, to see and be seen and to enjoy dancing to a live band. There was an admission charge of 50¢ and an additional charge of 10¢ a dance. Those who could not afford the fees could be found dancing out on the lawn. This was a popular place until it burned down in the 1930s. Another dance pavilion was constructed on Route 31, south of Main Street but it never attracted the same large crowds. (Courtesy of Patricia Schafer.)

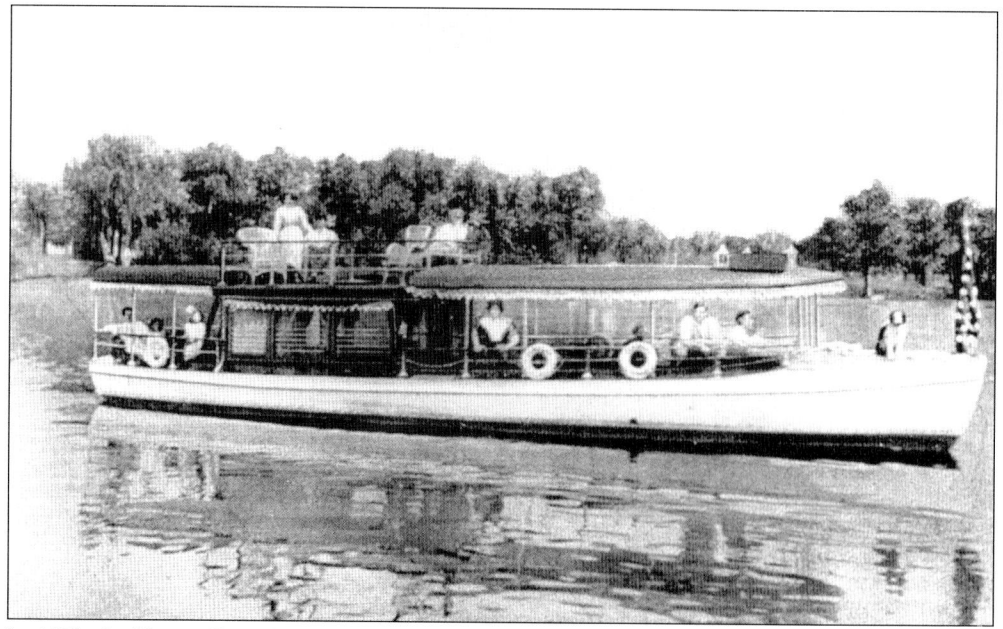

In 1912, the Hunter Boat Company launched passenger service daily up the Fox River to Pistakee Bay and to the lotus beds of Grass Lake. Round trip fare was 50¢. This boat, the *Gladene*, was one of the excursion boats that was built by the Hunter Company. (Courtesy of Shirley Klapperich.)

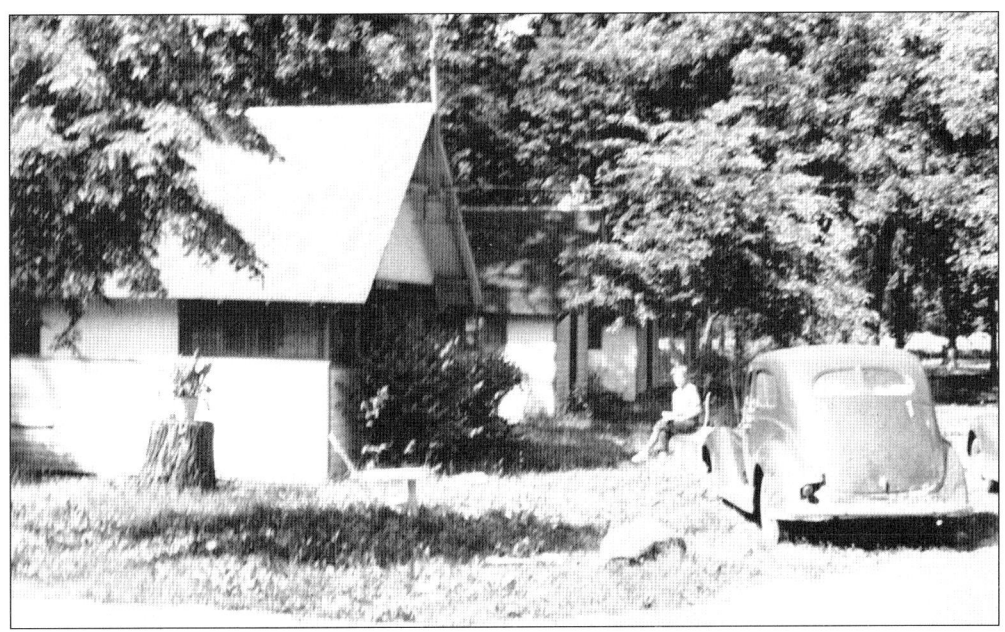

The influx of many summer and weekend visitors led to the growth of many resorts along the Fox River. Some were large and lavish; others were more moderate like these small cabins. The cabins along the river were rented out by the week, the month, or for the whole summer, or used by family members. Pictured above is the Rosedale Resort, one of the many small resorts along the river, with owner Evelyn Varese, sitting on the automobile on the right. The bottom photograph shows the same resort with the family home in the foreground. (Courtesy of Debra Gust.)

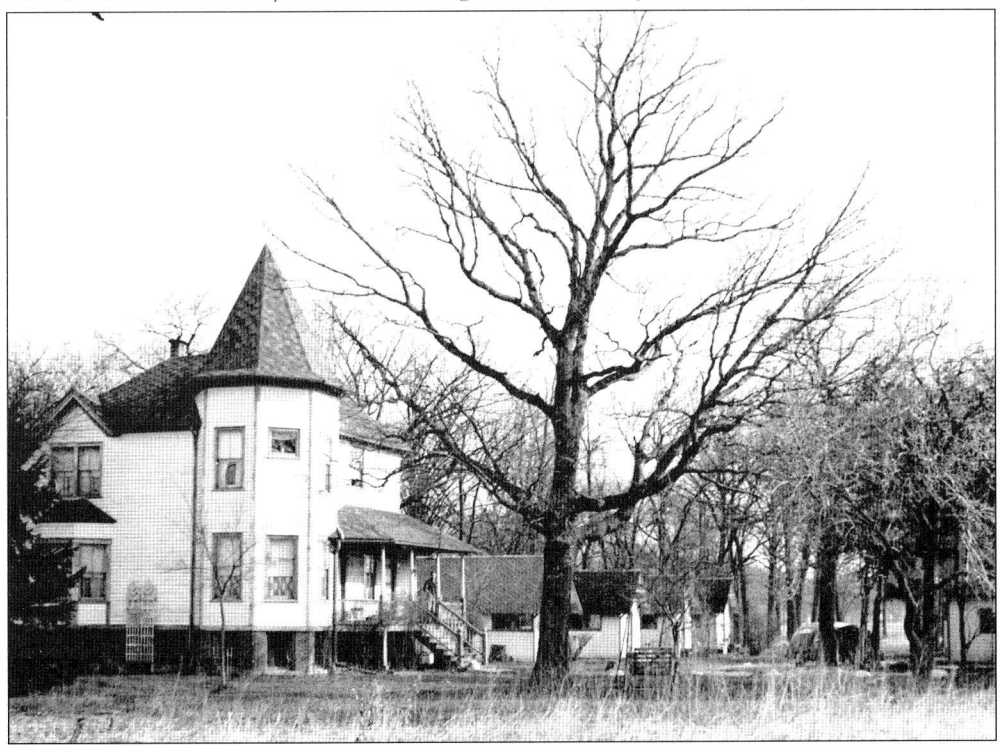

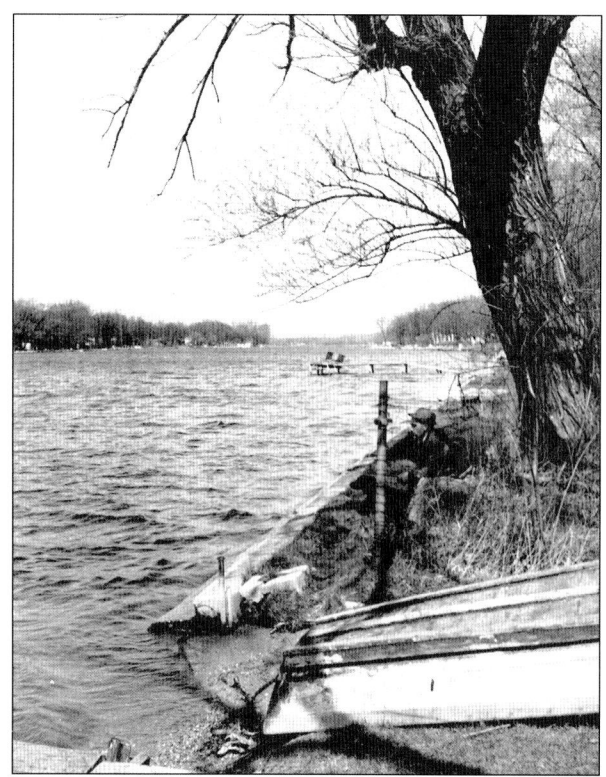

This view of the Fox River, looking north towards Pistakee Bay, shows a peaceful river as it stretches to the horizon. No boats are present at this time disturbing the waters with their wakes. It is a peaceful place for a man and his dog to sit quietly and appreciate the beauty and silence of nature. (Courtesy of Debra Gust.)

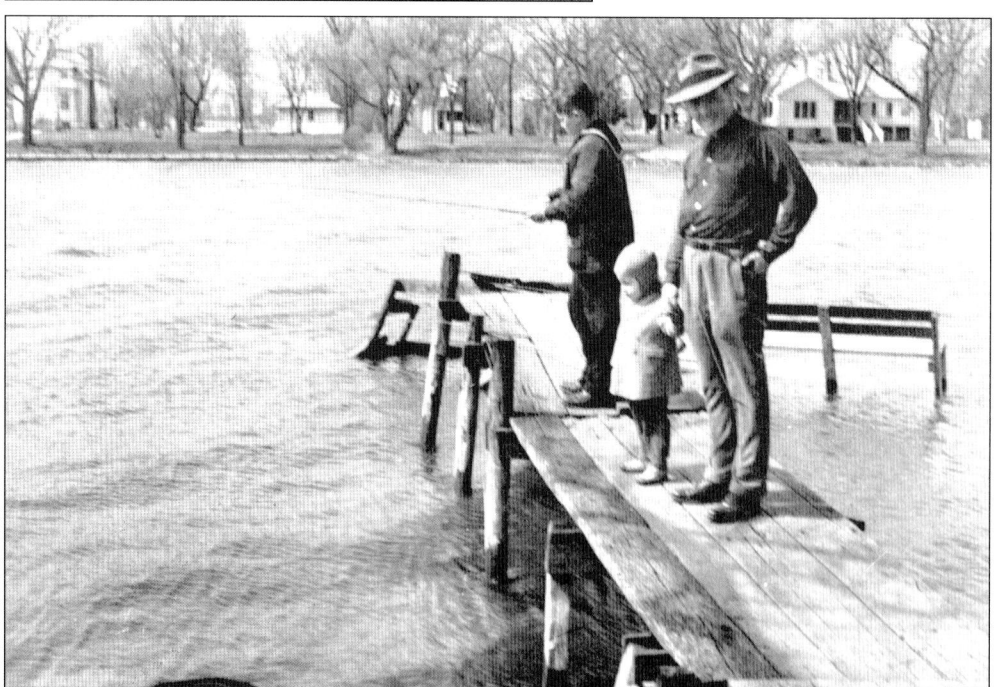

Along the Fox River there were many piers such as this one used to dock the owner's boats. It is a place to stand and view the river or to toss in a fishing line. Ralph Varese holds the hand of Billy Marquart as he peers into the river. (Courtesy of Debra Gust.)

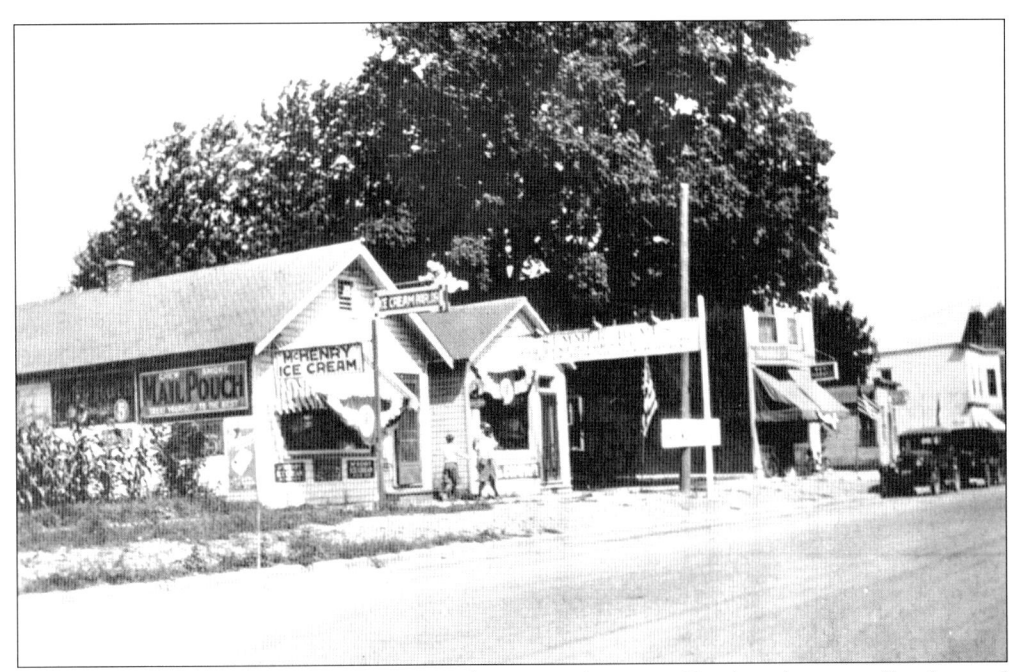

Looking to rent or buy a summer home in the 1920s? A visit to Kent's real estate office (second from left) on Riverside Drive was in order. Cottages along the river and some along McCullom Lake were available to visitors for their summer vacation. On a hot day, a stop at the ice-cream parlor (far left) was often needed. (Courtesy of the McHenry County Historical Society.)

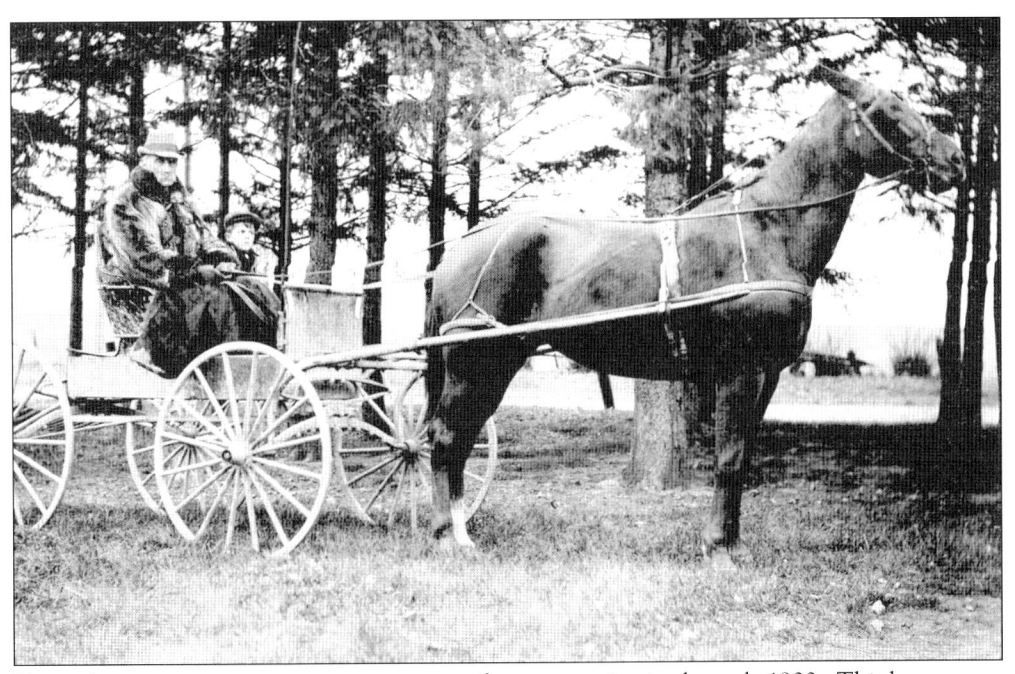

Horse-drawn carriages were common means of transportation in the early 1900s. This horse poses regally for his photograph. It must be a chilly day as the gentleman driving this carriage is wearing a fur coat. He is accompanied by a young boy, seen to his left. (Courtesy of Ilene Wiedemann.)

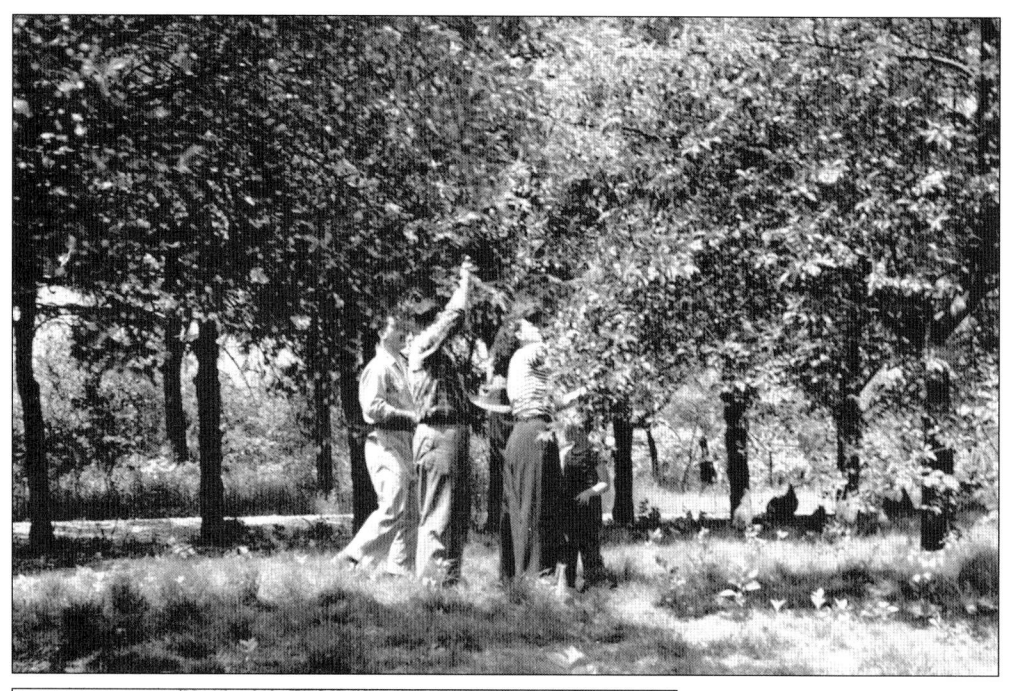

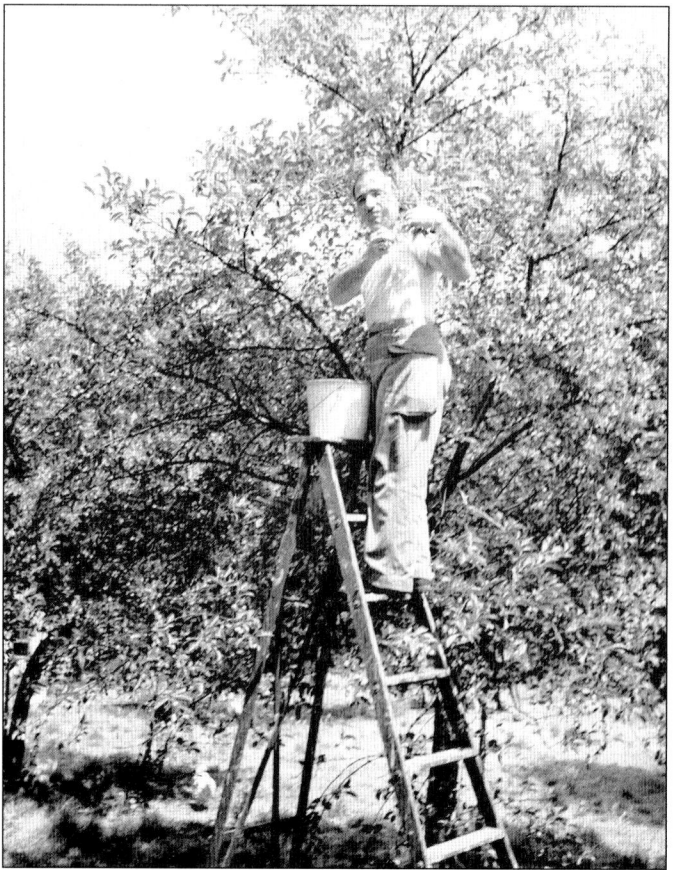

An orchard of apple and cherry trees grew well along the river. Picking the fruit when ripe was a family affair. Visitors from the city often joined in to harvest the fruit. The above photograph depicts, from left to right, John Varese, Ralph Varese, Neil Varese Baczynski, and Ralph Varese Jr. picking the apples. Can a hot apple pie be in the future? At left, Tony Varese, owner of the Rosedale Resort, climbs the ladder to pick cherries, a much more labor intensive job. Maybe it will be a cherry pie for dinner. (Courtesy of Debra Gust.)

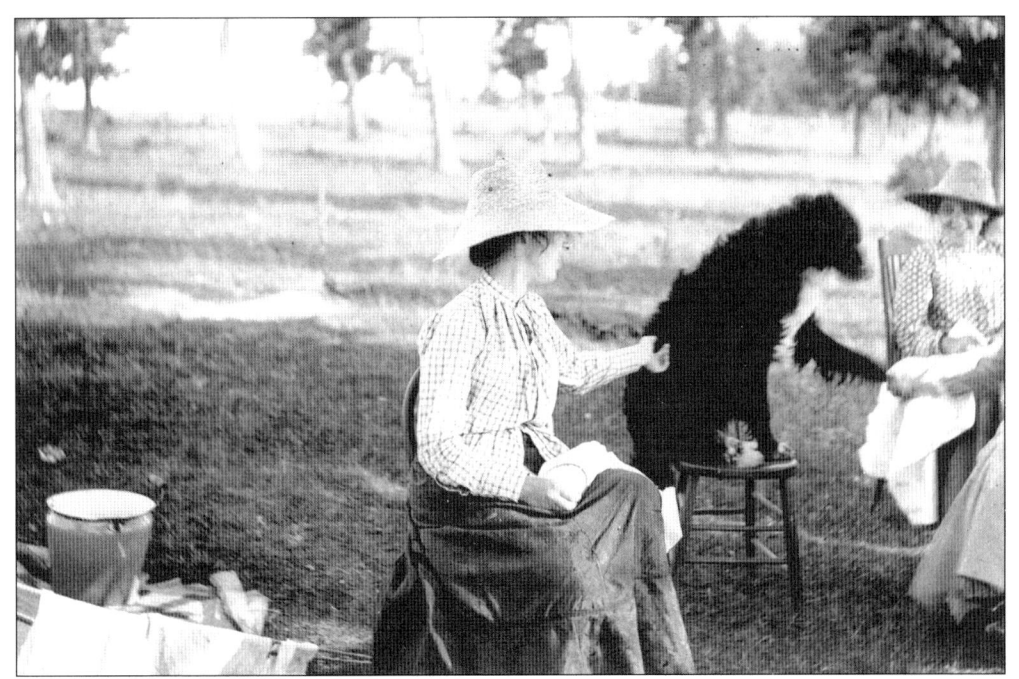

Summertime was a good time for a picnic in the country. Even the family dog was included in this outing. The large brimmed hats and long sleeved blouses kept the sun off the faces and arms of these women who spent their time visiting and working on their sewing projects. (Courtesy of the McHenry Public Library.)

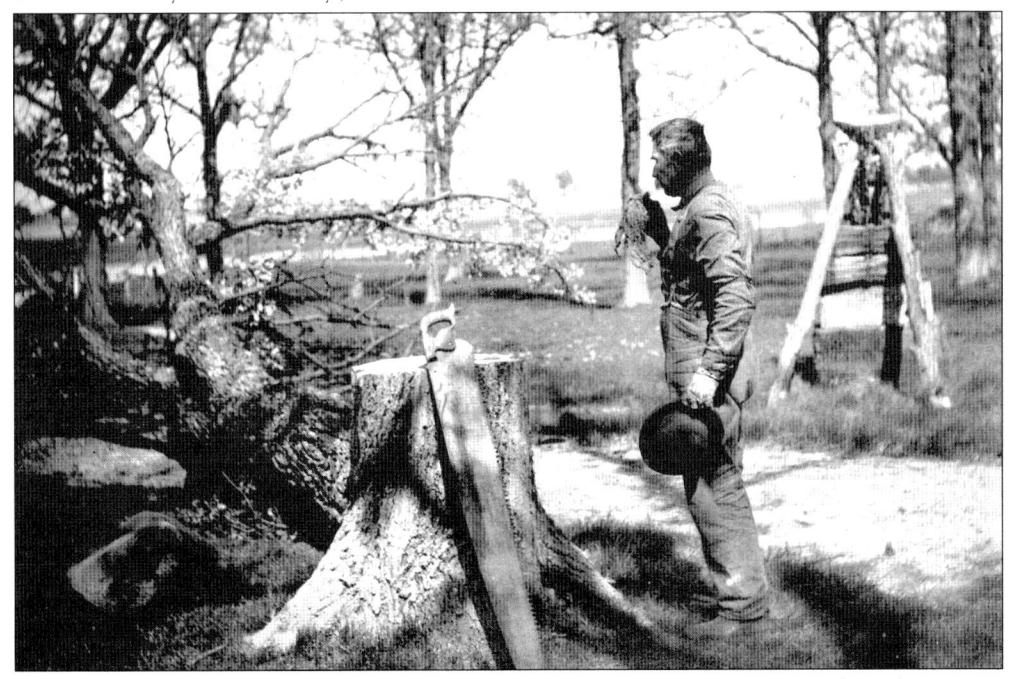

This gentleman seems to have had a busy day sawing down this large tree with nothing more than a handsaw. He is pictured taking a well deserved break and drink. This photograph was taken in 1900 along the Fox River. (Courtesy of the McHenry Public Library.)

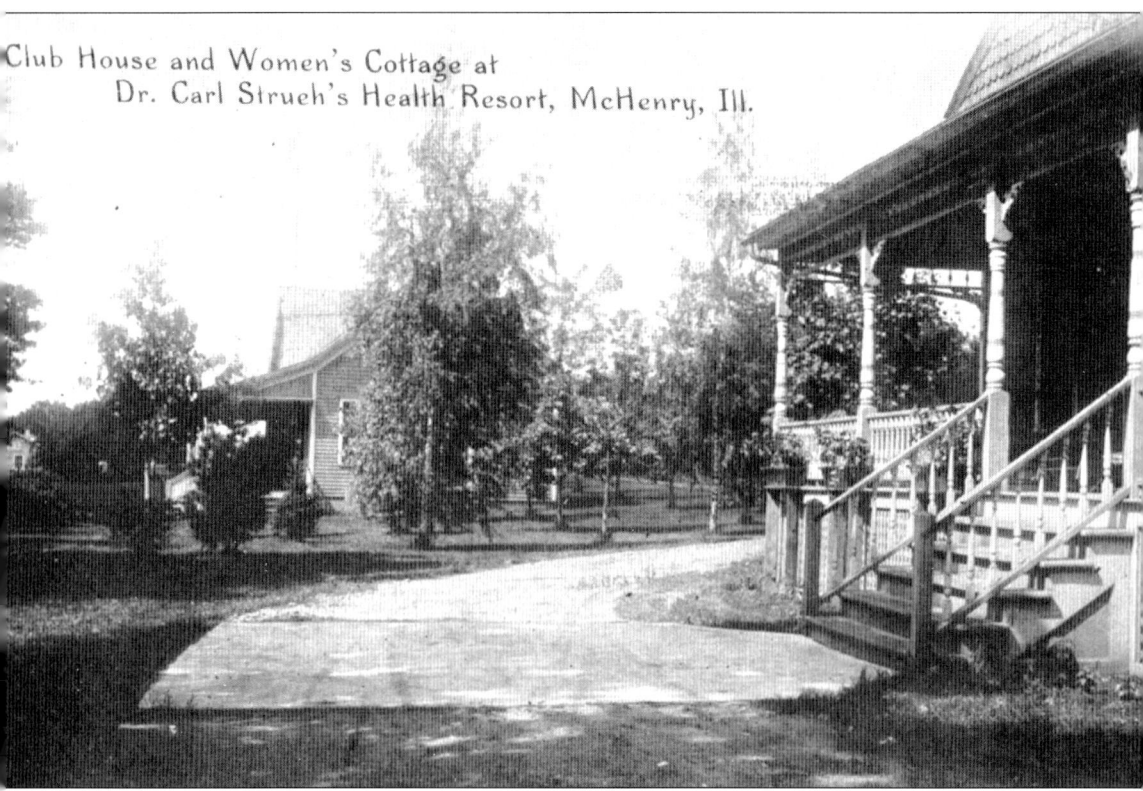

Club House and Women's Cottage at Dr. Carl Strueh's Health Resort, McHenry, Ill.

Located on the west side of the Fox River, slightly north of downtown McHenry, stood Dr. Carl Strueh's Health Resort. Strueh was a Chicago physician who believed that many illnesses could be treated with time in the country away from the dust and smoke of the city. He opened his health resort in 1907 and attempted to treat many health problems, including nervous disorders, gout, tuberculosis, allergies, obesity, drug poisoning, and stomach and bowel disorders. (Courtesy of Michael Clark.)

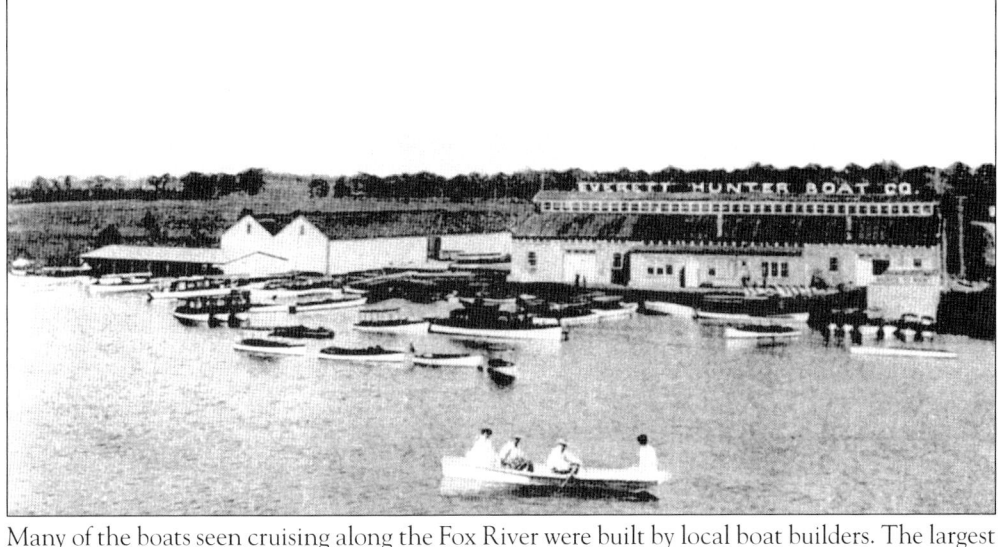

Many of the boats seen cruising along the Fox River were built by local boat builders. The largest among them was the Hunter Boat Company, known for their solid mahogany crafts. The large imposing building on the east side of the Fox River at Pearl Street was a familiar sight to those boating up and down the river. Hunter also built and ran the excursion boats that went up to Chain O' Lakes, employing many local people. In the summer, Hunter also sponsored boat races and supplied the trophies. Many of the boats that would participate in the races were Hunter products. (Courtesy of the McHenry County Historical Society.)

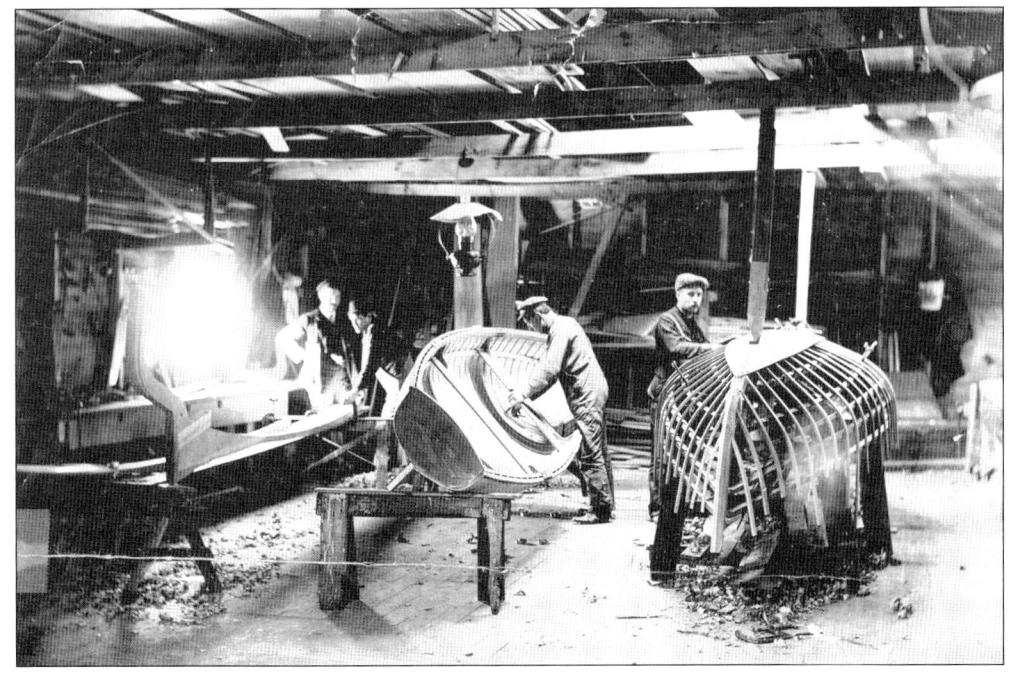

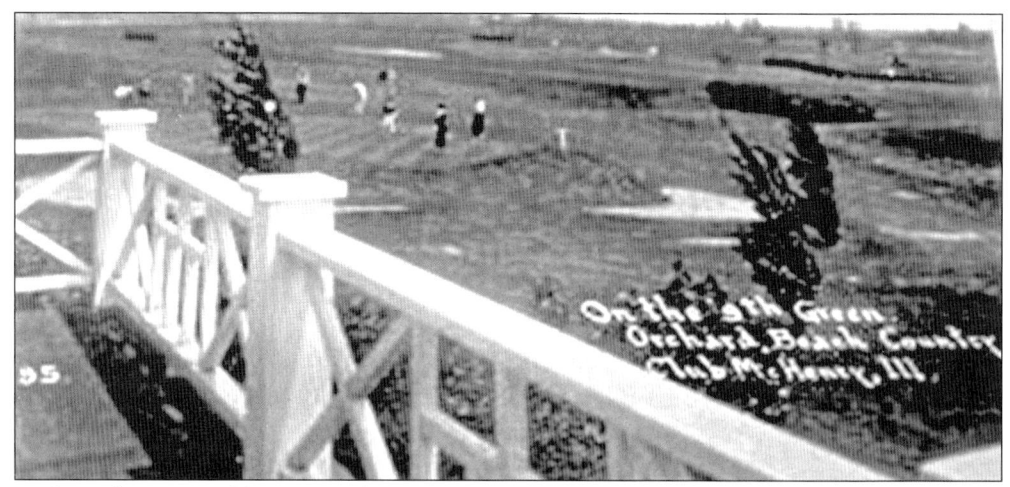

In the early 1900s, golf was a popular activity in McHenry. Many of the popular resorts attracted visitors because of the presence of their golf courses. This view of the ninth hole shows a group of golfers out on what appears to be a very windy day. Note the trees bending to the left. (Courtesy of Michael Clark.)

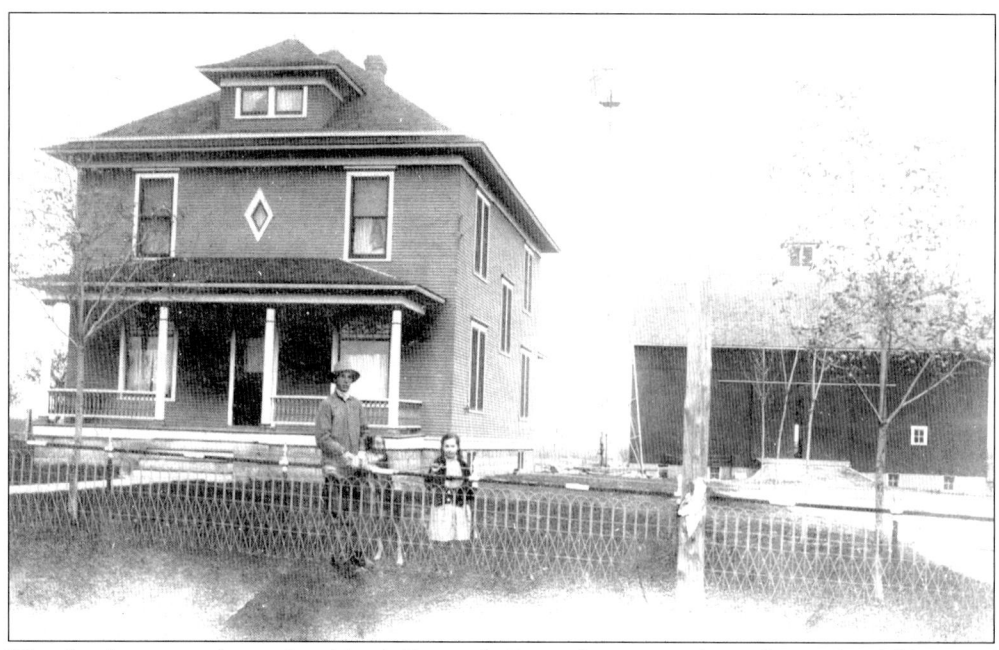

This farmhouse was located on North Riverside Drive. It was transformed into the clubhouse of the Orchard Beach Golf Club and Resort. The golf club was a popular place for visitors to stay and play during the early years of the 1900s. (Courtesy of Henry Buch.)

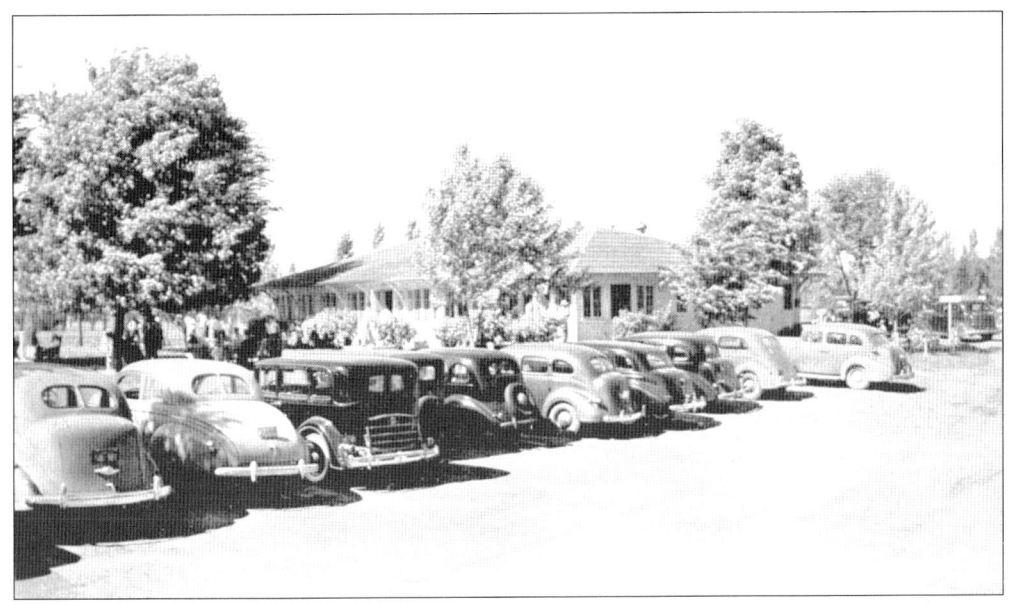

McHenry Country Club has been part of the McHenry scene since 1922, when it was established as a private nine-hole golf club. The original clubhouse was a 14-by-30-foot structure that was erected in one day by three men. It contained a lunch counter and restrooms. In 1926, an additional nine holes were added, making it a full 18-hole course. The current clubhouse was built in 1953 and continues to undergo remodeling as needed. (Courtesy of Patricia Schafer.)

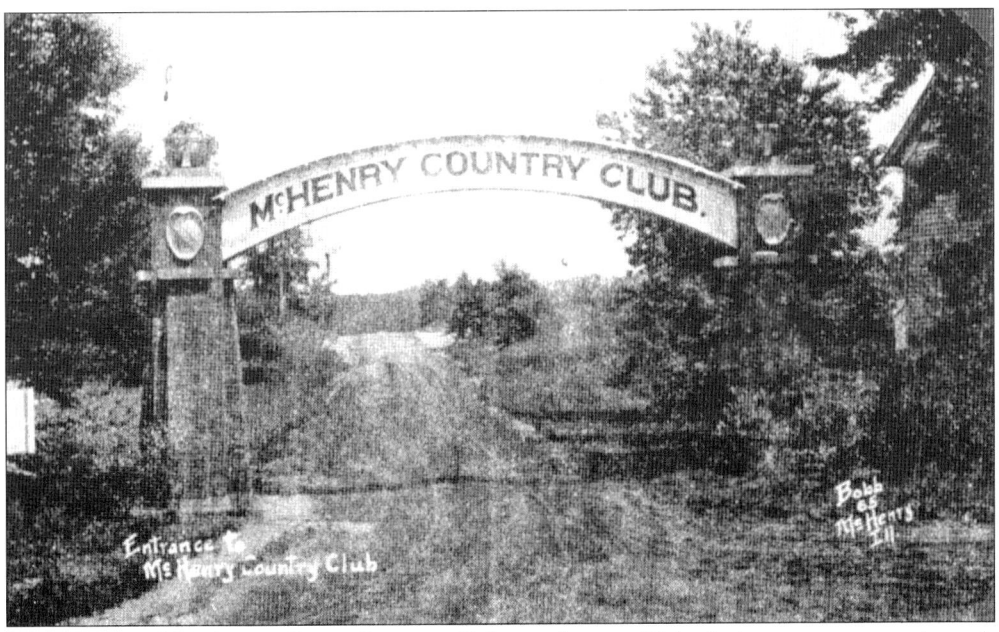

In the 1920s when the McHenry Country Club was first established, the entrance was through this wooden arch. The street is John Street, which was unpaved and often presented a muddy entrance to the club. (Courtesy of John Baumgartner.)

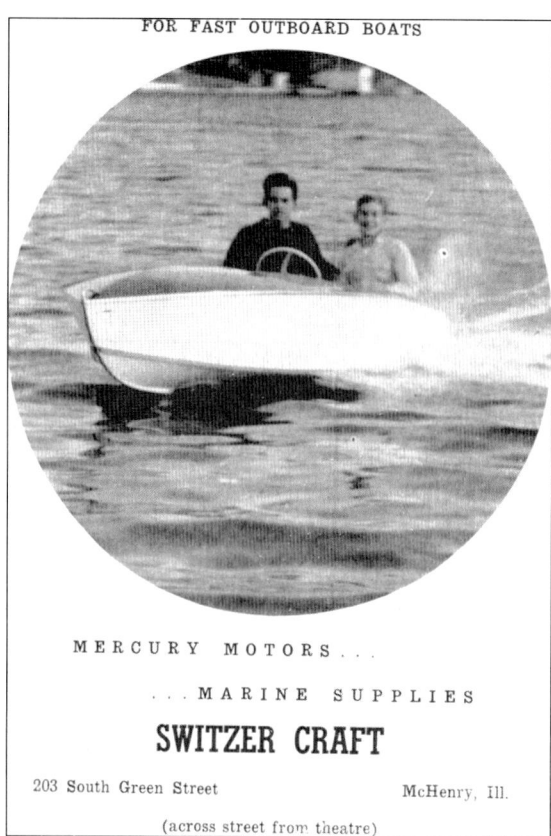

The Hunter Boat Company was not the only boat company in town. The Switzer Boat Company built their boats in the basement of Gladstone's Department Store. This Switzer advertisement is from the 1940s. (Courtesy of Joan Wirtz.)

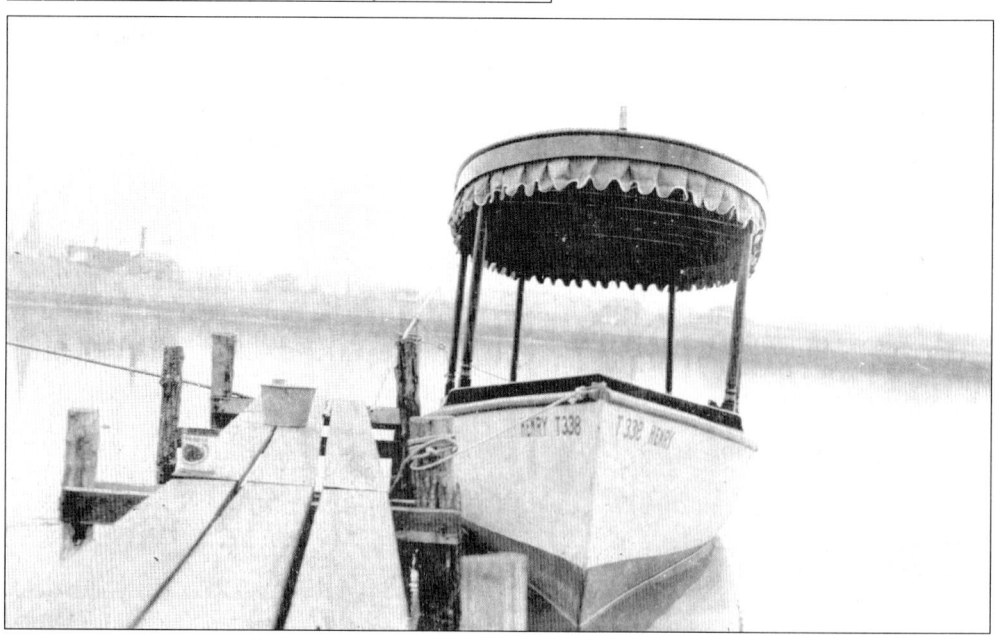

This pleasure boat is tied up at the dock, waiting for visitors to take a ride. In the late 1800s and early 1900s, many of these boats could be found cruising up and down the river. The awning on top helps to keep the hot summer sun off the riders. (Courtesy of Henry Buch.)

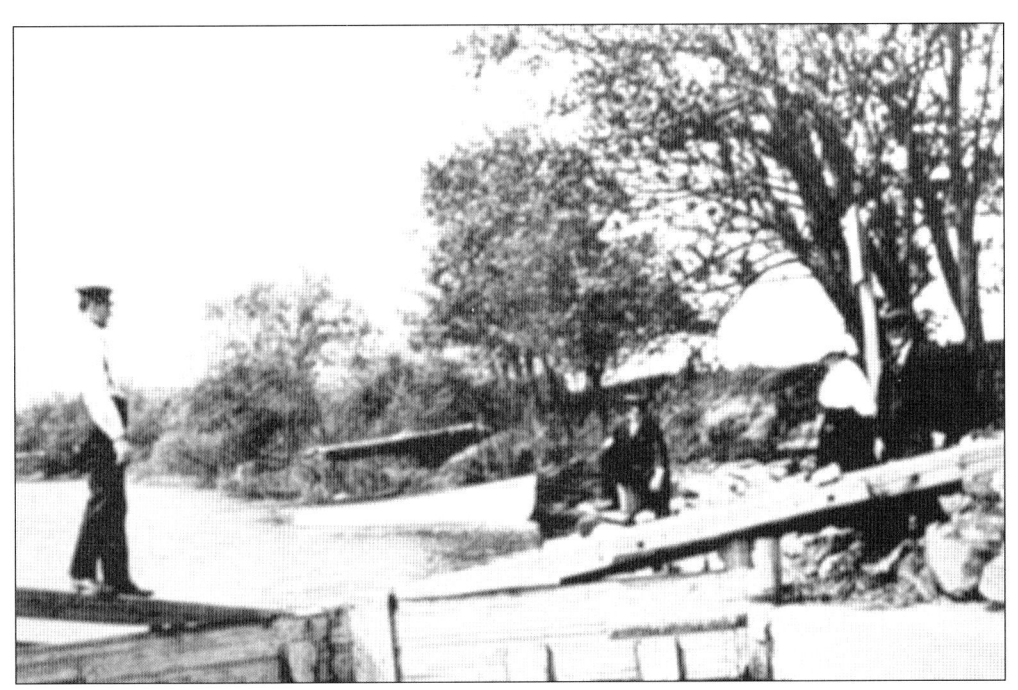

The dam was first built of wood about three miles south of McHenry in 1907 by the Fox River Navigable Waterway Association. The cost of operating the dam was beyond the financial abilities of the group. In 1923, they deeded it over to the State of Illinois. By the late 1930s, this dam became unstable. The State of Illinois contracted for a concrete structure to replace the old dam in 1939. By 1957, increased boat traffic along the river along with public interest in using the river for recreational purposes, led to a public hearing on building a lock. In 1960, the new lock was opened and remains one of the busiest in the state. (Above, courtesy of Michael Clark; right, courtesy of Priscilla Rutter.)

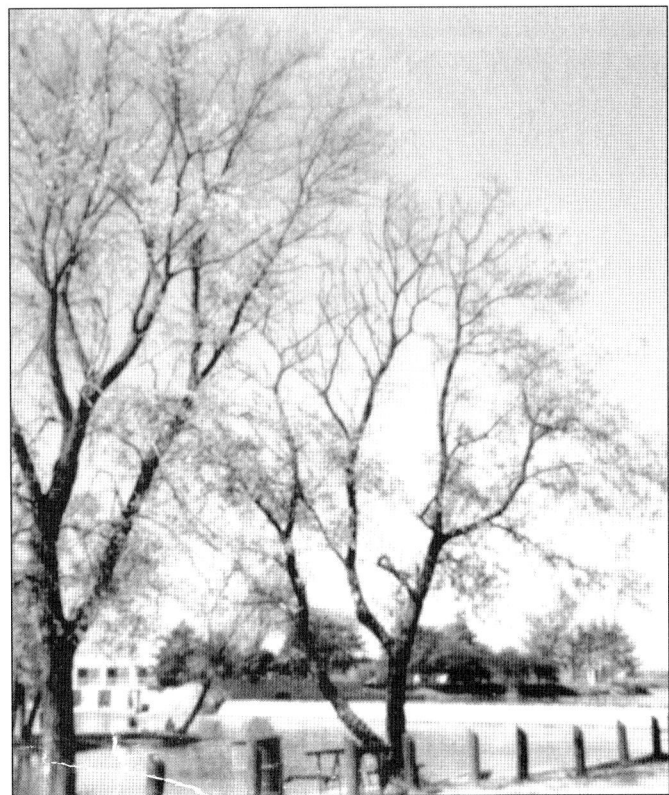

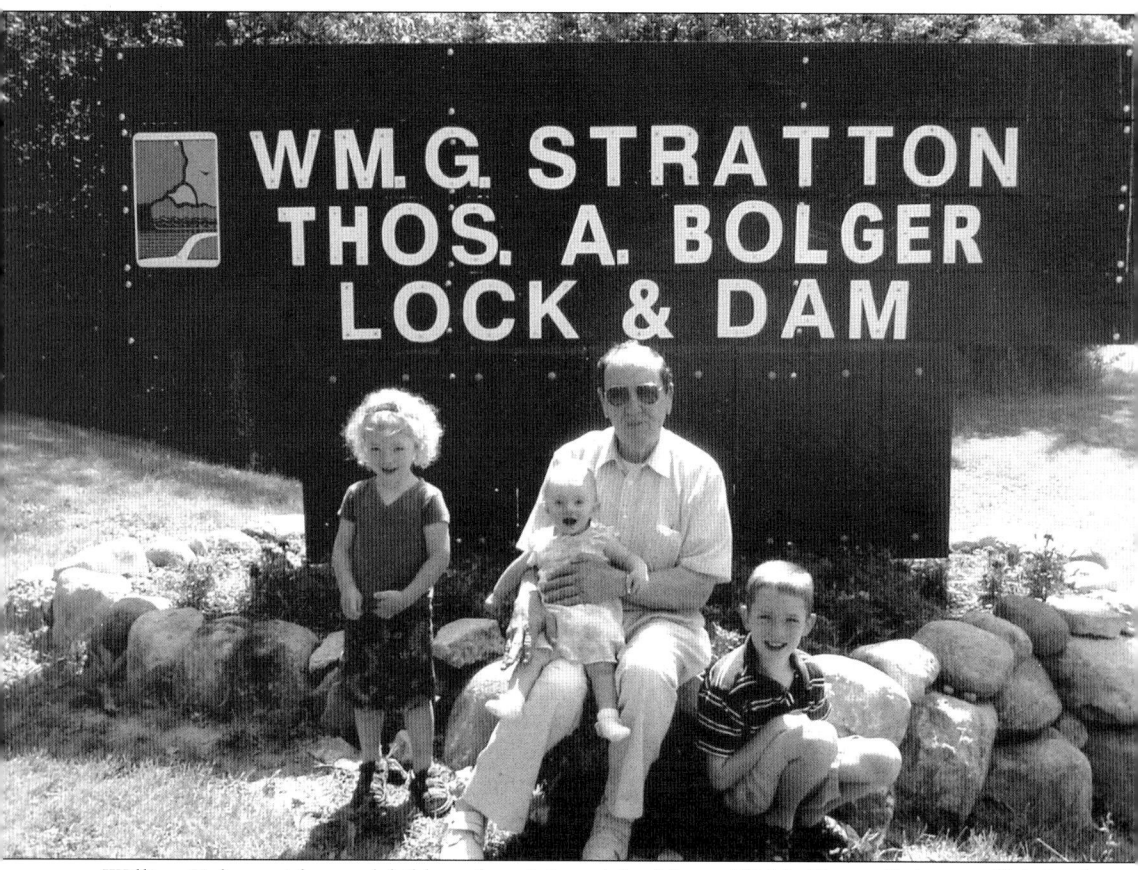

William Bolger, with grandchildren, from left to right, Megan Walsh, Trinity Bolger, and Michael Walsh, sits in front of the sign that commemorates the naming of the McHenry Lock and Dam after former governor William G. Stratton and Bolger's father, Thomas A. Bolger. Thomas A. Bolger was a longtime state senator. (Courtesy of William Bolger.)

Four
SERVING THE PEOPLE

While the City of McHenry has run summer recreation programs since the 1930s, it was not until August 1979 that the city officially created the McHenry City Parks and Recreation Department with Pete Merkel as the director, a position he still maintains. During his tenure, the department has continued to acquire more parklands and has started new programs and festivals to serve the people of McHenry.

The McHenry Fire Protection District was officially formed in 1939. It began as a volunteer district and today remains staffed with part-time fire fighters. Since its founding in 1939 with Gus Freund as the first fire chief, its current chief, Wayne Amore, is only the sixth person to hold the position. It has grown from one fire truck housed at city hall to three fire stations with 27 pieces of firefighting and rescue equipment.

The police department has evolved from one man, Jack Walsh, walking the streets to preserve order, to a department equipped with modern-day technology. Despite the growth of the city, McHenry still maintains a very low crime rate. The hometown feeling is preserved as bicycle and foot patrols can be found throughout the city in the summer. Chief Thomas J. O'Meara is the 17th chief to serve the city in over 100 years.

The McHenry Public Library has come a long way from its first home in a classroom in the McHenry High School. When the library was formed by members of the Mother's Club, they could only dream that someday they would serve over 20,000 people, providing books, videos, and computer access.

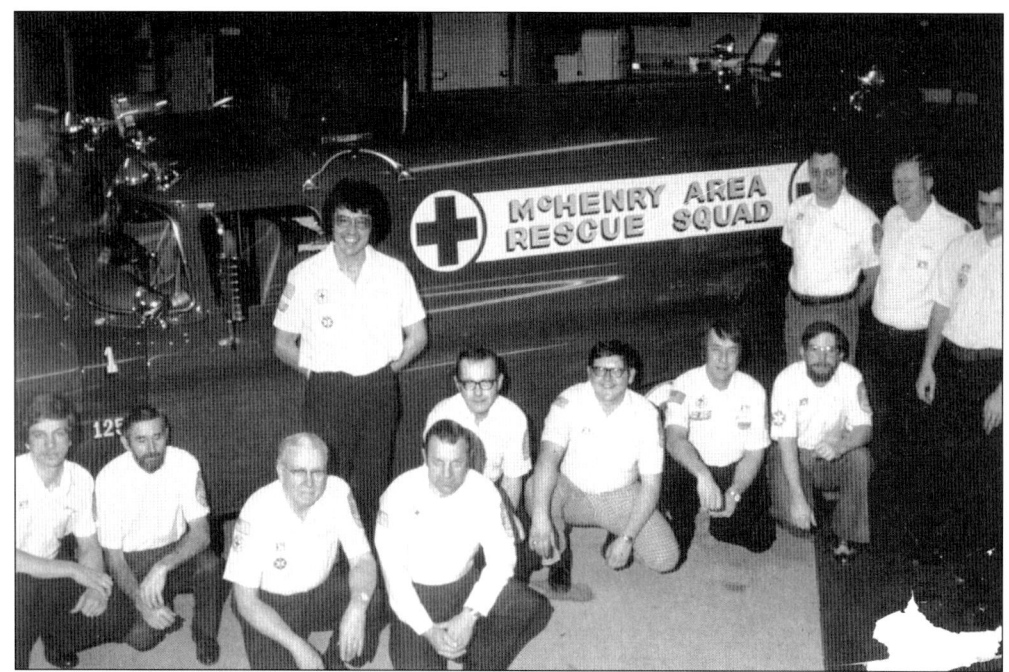

Although a tax-supported fire district had been formed, they did not provide ambulance service. That service was provided by the funeral homes. On January 10, 1972, a group of men established the McHenry Area Rescue Squad to provide immediate temporary care to the people of the McHenry area. In 1983, the rescue squad merged with the fire department. Three founding members continue to be involved with the fire department: Phil Gust, Ron Schaefer, and Mark Justin. (Courtesy of the McHenry Fire Department.)

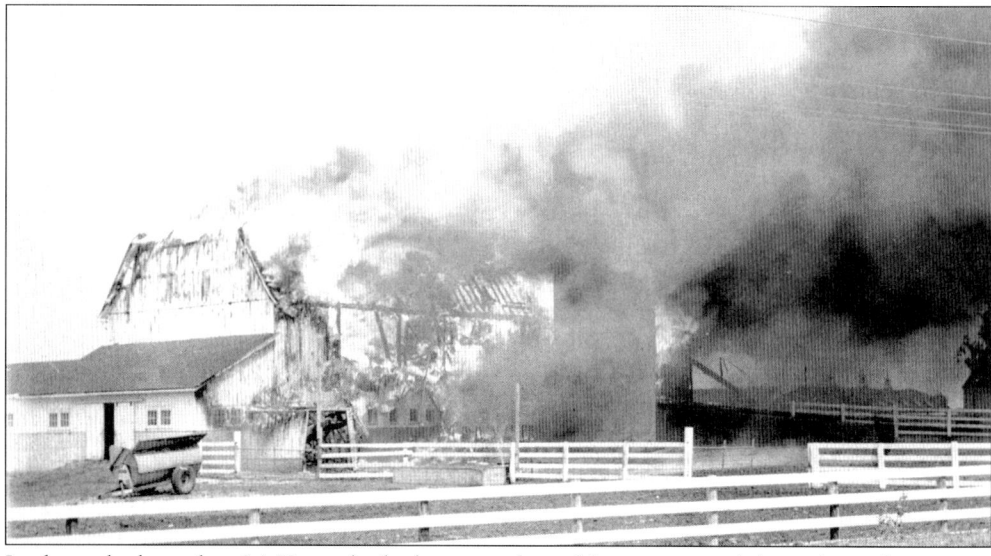

In the early days when McHenry had a large number of farms scattered throughout the county, fighting fires was difficult. All firemen were volunteers who had to leave their regular jobs when the siren alarm sounded. In the beginning, volunteers were not paid for this service, but in 1971, they were given $6 a call. Barn fires were common. Along with fighting the fire, animals had to be removed and quieted. (Courtesy of the McHenry Fire Department.)

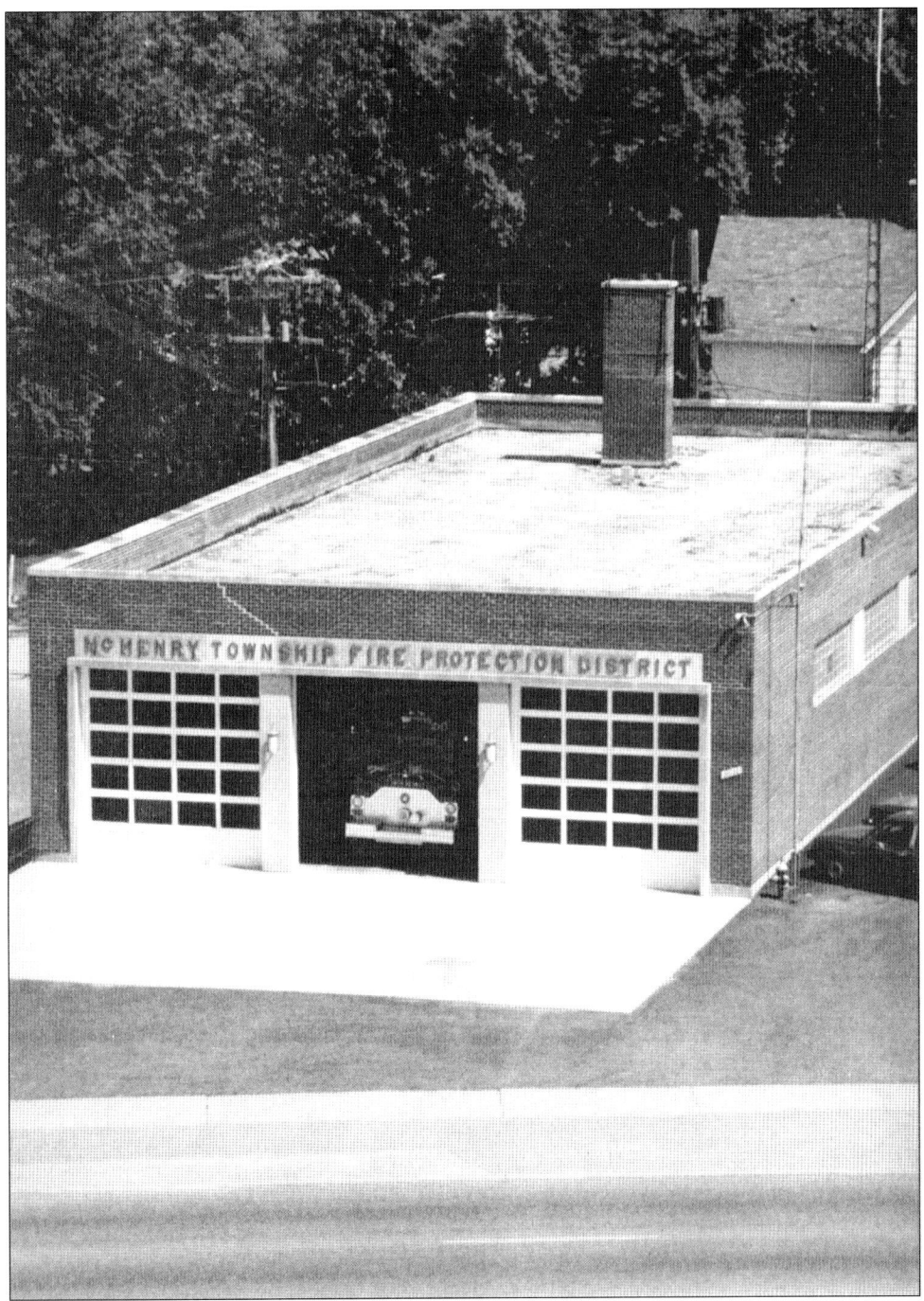

Even though the McHenry Township Fire Protection District was formed in 1939, it was not until 1955 that this fire station was built on the corner of Routes 120 and 31. Prior to that time equipment was housed at city hall on Green Street. Originally the department consisted of volunteers who were alerted of a fire by the blowing of a steam whistle from a factory on Borden Street, or a siren blowing at the fire station. Gus Freund was appointed the first fire chief and served from 1939 to 1949. (Courtesy of the McHenry Fire Department.)

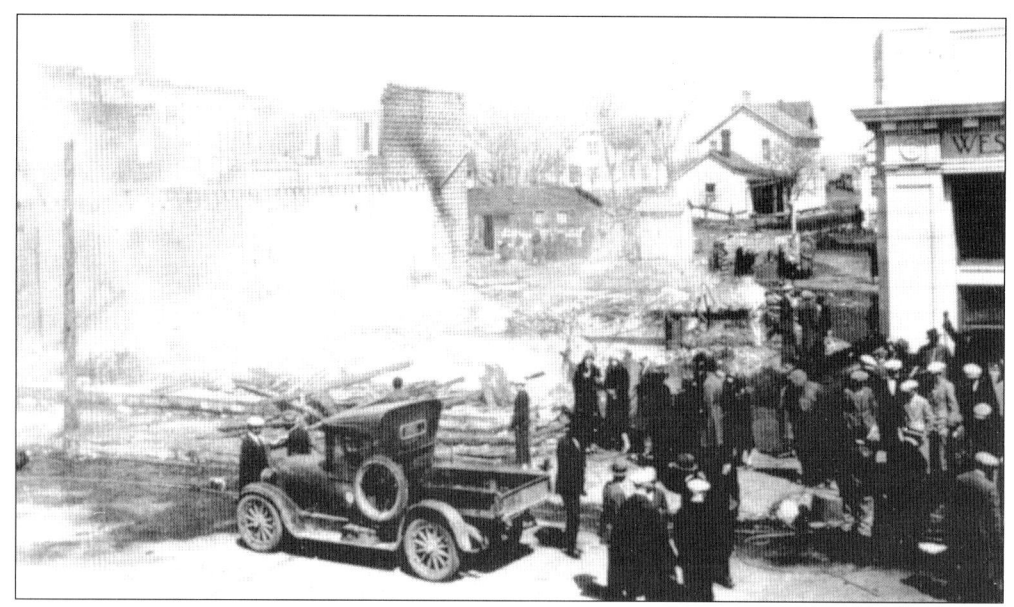

The N. R. Justen Furniture store, which was located on Main Street, suffered the same fate that would later befall the successor Justen Furniture store on Green and Elm Streets. The store, a wood building filled with flammable materials from building furniture and caskets, burned to the ground on April 11, 1926. (Courtesy of the McHenry Public Library.)

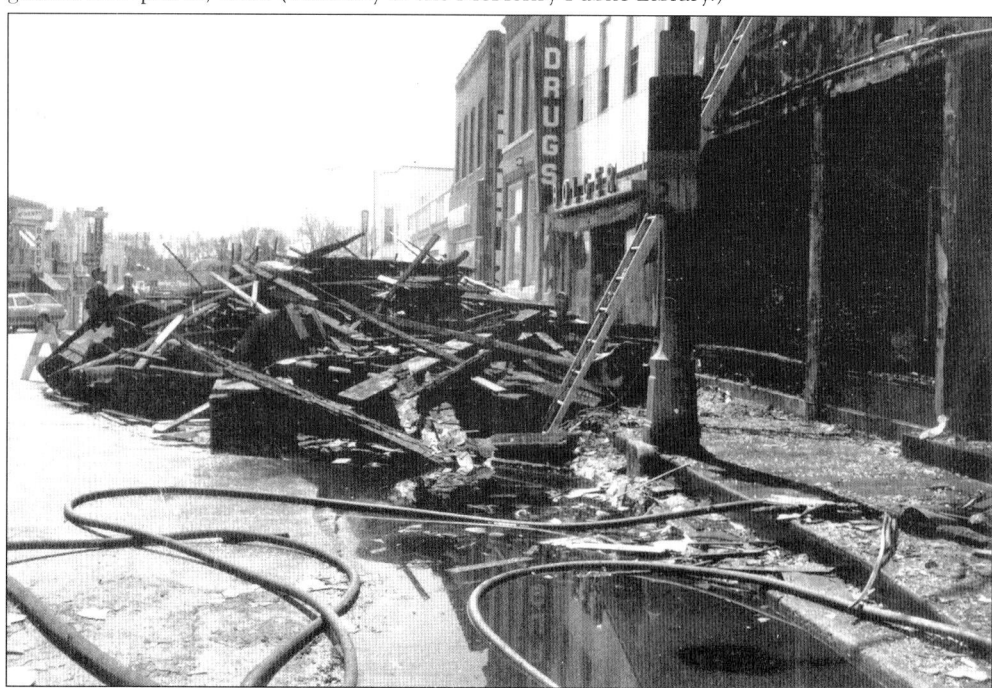

On April 24, 1969, the Justen Furniture store, a fixture on Green Street since the late 1800s, burned. The building, located on the corner of Elm and Green Streets, stood between the Justen Funeral Home on Elm Street and Bolger Drug Store on Green Street. A fire wall between the pharmacy and furniture store saved it from also succumbing to the fire. It was estimated that the fire caused approximately $70,000 in damage. (Courtesy McHenry Fire Department.)

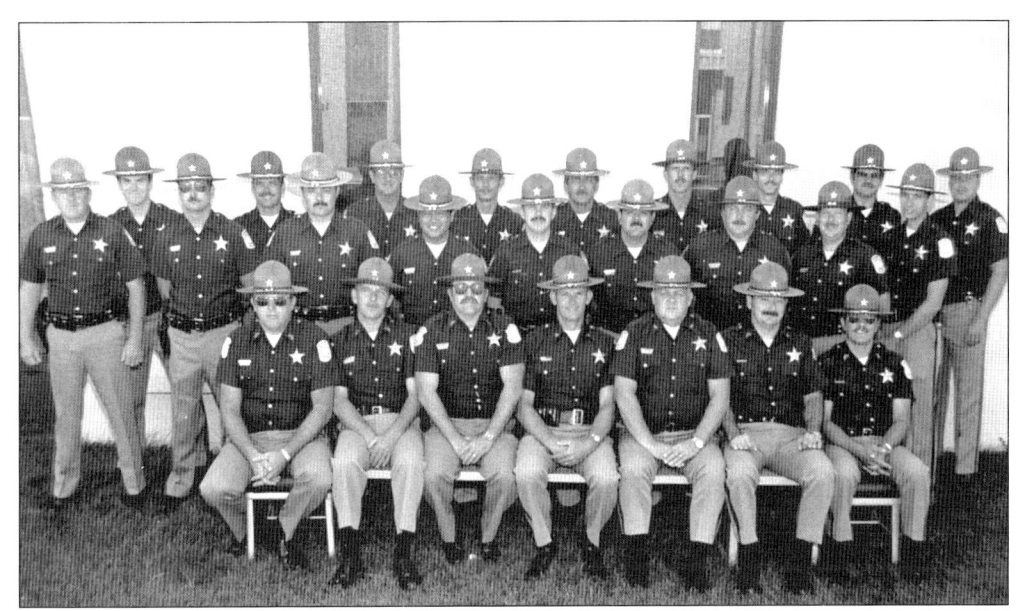

Today's police officers face a very different type of work than Jack Walsh, the first police chief and the first policeman in McHenry. Originally hired to control the fights that inevitably broke out in the many saloons, he began walking the town and became known not for arresting criminals but for preventing crime. He earned $48 a month and was on duty 24 hours a day. He served as police chief from 1890 to 1933. (Courtesy of the McHenry Police Department.)

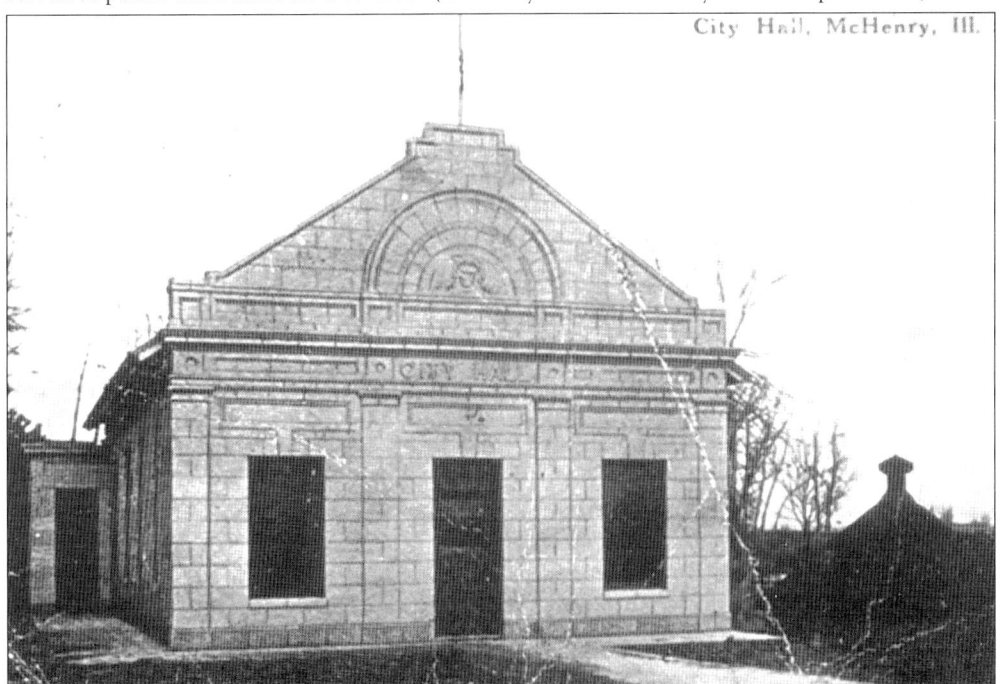

The original city hall, which was built in 1875 as a cheese factory, was replaced by this solid building in 1920. It was an impressive building, faced with white terra-cotta stone from the local American Terra Cotta Stone plant on Route 31. Located on Green Street, this building served as both the city hall and the police station. (Courtesy of John Baumgartner.)

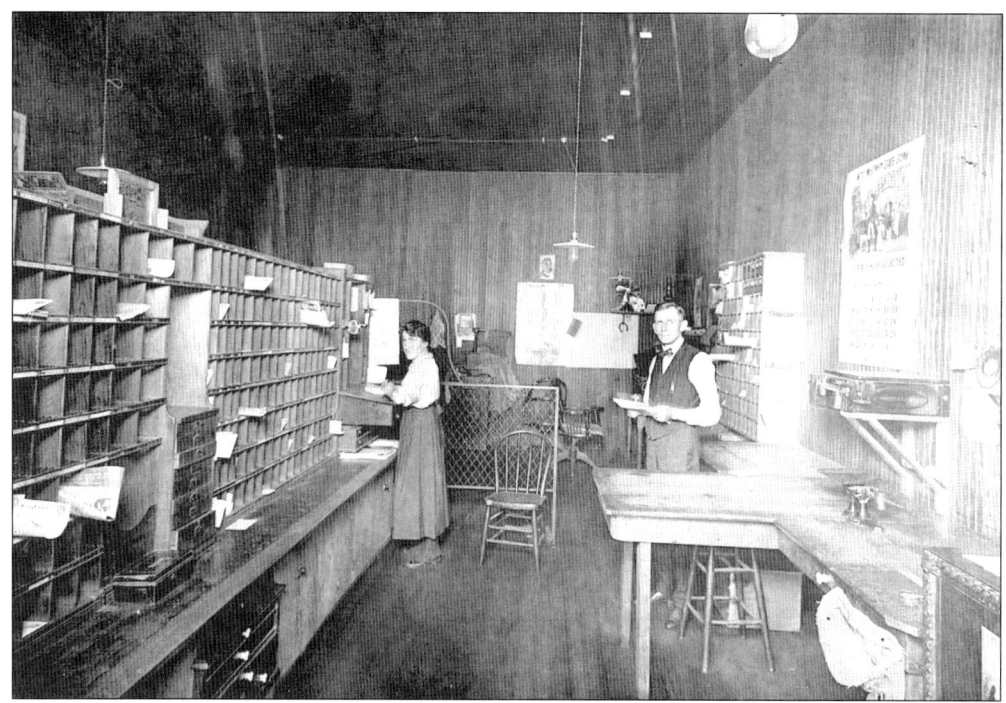

This 1917 photograph was taken inside the West McHenry Post Office. Clerk Therese Knox sorts mail for later delivery. Standing to the right is postmaster E. E. Bassett who served in this capacity from 1914 to 1935. During his tenure, the postmaster was paid $720 a year for his services. (Courtesy of Ilene Wiedemann.)

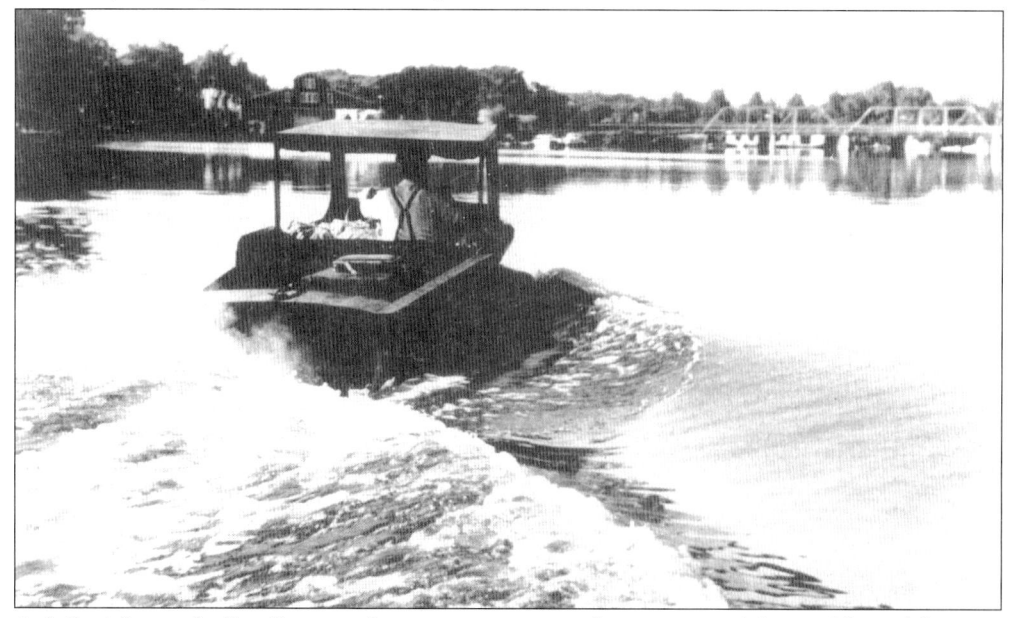

A daily sight on the Fox River in the summertime was the presence of the mail boat delivering mail to the many houses and cottages that lined the river. This photograph catches the mailman, "Skipper" Bill Schaefer, as he heads north up the river on his daily route. (Courtesy of Ilene Wiedemann.)

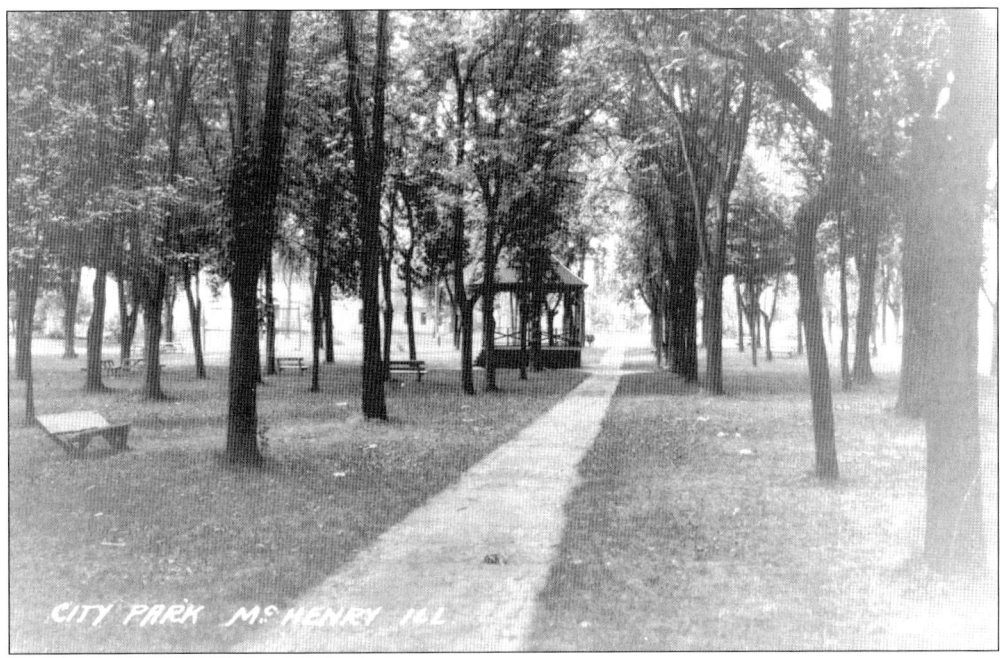

The original gazebo from the early 1900s is pictured in this view of the city park located on Pearl Street. This park was the scene of the early city festivals and concerts. Marine Days events were held here. Although the name of Marine Days has been changed to Fiesta Days, the park is still an important part of festival activities. (Courtesy of Shirley Klapperich.)

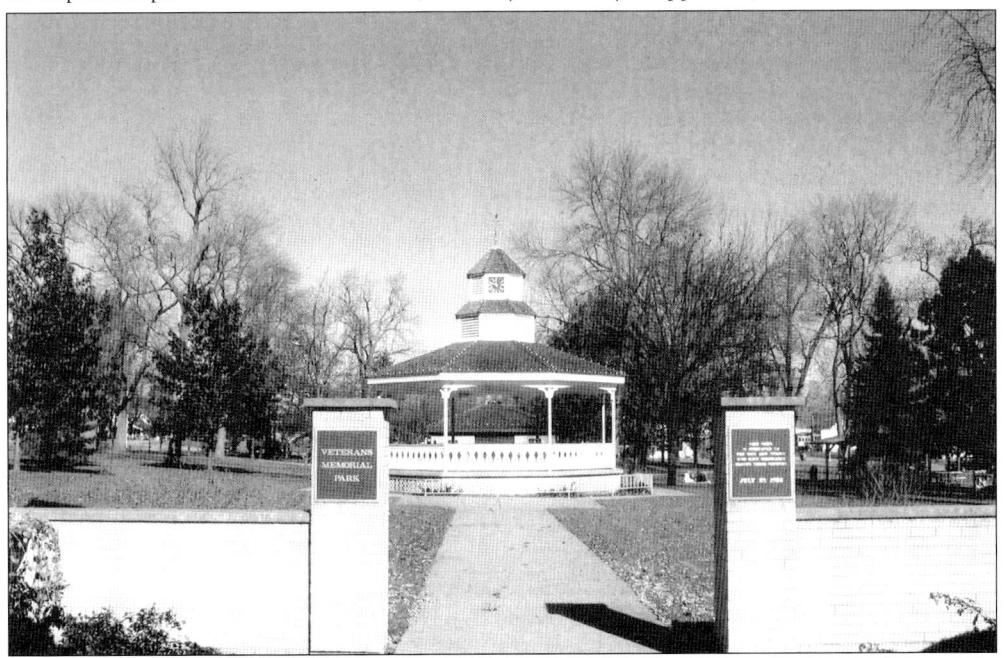

Very different from the earlier gazebo in Veteran's Memorial Park, this large white structure was built in 1985 to commemorate the 150th anniversary of McHenry. The structure is large enough to accommodate the bands and musical groups that are often part of the summer celebrations in the park.

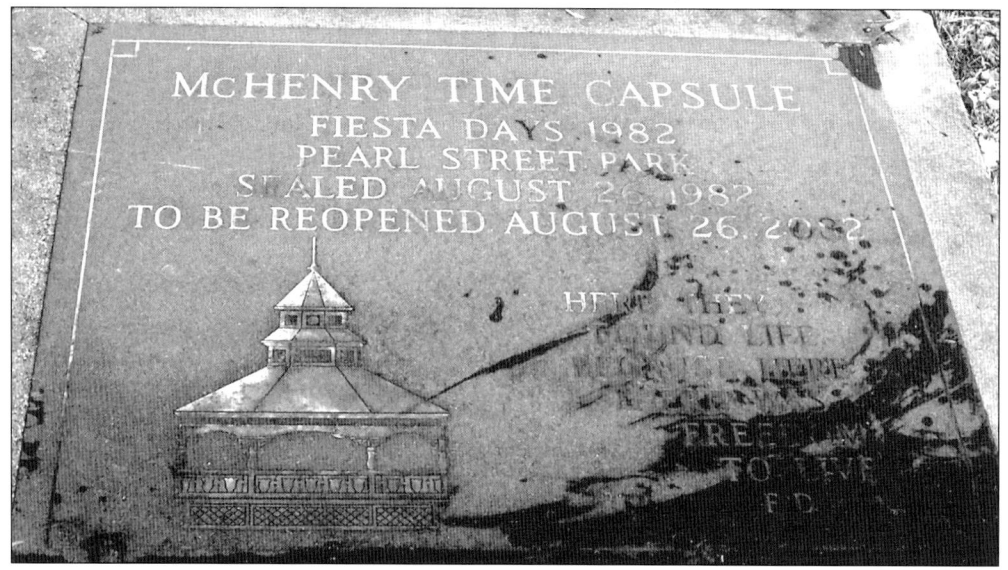

At the Pearl Street entrance to Veteran's Memorial Park, there is a marker that bears an inscription stating that a time capsule was buried in this spot. In 1982, the year which marked the 15th anniversary of the Senior Citizen's Club, Pres. Roland Grayson obtained permission from the city to prepare a century vault. Items interred included skateboards, clothing of the period, toys, and an album of the city's rescue squad activities. A burial vault was provided by Mark Justen. (Courtesy of Priscilla Rutter.)

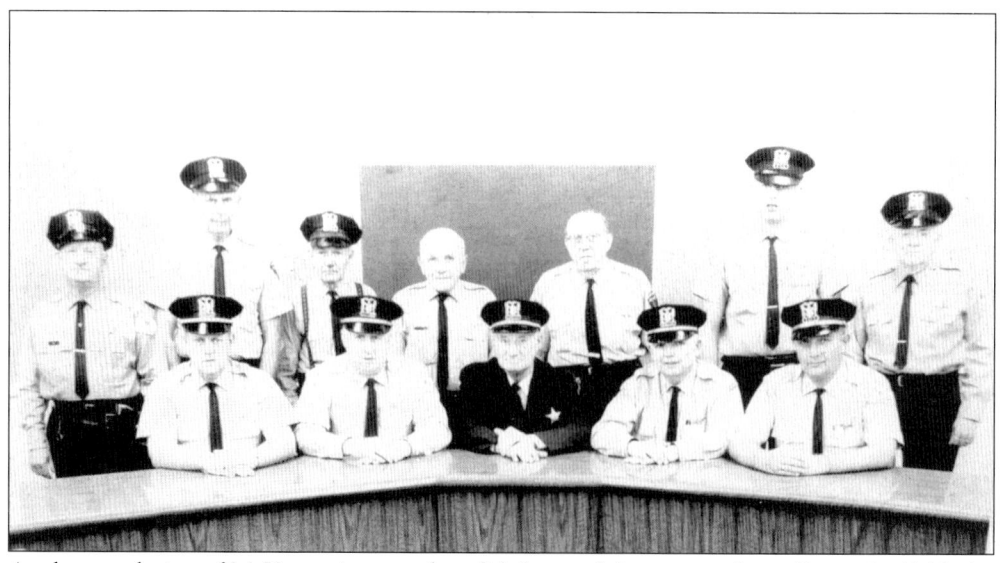

As the population of McHenry increased so did the need for more police officers. In 1966, the entire police department posed in their uniforms for this department photograph. With two highways intersecting through town, traffic control remains a major concern. (Courtesy of the McHenry Police Department.)

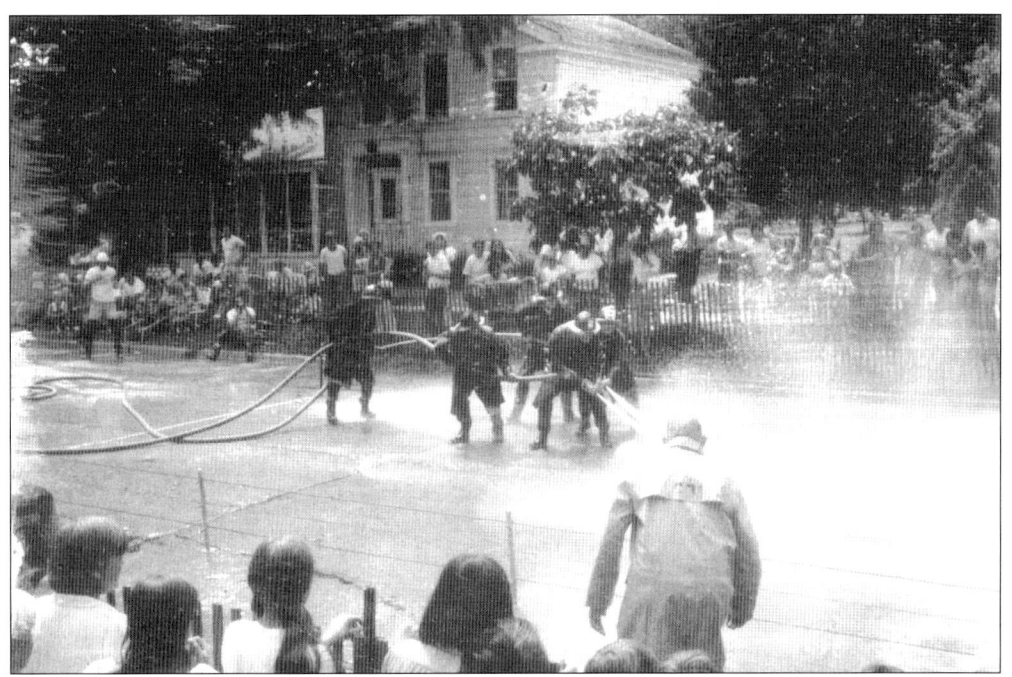

For many years, one of the highlights of the summer was the water fights of the McHenry Fire Department against neighboring firefighters. Bystanders could expect to get soaked as the firefighters' hoses often sprayed the crowds as much as they sprayed their opponents. (Courtesy of the McHenry Fire Department.)

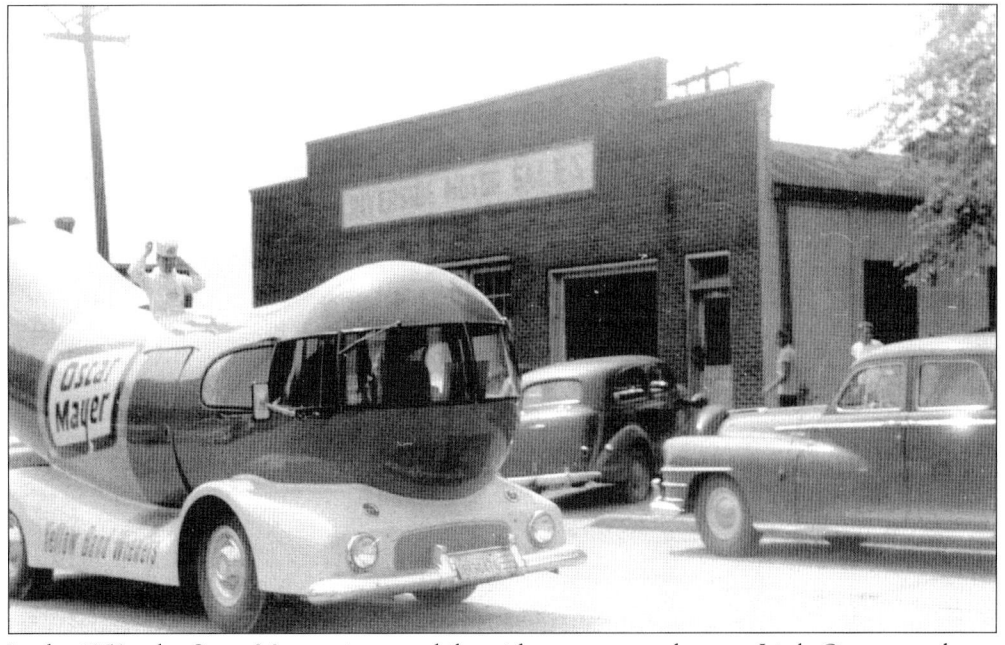

In the 1950s, the Oscar Mayer wiener mobile, with company spokesman Little Oscar was always a hit at local parades and festivities. Children would flank around the giant hot dog as it passed through town. The hot dog was one of America's favorite fast foods, long before the proliferation of the current fast food choices. (Courtesy of Patricia Shafer.)

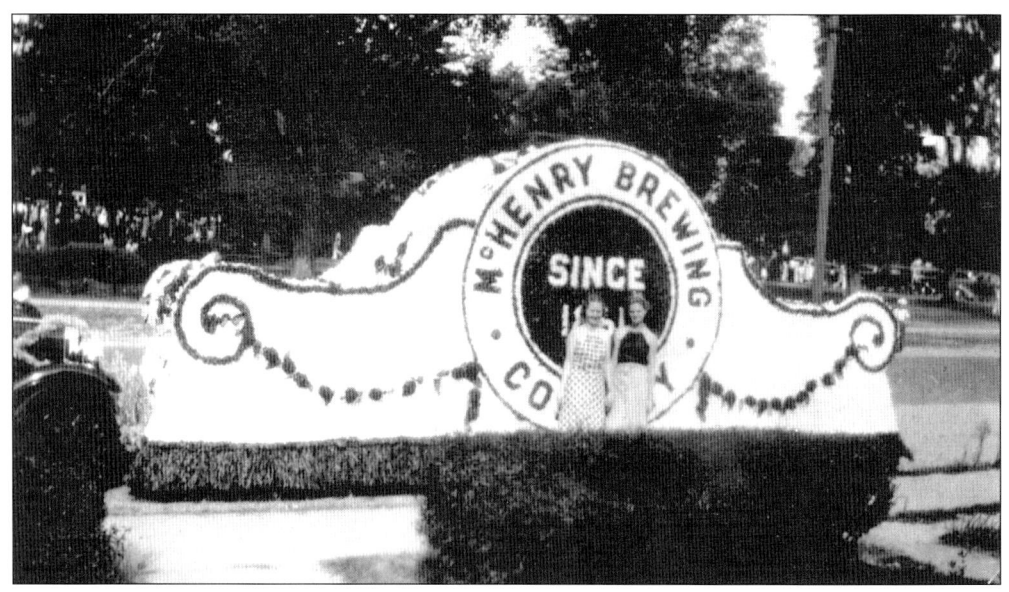

One hundred years is a milestone. In 1936, the city celebrated the 100th anniversary of its founding. This float, sponsored by the McHenry Brewery, was one of many participating in the centennial parade. Standing in front of the float are Lucille Smith (left) and Mildred Rickman. (Courtesy of Joan Wirtz.)

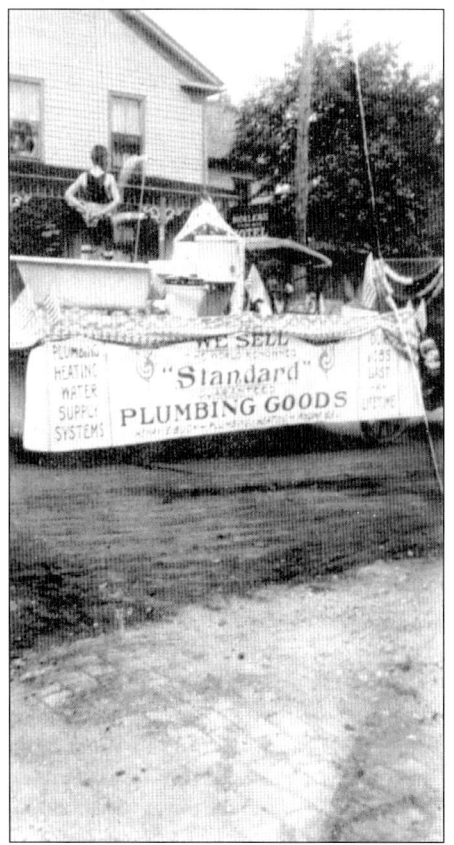

Parades have always been a part of life in McHenry. This 1919 float for Buch's Plumbing contains all the fixtures a well-appointed bathroom of the time would contain. The gentleman in the tub seems to be ready to go for a swim rather than to take a bath. (Courtesy of Henry Buch.)

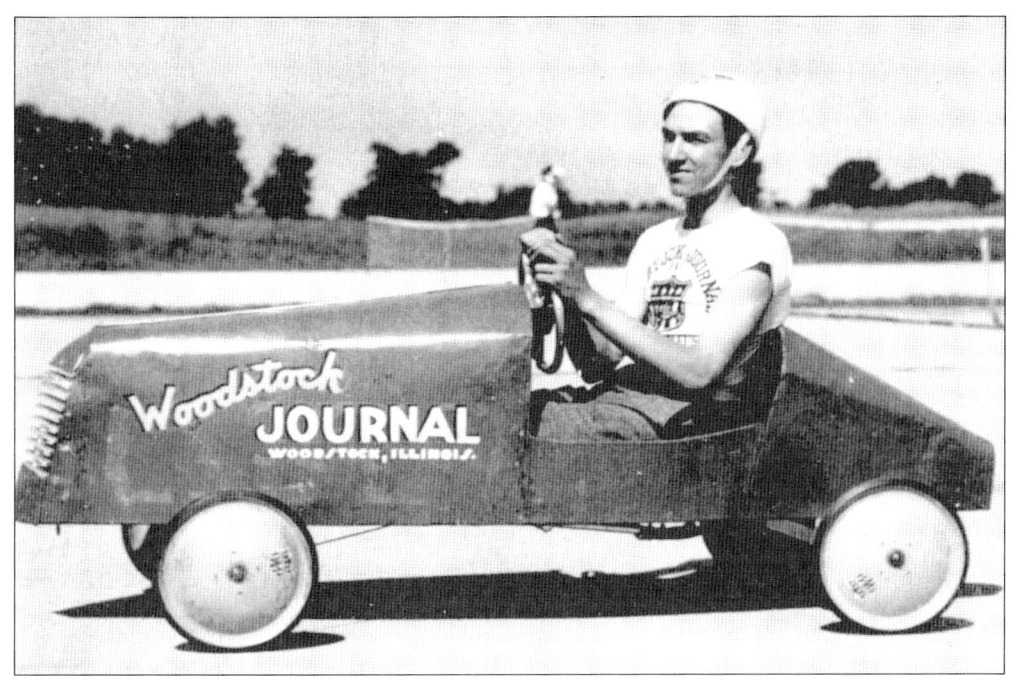

Henry Buch was 16 years old when he won the soap box derby with this car in McHenry in 1939. He later participated in another derby and was sponsored by the Woodstock Journal, requiring him to paint his car and place the sponsor's name on the car. (Courtesy of Henry Buch.)

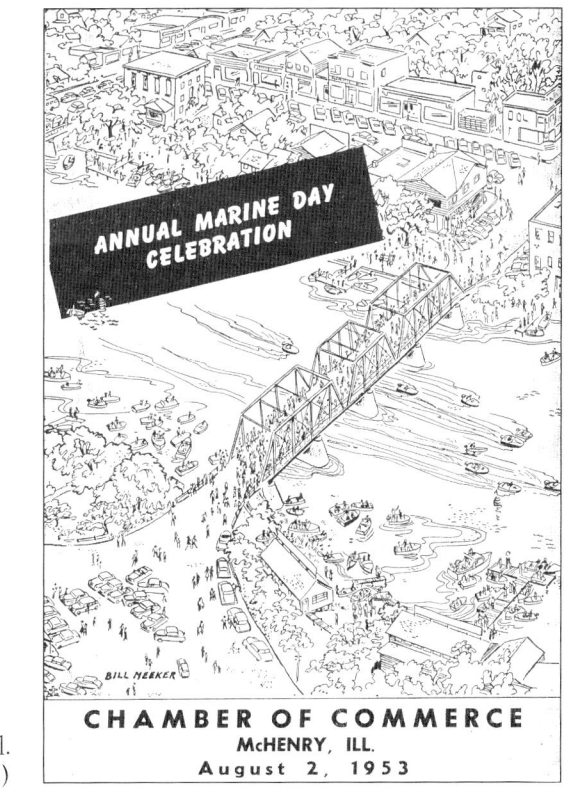

This chamber of commerce poster from 1953 advertises the annual Marine Days celebration. Marine Days was an annual festival originally held at the waterfront. A parade, boat races, and band concerts in the park were all part of the festivities. Each year many of the local teenage girls competed to become queen of the festival. (Courtesy of the Landmark Commission.)

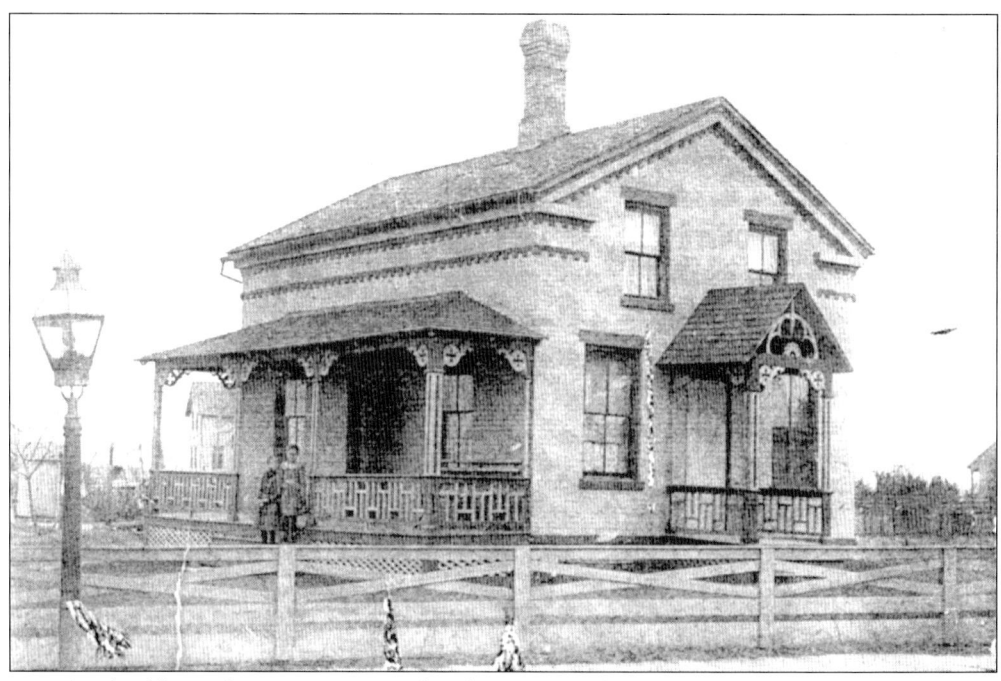

In 1952, the library, having outgrown the classroom at the high school, purchased the former Tesch residence on Green Street as a permanent home for their book collection. Remodeling was necessary to make it into a proper library. Pictured below are the volunteer local craftsmen who completed the remodeling in 1953. Seen here from left to right are (first row) Floyd Freund, Knute Johansen, and Arthur Harndson; (second row) Floyd Cooley, Chris Zauk, Joe Brefeld, Harold Jensen, Lee Larson, and Al Bienapfl. (Courtesy of the McHenry County Historical Society.)

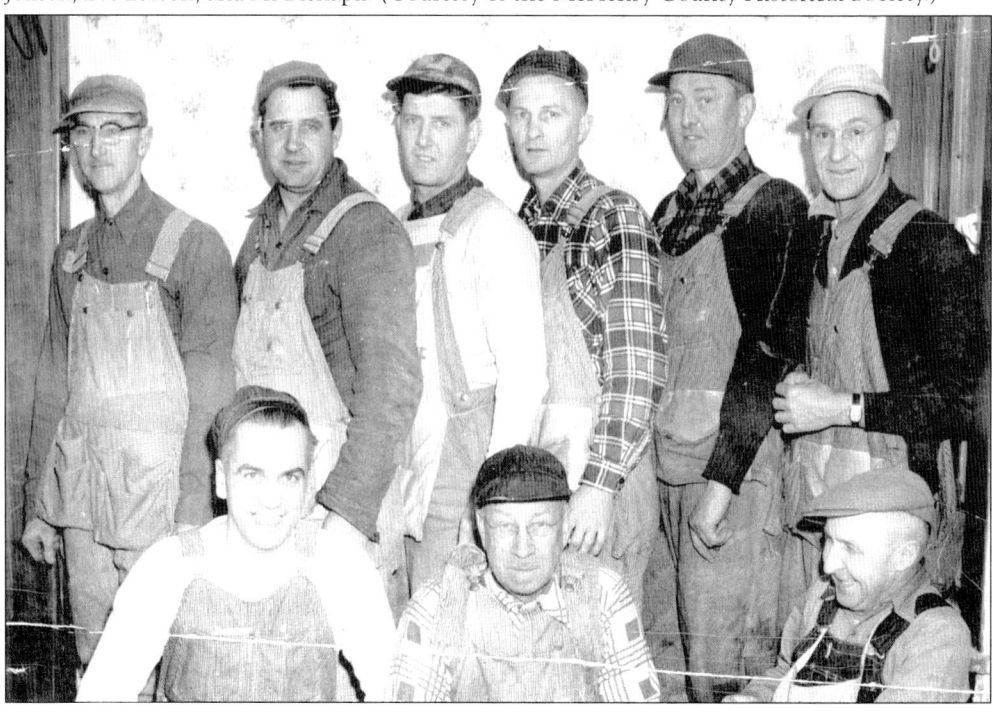

Five

BUILDING BUSINESS

As McHenry grew in population, so too did the needs of the people for food, household supplies, and clothing. Hardware stores, pharmacies, grocery stores, restaurants, and local saloons opened in each of the three separate business districts.

Other types of businesses developed making use of the area's resources. Farmer's crops were sold to local stores and also shipped to the city of Chicago. Milk from the dairy farms was collected, processed, and sold locally or transported by train to other areas. The high gravel and stone content of the soil provided gravel for roads and other construction and granite for cemetery monuments.

With the city's prominence on the river, boat builders found their way to McHenry. Lumber yards used the train and the river to transport timber into the area to meet the construction needs of the growing city. Ice cut out of the millpond and McCullom Lake provided refrigeration locally and in Chicago and for cooling products such as milk that required transportation into Chicago. A short-lived pearl-growing business made its home at the side of the river.

While some of these businesses have moved on to other locations, others have taken their place. Some, such as the ice harvesting, became outdated with the appearance of electric powered refrigeration. Many of the original businesses are still owned by descendants of the original owners.

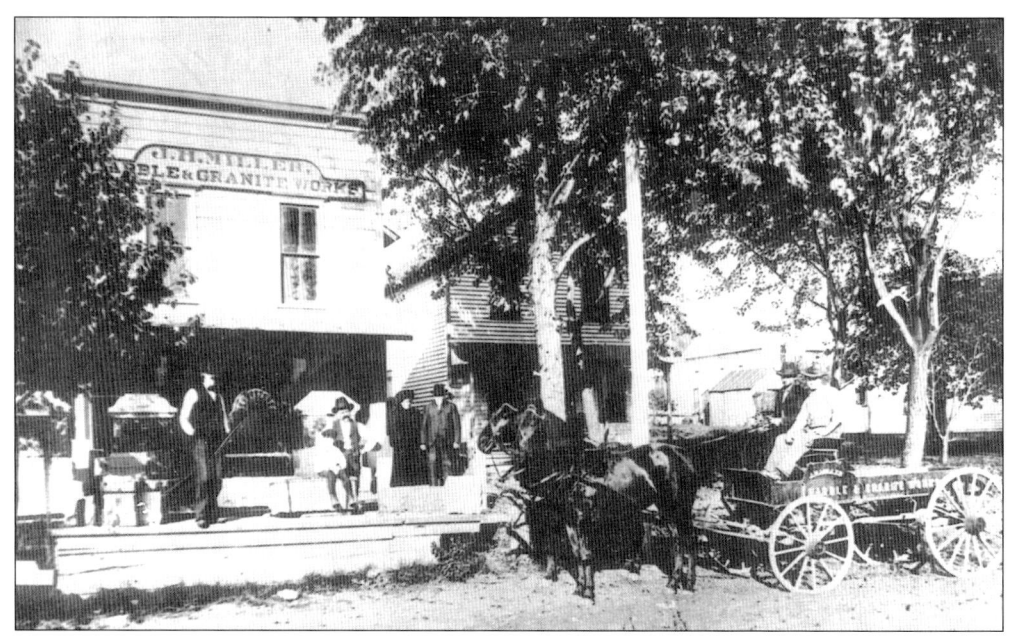

In 1868, Henry Miller, an immigrant from Germany, started the J. H. Miller Marble and Granite Works. Since work was done on-site, each stone was an individual design. This photograph of his store on Elm Street was taken in 1890. At that time, the hand-carved monuments were moved by horse and wagon to the cemeteries. The business continues at the same location. It is considered to be the oldest continuous McHenry business still owned and operated by the same family. (Courtesy of John Henry Miller.)

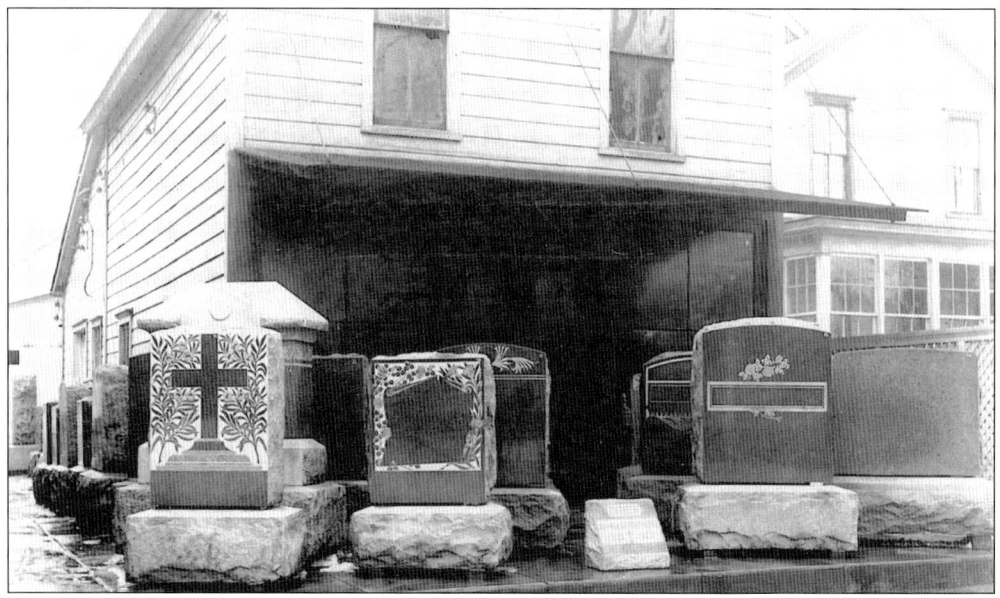

The monuments in this photograph, on display in front of the Miller store, show the craftsmanship and design in each individual monument. The Miller Monument Company continues to supply monuments for the cemeteries in the area but the business has changed. Today the engraving is completed at the quarries while the monument company is responsible for selling the stones and setting them at graveside. (Courtesy of John Henry Miller.)

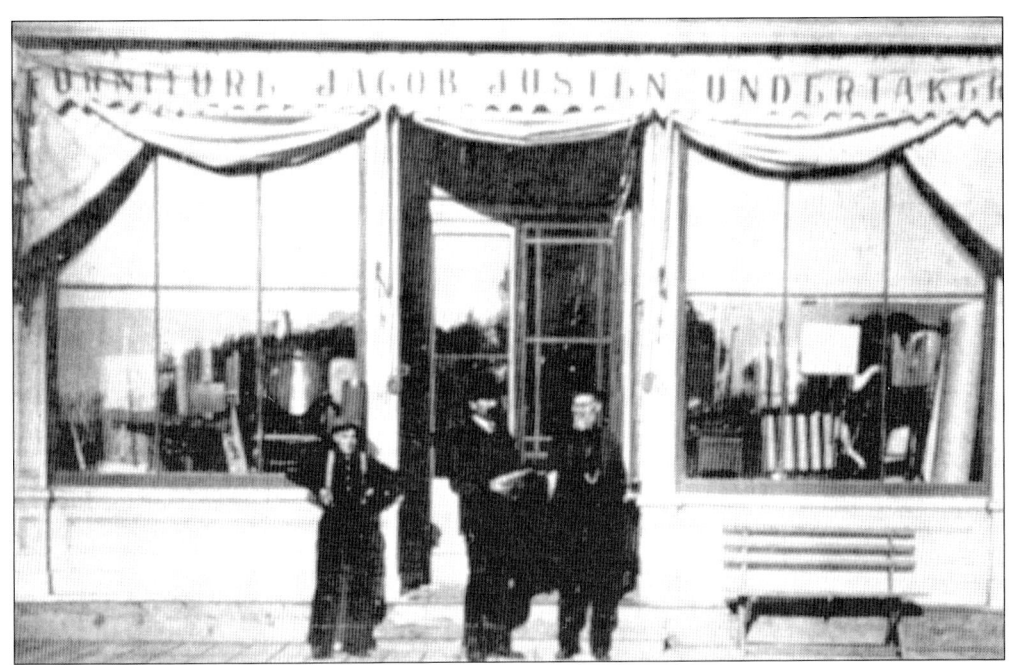

In 1882, brothers Jacob and Nick Justen opened the first funeral home on Main Street in West McHenry. After several years, the partnership split. Nick maintained the business on Main Street, while Jacob opened another funeral home and furniture store on the south side of Elm Street. (Courtesy of Mark Justen.)

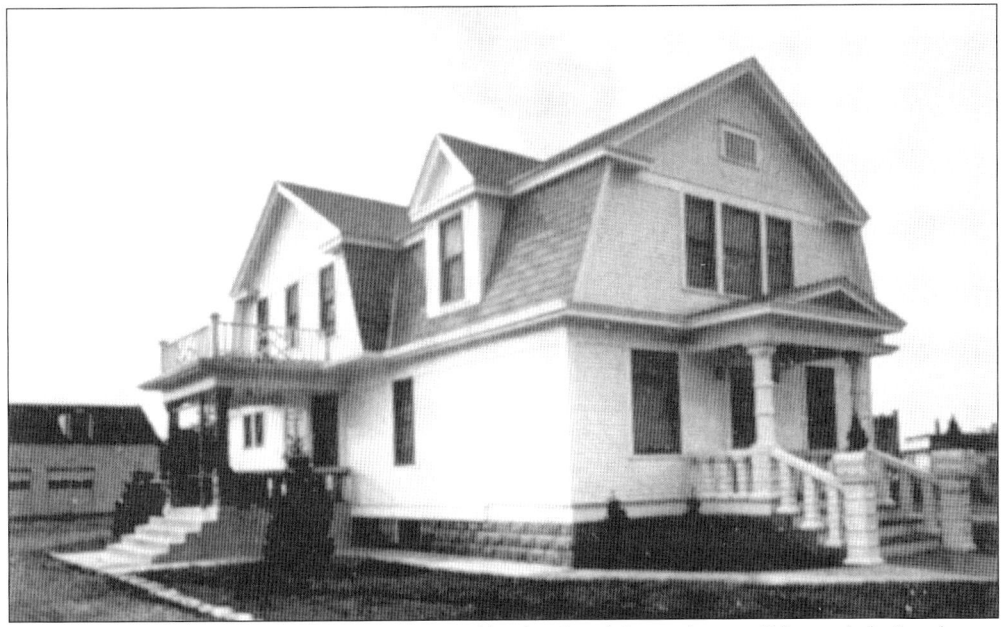

The funeral home on Elm Street was actually the family's residence. Often while Jacob was attending to the burial, family members were replacing the family furniture in the parlor. While the name was changed to George Justen and Sons Funeral Home, it continues to be operated by family member Mark Justen, making it the city's second oldest business continued by the same family. (Courtesy Mark Justen.)

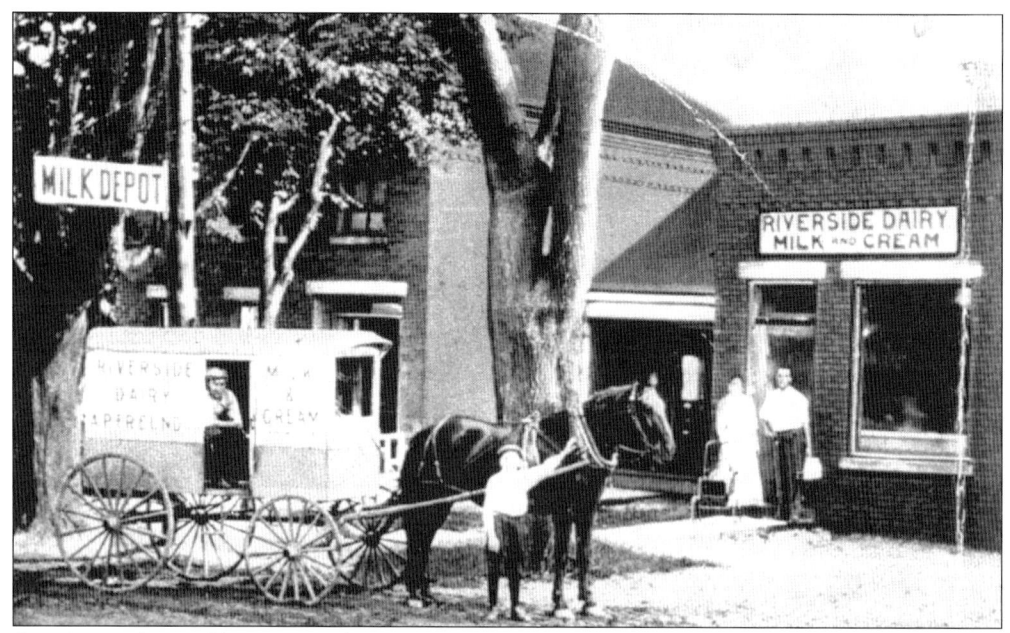

Standing in front of their Riverside Dairy on the south side of Elm Street are Anton P. and Margaret Freund with their infant daughter Leone in 1915. The milk delivery wagon's horse, Molly, is being held by Donald Givens, while John Givens remains in the truck. Milk depots, such as this one, were collection points for various farmers to sell their milk. (Courtesy of Barbara Gilpin.)

"Milk Is Only As Good As The Care It Gets"

Our bottles are thoroughly washed by machine and sterilized.

Our Milk is filtered, pasteurized and handled in a strictly sanitary manner.

"A BOTTLE OF MILK IS A BOTTLE OF HEALTH"

Riverside Dairy, McHenry

Raw milk was brought to the local dairies by the farmer to be processed and bottled. Fast, hygienic bottling was required to prevent spoilage. In the 1920s, the time of this advertisement for the Riverside Dairy, electric refrigeration was not available in most homes. Riverside Dairy prided itself on producing a clean, bacteria-free bottle of milk, as evidenced by this advertisement. (Courtesy of Ilene Wiedemann.)

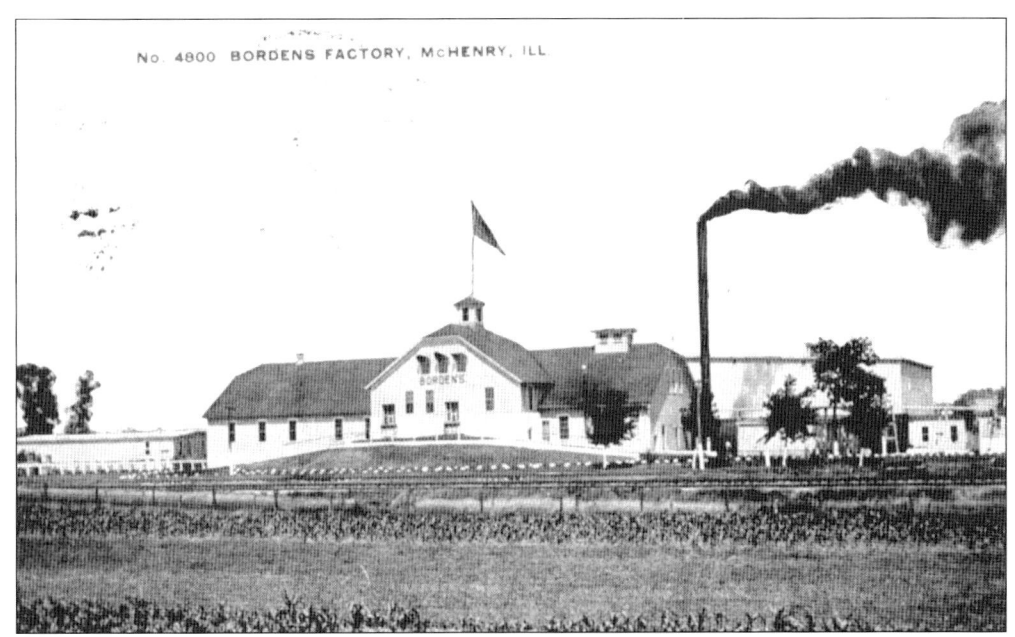

Borden Milk Factory opened in the early 1900s on Borden Street in West McHenry. Farmers from the area brought their milk to the processing plant by wagon pulled by horses. When the weather was really snowy, the trip would be made by sled. The milk was taken to this building, where it was processed and shipped by rail to Chicago. Ice from the pond was harvested in winter and used to keep the milk refrigerated. (Courtesy of Patricia Schafer.)

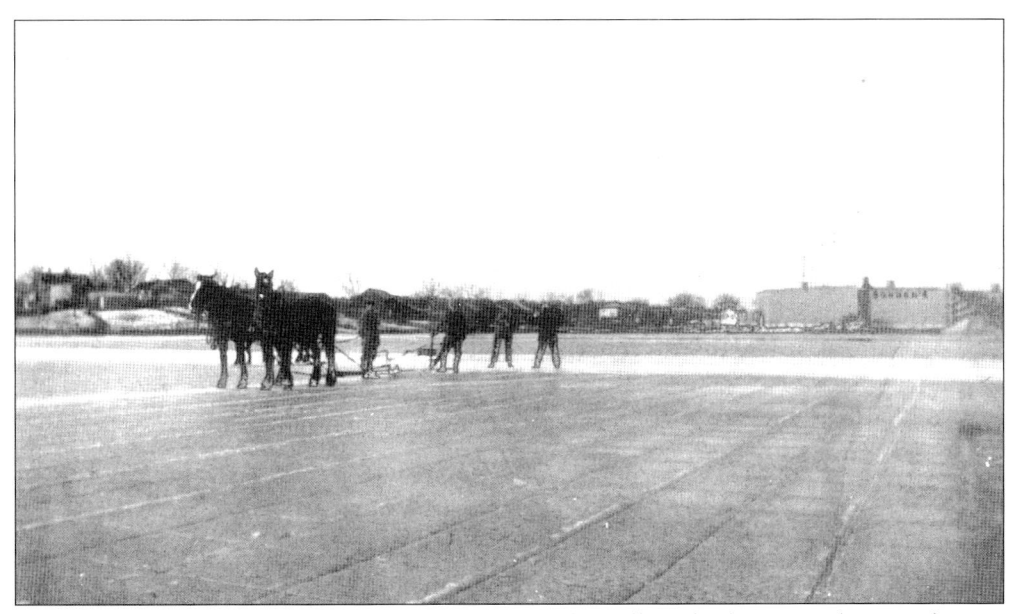

These men spent their winter days cutting ice out of the millpond. The ice was harvested to use locally or be transported to Chicago in the days before electric refrigeration. The Borden plant in the background used the ice to transport their milk products. This photograph was taken in the early 1900s. (Courtesy of James Althoff.)

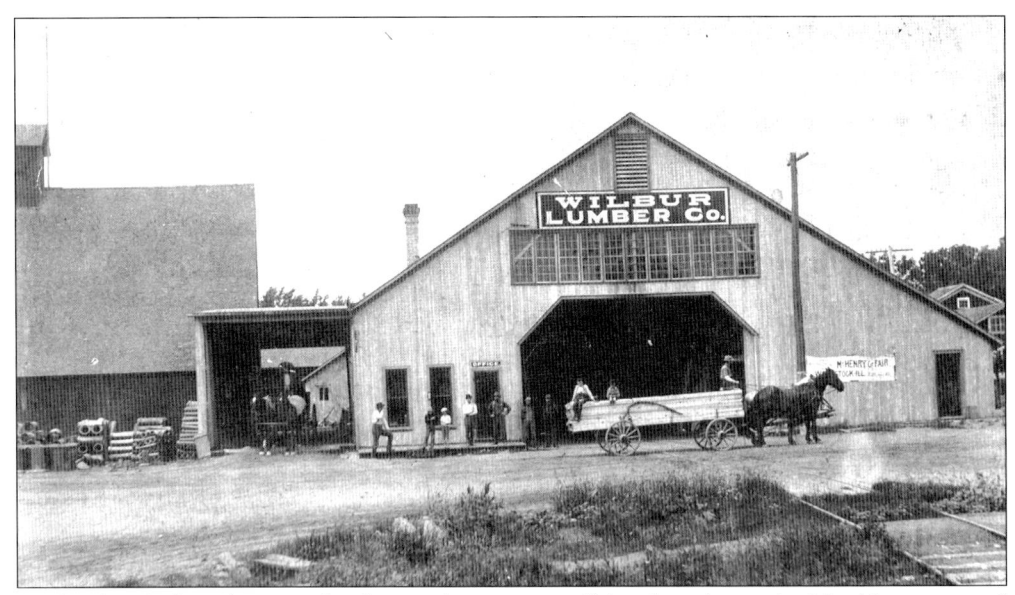

In the days before the mega lumber yards, many small local yards supplied building material for homes and barns. These yards were often built close to the railroad lines for easy transport. Pine was the most common lumber used because it was plentiful in Illinois forests. The original Wilbur Lumber Yard was located on Main Street, along the railroad. This photograph was taken in the early 1900s. Wilbur Lumber Yard was later purchased by Alexander Lumber Company. (Courtesy of the McHenry Landmark Commission.)

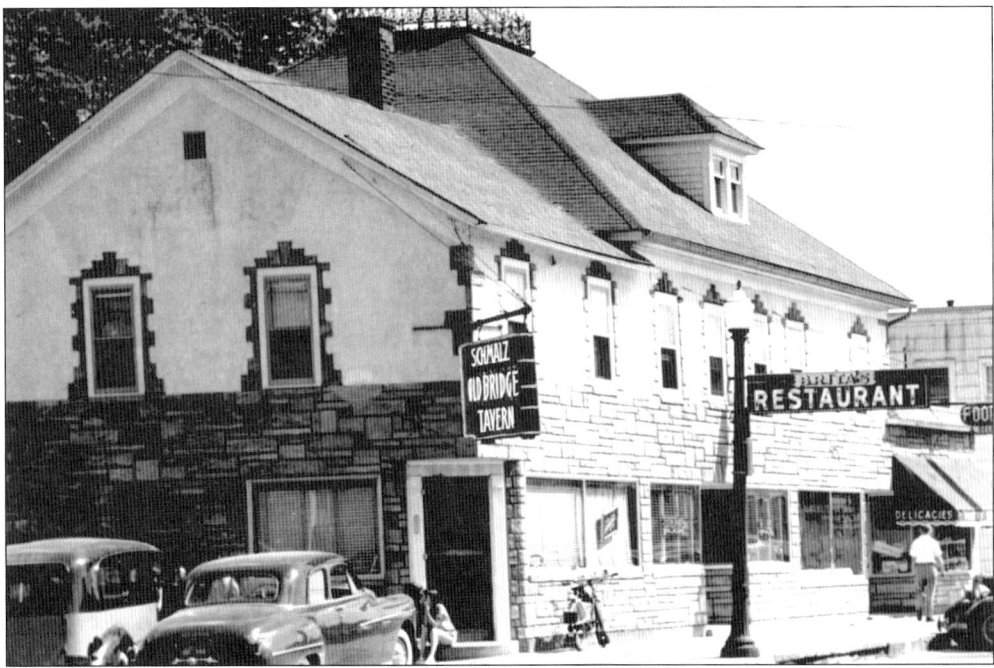

This historic building, located on the corner of Pearl Street and Riverside Drive, is the oldest frame structure in McHenry. The ornate metal at the top of the roof was removed during World War II. In the 1950s, the owner of this tavern would anchor a Christmas tree in the center of the river, near the bridge, complete with electric lights. (Courtesy of the McHenry County Historical Society.)

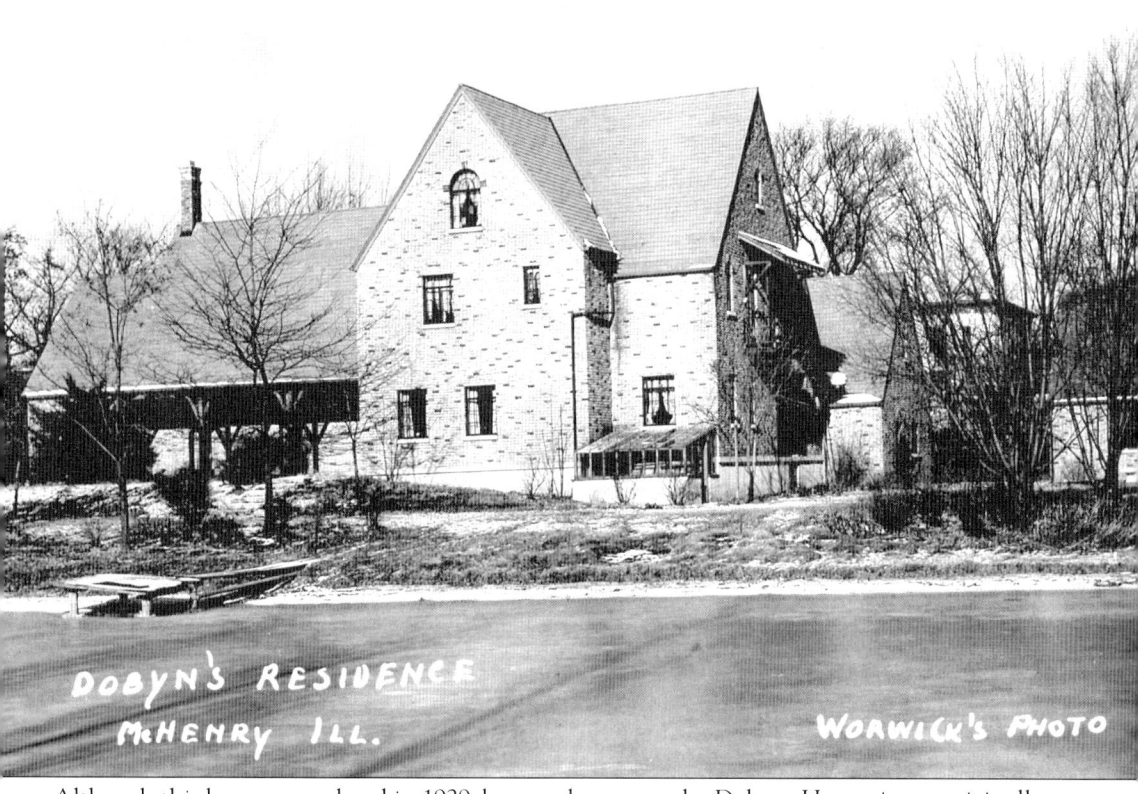

Although this house, completed in 1929, became known as the Dobyns House, it was originally built for a Dutch immigrant named Julius Kaig. Kaig was responsible for straightening Boone Creek. Because the land was swampy, it had to be built on a floating foundation. Kaig drained the millpond allowing development along Route 120. In 1938, the house was acquired by the Dobyns family who established an antique shop in the carriage house. The antique shop closed in 1968, then was reopened by Grace Dobyns in 1970. It remained in business until 1989, when Chuck Miller purchased the house and after renovations and restoration opened the Dobyn's House Restaurant. He ran two cruising boats, the *Flossie Belle* and the *Anna Marie*. Today the house is known as the restaurant Joey T's On the Fox. (Courtesy of the Landmark Commission.)

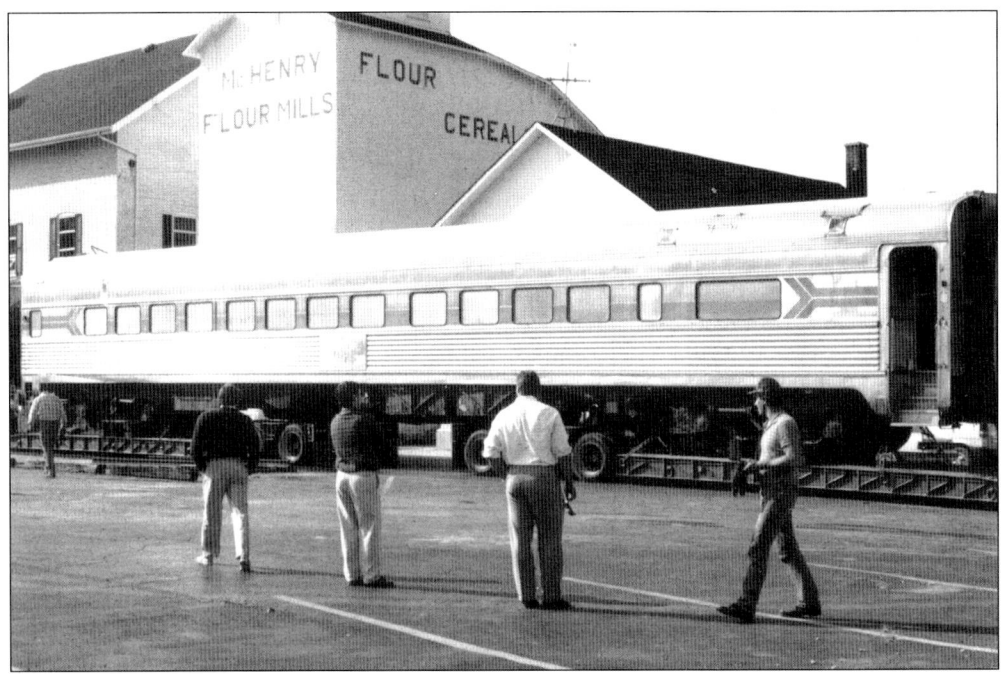

Located on Crystal Lake Road, this three-story building, built in 1870, was the original site of the Champion Brick Yard operated by A. H. Hanly. In 1875, it became the McHenry Flour Mill, which operated well into the 1900s. Flours such as, graham, whole wheat, and self-rising buckwheat were among those milled here. Flour was produced until just prior to the start of World War II. Gary Adams, founder of the TaylorMade Golf Company and designer of the metal wood golf club, used these buildings for his company in the late 1970s. The train car was purchased by building owner James Althoff and moved to the site when TaylorMade needed more space. The railroad car was used as a sales display room. (Courtesy of James Althoff.)

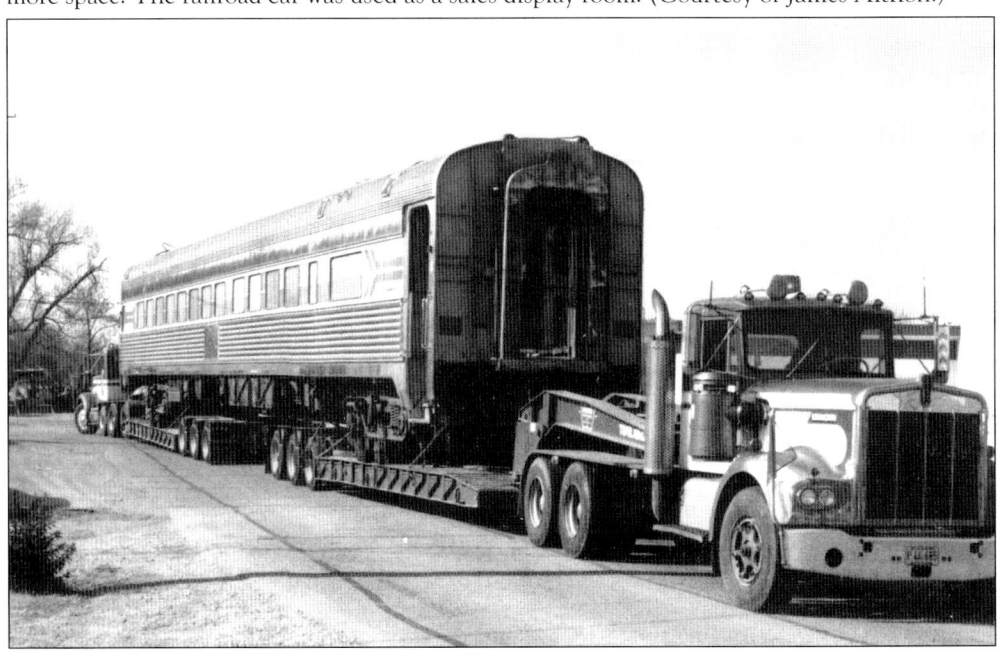

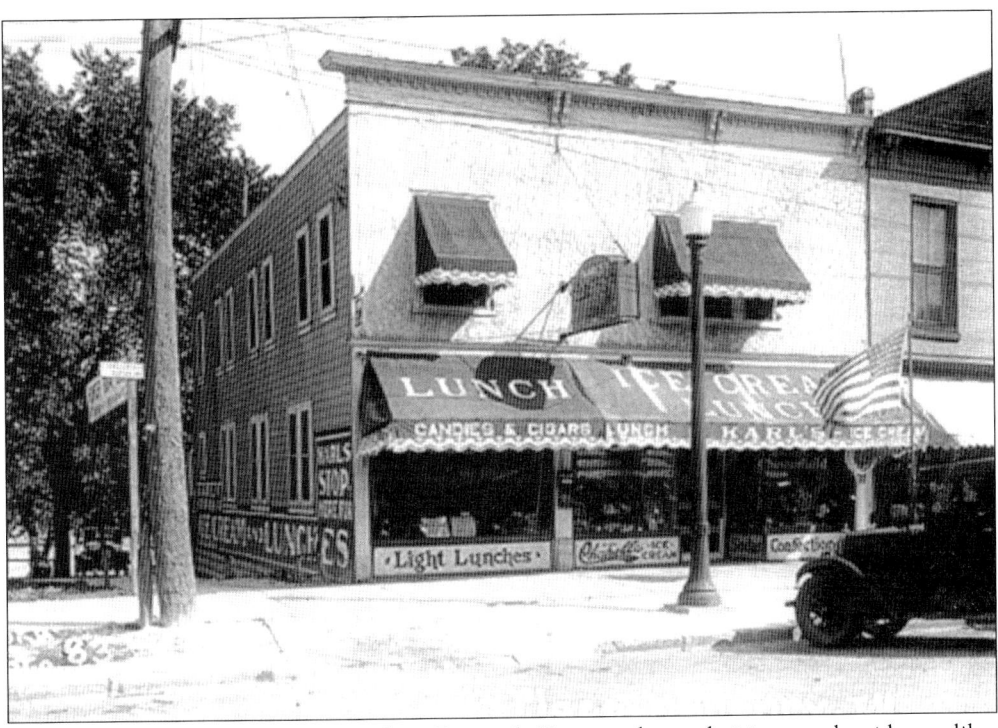

Karl's Place, one of the restaurants along Riverside Drive, welcomed visitors and residents alike. Lunch, ice cream, candies, and cigars were all available here. (Courtesy of Shirley Kapperich.)

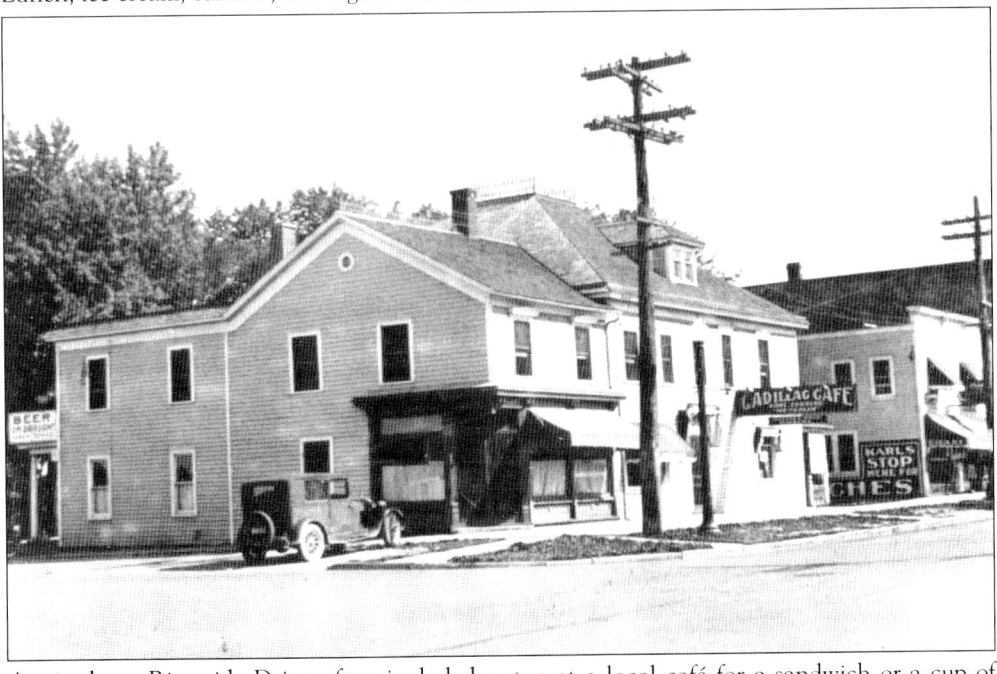

A trip down Riverside Drive often included a stop at a local café for a sandwich or a cup of soup. The café was the place local residents stopped not only for their coffee but to exchange all the local gossip. This photograph of the Cadillac Café was taken in 1920. The café is still in existence as the Little Chef. (Courtesy of Shirley Klapperich.)

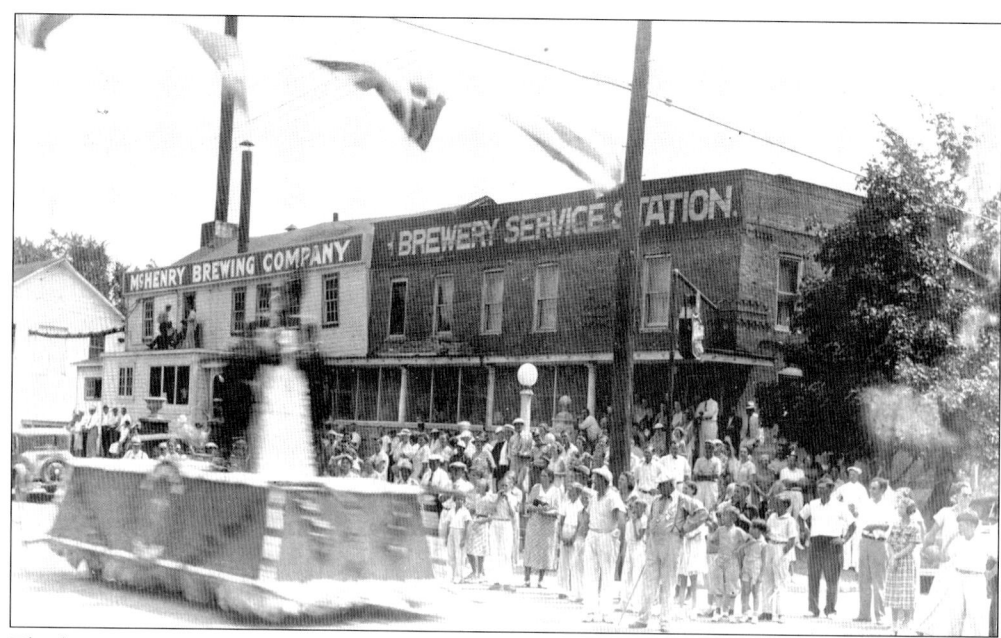

The brewery, located on the southeast corner of Green and Pearl Streets, at 3425 Pearl Street, was opened by George Gribbler in 1868. Beer was manufactured here and sold under many different labels. At one time, this brewery produced 1,200 barrels of beer per day. Gottlieb Boley purchased the brewery in 1880. It continued to be operated by his descendant, Patsy Boley, until the 1930s. When Prohibition came, the brewery produced malt and a beer that had the alcohol removed. Local townsfolk would purchase the malt and take it home, add sugar and yeast to produce their own illegal beer. The 1936 centennial parade is passing the brewery in the above photograph. The photograph below is one of the McHenry Beer labels. (Above, courtesy of Shirley Klapperich; below, courtesy of Michael Clark.)

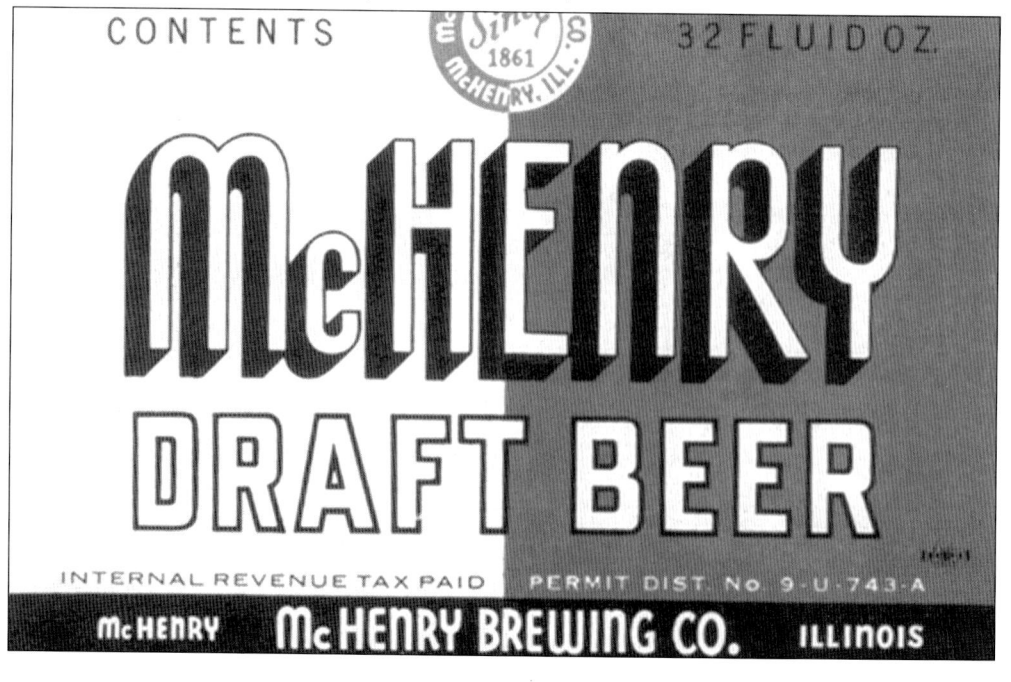

With $25,000 capital, P. S. Webster founded the West McHenry State Bank in 1906. It was originally located on the south side of Main Street. By 1916, the bank moved into this stone and granite building on the north side of the street, where it remained for 40 years. The bank changed its name to McHenry State Bank. The bank later moved to Elm Street and is now known as First Midwest Bank. (Courtesy of Ilene Wiedemann.)

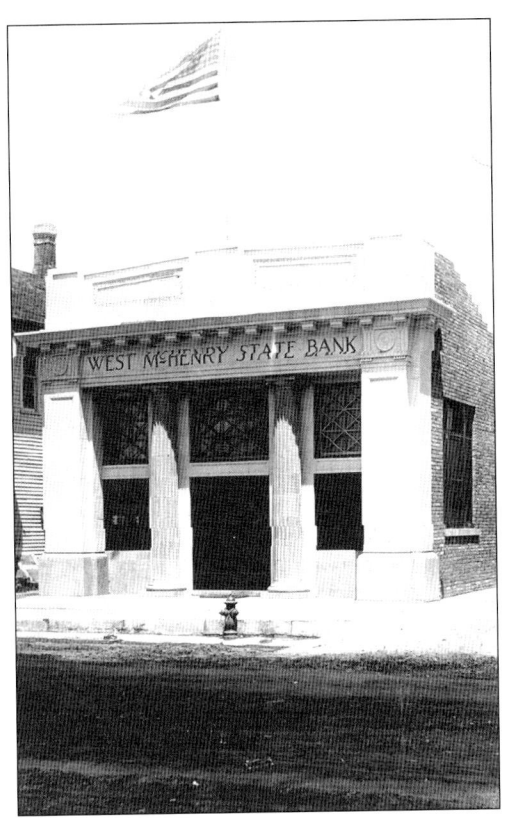

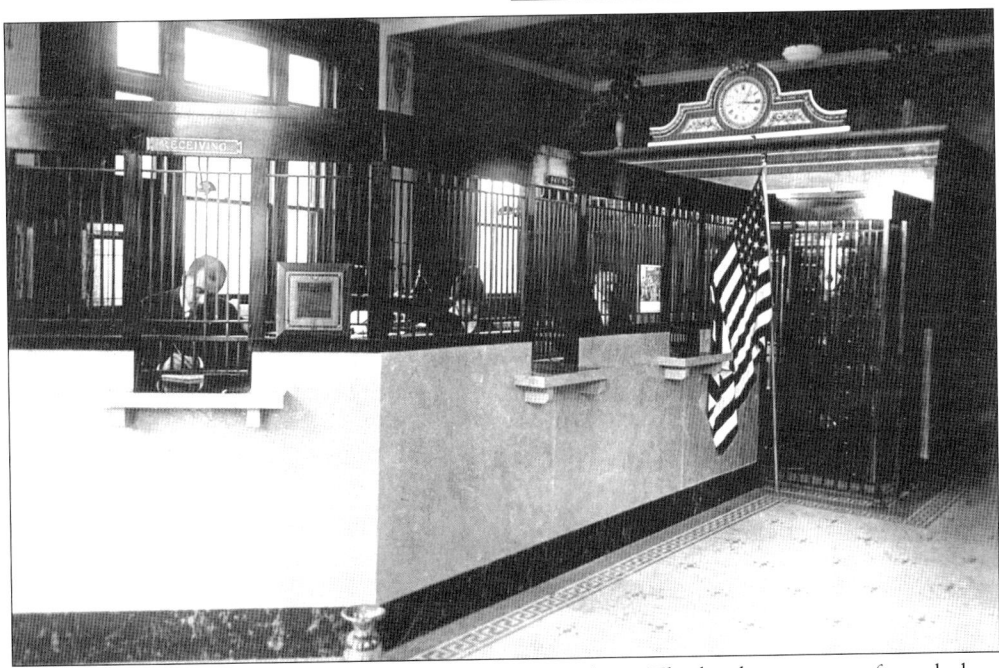

The inside of the West McHenry State Bank is shown here. The bank was a very formal place where attendants remained separated from customers by barred teller cages. Note the spittoon in front of the teller's window. (Courtesy of Ilene Wiedemann.)

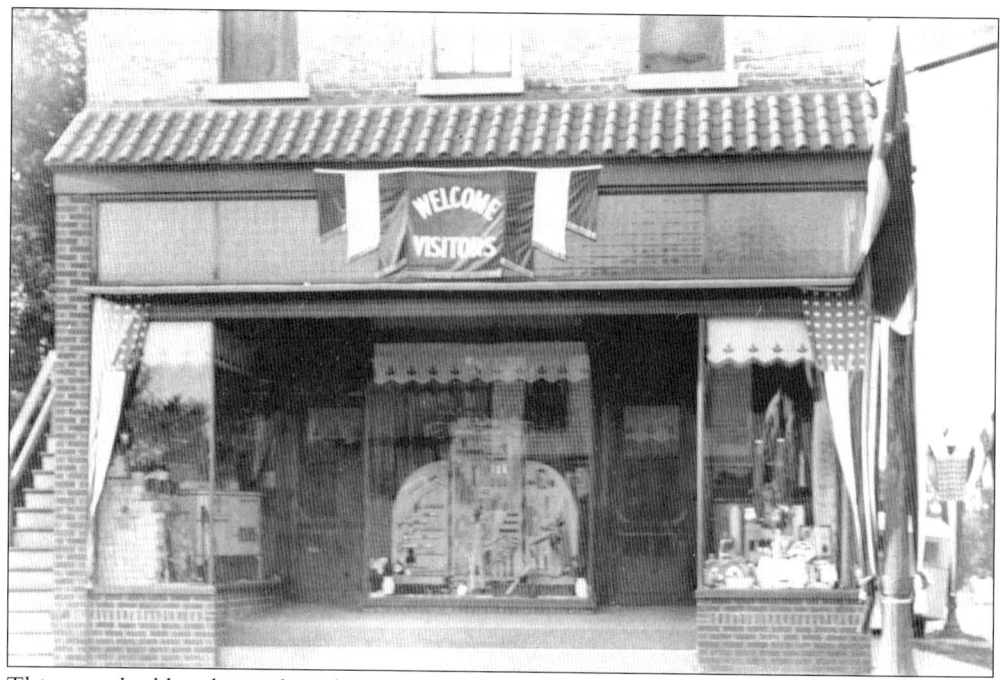

This stone building located on the northwest corner of Main Street and Route 31, was the home of Althoff's Hardware Store. Along with the hardware store, the Althoffs operated a sheet metal business in the basement. (Courtesy of James Althoff.)

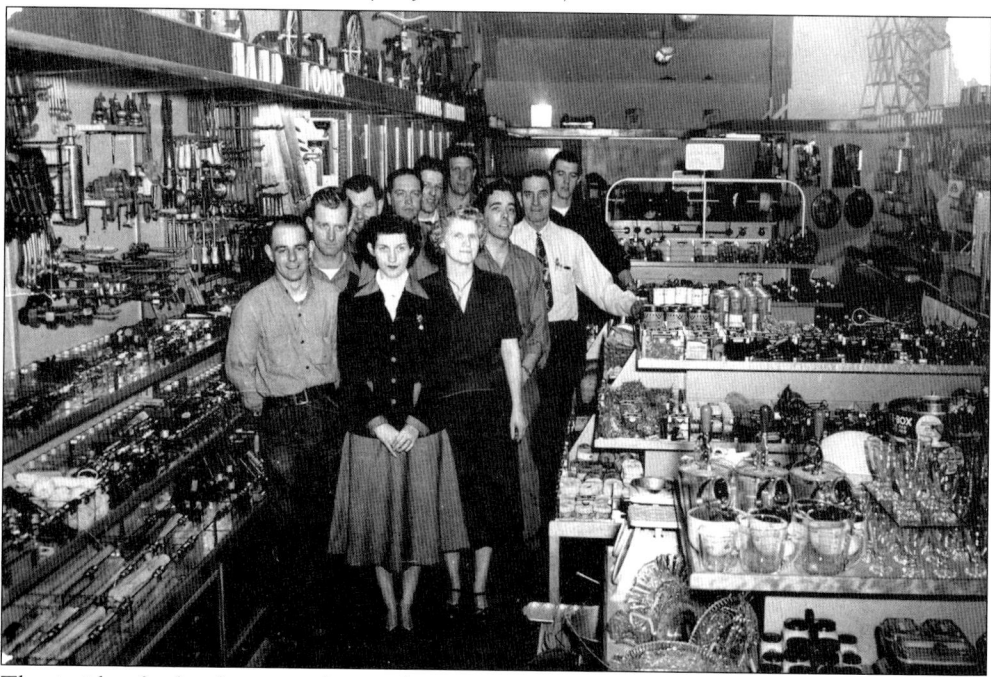

The inside of a hardware store was always an interesting place to shop. Whether the need for a tool or a new crystal bowl for the dining room table, it can be found here. The inside of Althoff's Hardware makes use of every inch of space. Pictured is the Althoff's staff taken in the mid-1900s. (Courtesy of James Althoff.)

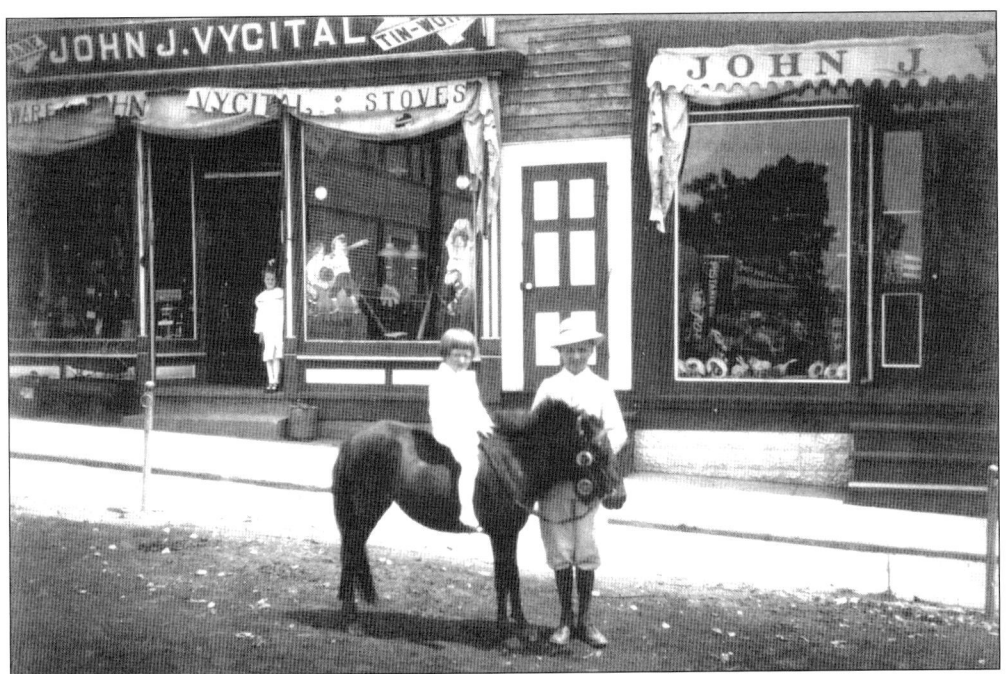

Vycital's Hardware was located on Green Street. Originally it sold only hardware, but quickly expanded, adding additional items such as housewares and gift items. By the 1920s, many of the owners of small farms purchased additional farm equipment, brooder houses, and material for chicken coops here. Builders also came to Vycital's store to purchase building supplies. (Courtesy of the McHenry County Historical Society.)

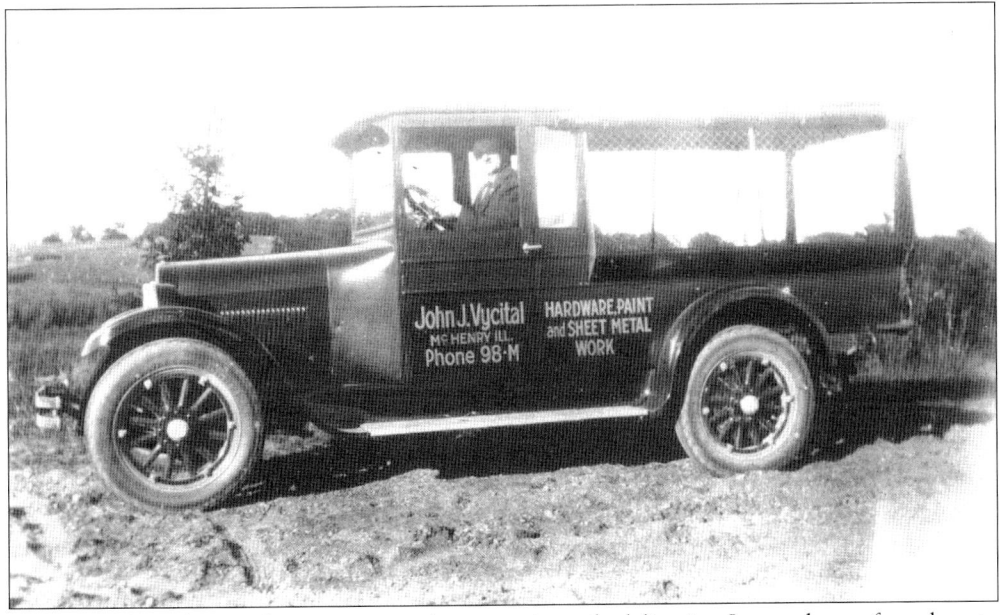

The Vycital truck was often seen around town as it made deliveries. It was the perfect place to advertise the store. Note that the store also provided hardware, paint, and sheet-metal work as lettered on the truck. Telephone numbers were far simpler than current 10-digit numbers. Vycital's number is noted to be 98-M. (Courtesy of the McHenry County Historical Society.)

85

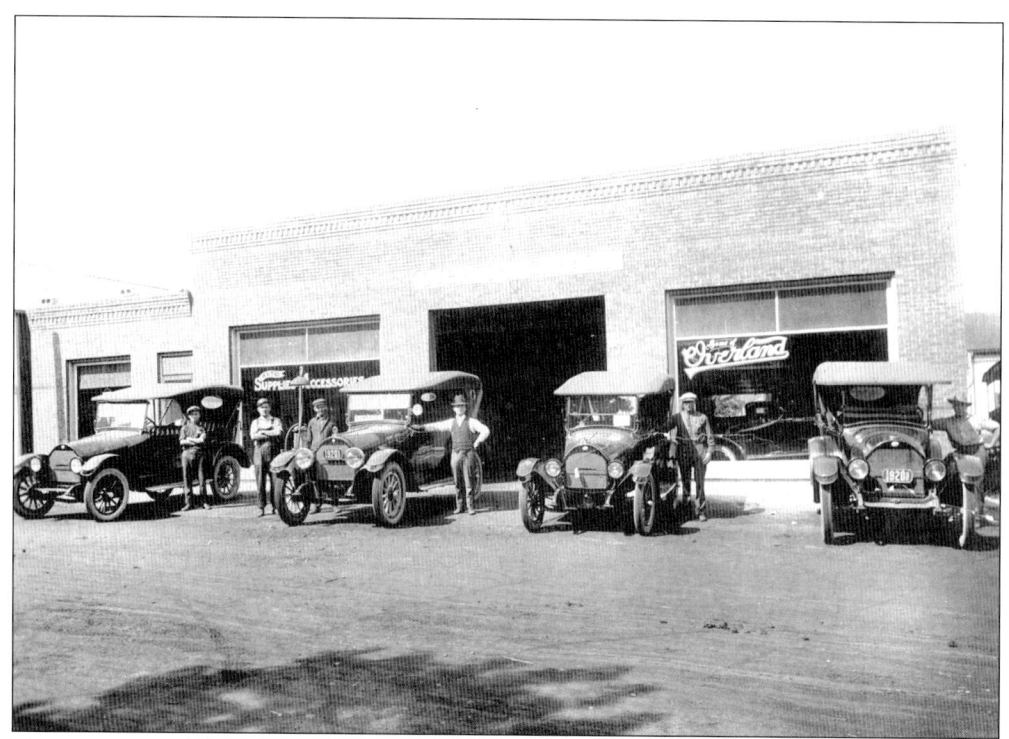

No mega automobile mall here. A new car was a reason to visit a local dealer, such as Overton's in West McHenry. New models in stock included all the popular colors: black, black, and black. Standing in the center is Richard Overton. The man third from the left is identified as Arthur Edstrom, an employee of Overton. (Courtesy of Katherine Edstrom.)

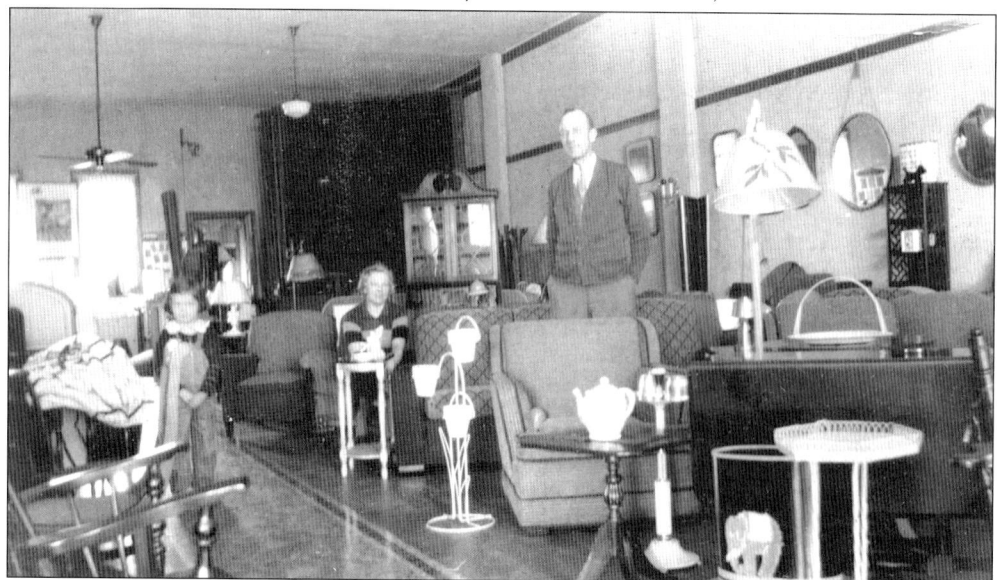

Justen's Furniture store had a wide selection of household items. Whether a shopper was looking for a roomful of furniture, a smaller piece such as an end table, or even just a tea pot, Justen's store probably had whatever was needed. This photograph of the inside of the Justen store on Elm Street was taken in 1950. (Courtesy of the McHenry Public Library.)

The neighborhood tavern was a popular place for working men to gather. It was not a fancy cocktail lounge, but rather a place known for serving a shot of whiskey or a beer and a place to share the neighborhood gossip. This tavern on the southwest corner of Main Street and Route 31 is pictured in the late 1800s. (Courtesy of Katherine Edstrom.)

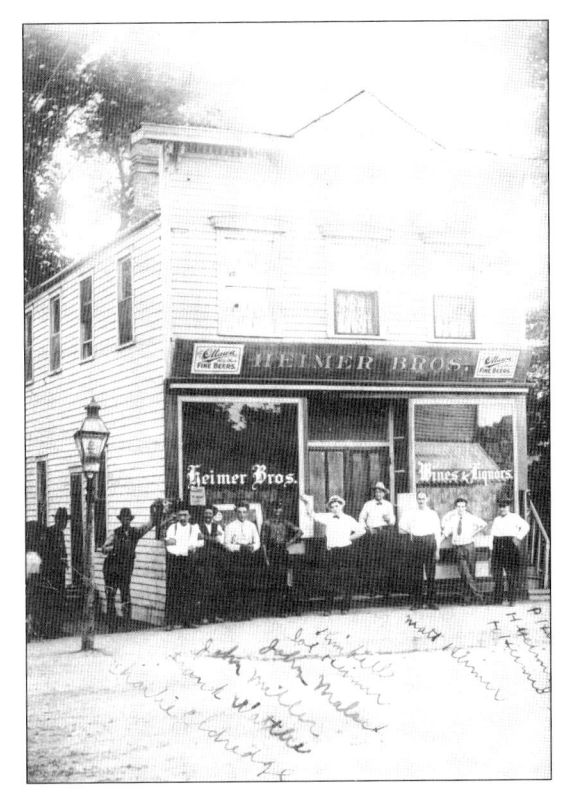

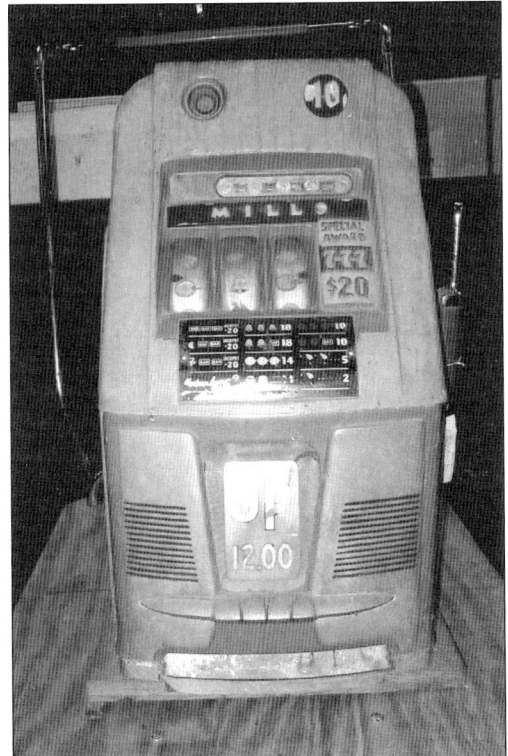

This slot machine is one of many that could be found in local business from taverns to pharmacies. One resident remembers accompanying her father and grandmother to the local tavern so father could have a beer and grandmother could play the slot machines in the women's bathroom. A raid by the state police in the mid-1900s finally removed the machines from local businesses. (Courtesy of the McHenry County Historical Society.)

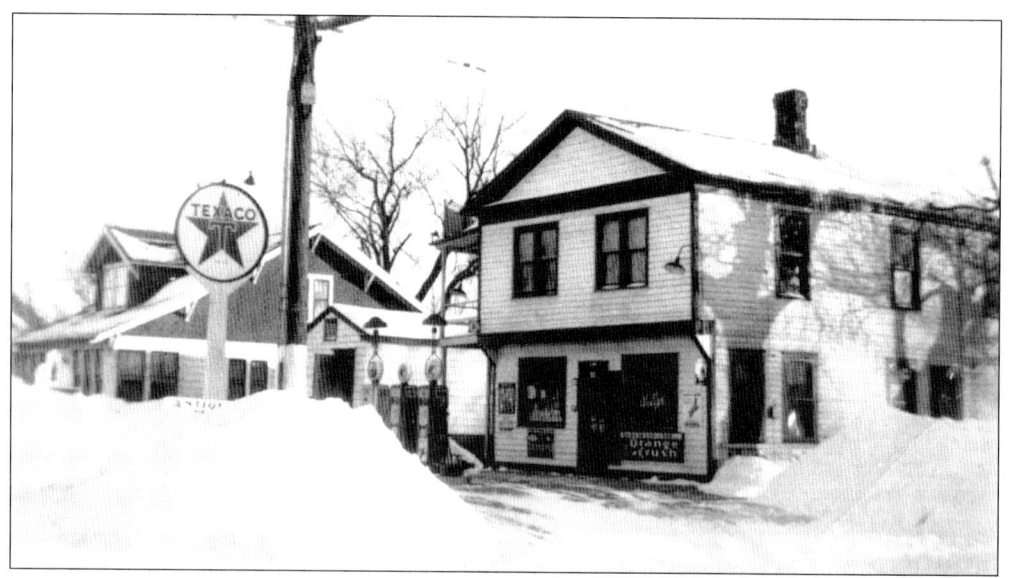

Believed to have been built around 1890, this two-story building on the southeast corner of Elm Street and Riverside Drive, opened as Holly's Filling Station and Ice House in 1934. Warren Holly operated the station until 1974. In 1976, Harriet Whitman with Don and Kathy Schramm tore out some of the existing building and opened a pancake house on the site. The restaurant, Windhill, continues in operation today with a gift shop occupying the original building. (Courtesy of the McHenry County Historical Society.)

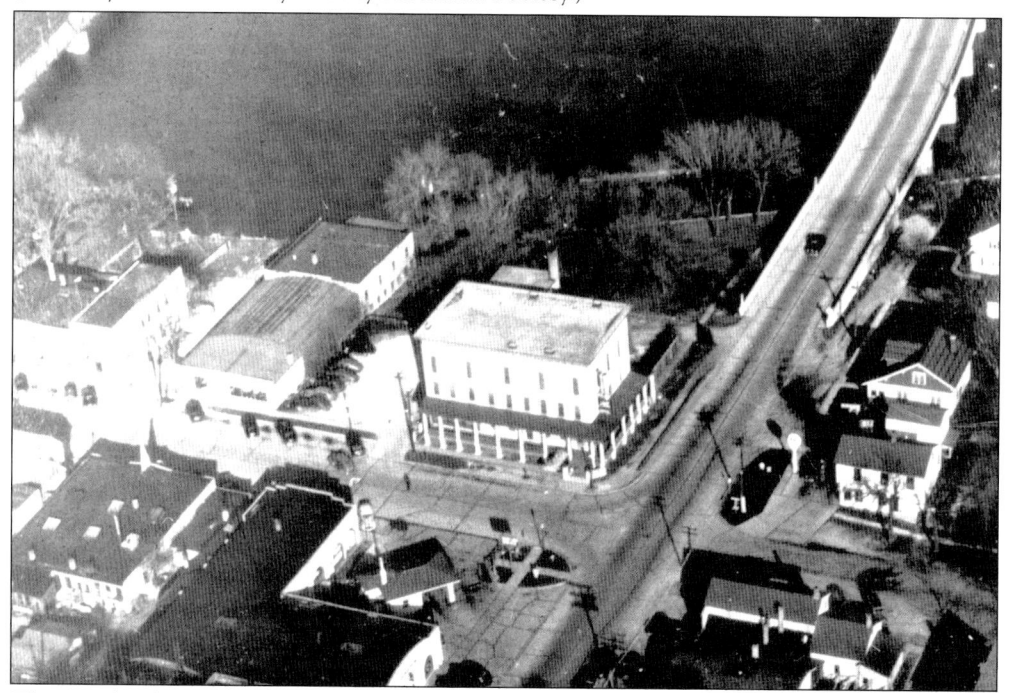

This overhead view of the bridge at Elm Street and Riverside Drive was taken around 1940. Holly's Texaco Station can be seen on the lower right corner, across from the Riverside Hotel. In the upper left corner a portion of the old iron Pearl Street bridge can be seen. (Courtesy of the McHenry County Historical Society.)

At Harvey Nye's shop on Pearl Street, he and Albert Blake (rear) work on charging a large batch of batteries. In the 1920s, the batteries were built locally and had to be returned to the shop to be charged. These batteries were used in radios and automobiles. (Courtesy of Patricia Schafer.)

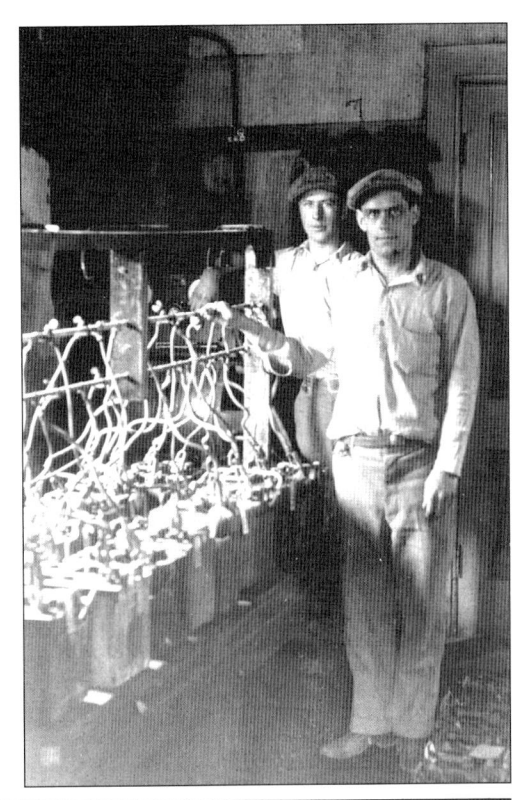

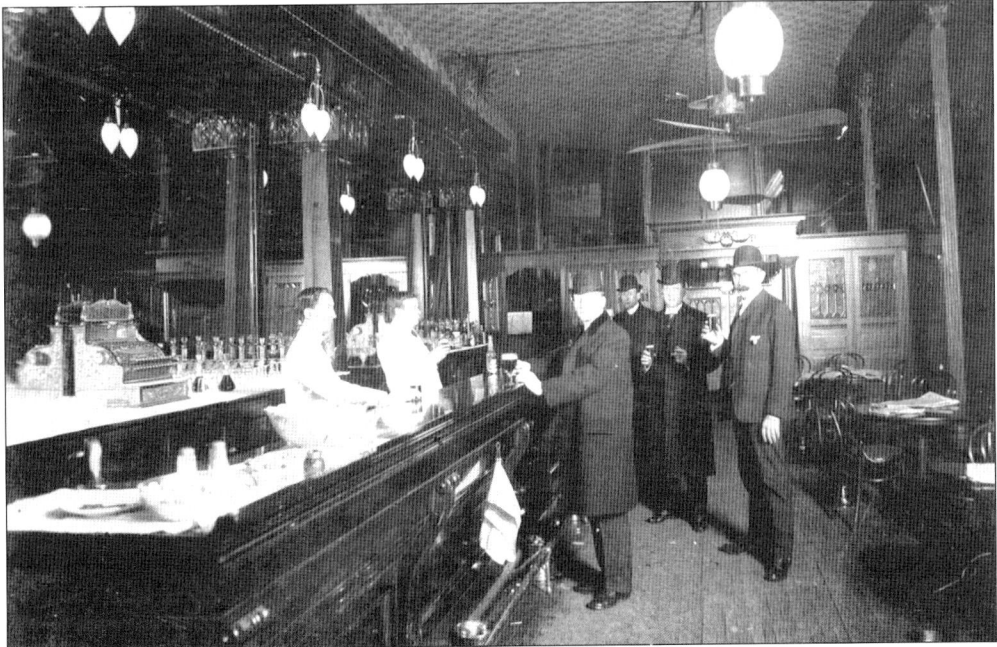

These unidentified gentlemen, dressed in hats and topcoats, are enjoying a beer in one of the local taverns. Note the spittoons placed along the floor near the bar. This tavern is believed to be on Riverside Drive and may have been the interior of the Barbian store. (Courtesy of Patricia Schafer.)

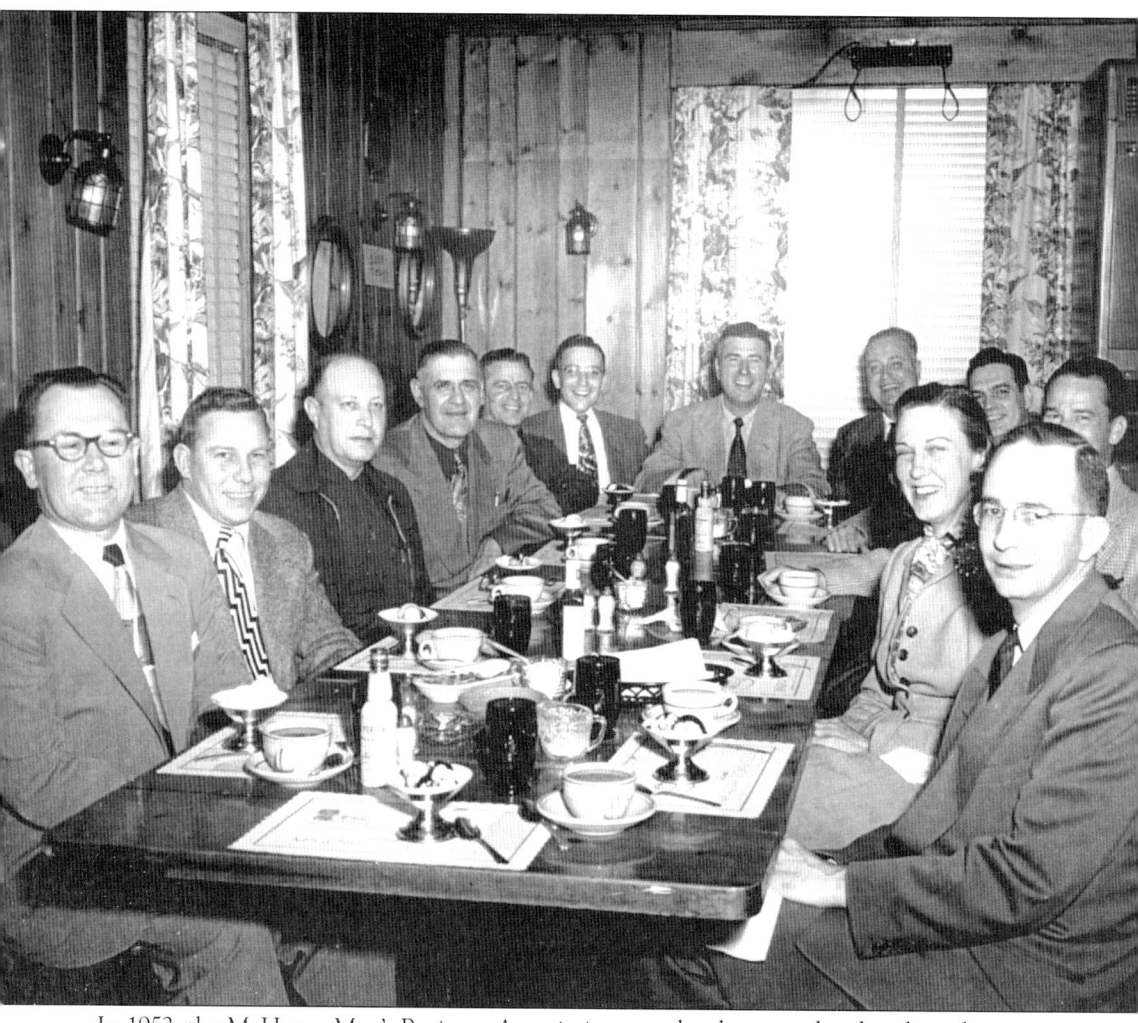

In 1952, the McHenry Men's Business Association voted to become the chamber of commerce. The first meeting of the newly formed chamber was held at the Bickler McHenry House under the direction of Pres. Albert Blake. Pictured here, clockwise from left to right, are Tony Wirtz, John Terrence, Augustine Freund, Jack Thies, Richard Hester, Dan Justen, Albert Blake, Russell Switzer, Jack Buchie, John Looze, Mildred Holman, and Dr. Eugene Saylor. (Courtesy of Patricia Schafer.)

Six

CHURCHES, SCHOOLS, THE HOSPITAL, AND SPORTS

For the majority of people who settled in the McHenry area, whether from the East Coast or from Germany and Ireland, belief in God was an important part of their lives. Churches began to be formed very soon after their arrival.

Rev. Joel Wheeler, who came to the area from New Hampshire in 1837, founded the first church, a Baptist church. The early church services were held in the main room of his house. In 1838, he opened a boarding school in his home. It is believed that a number of the early prominent people of the county were his students.

The year 1840 brought two additional churches to McHenry. The Methodist church began as a prayer group of approximately eight people who met in the Ira Colby home. St. Patrick's Catholic Church also started in much the same way. A visiting priest would celebrate mass in the home of the Sutton, Frisby, or Wall families, prior to the building of the first church in 1853. The first Lutheran church was founded in 1876 and held services using the Baptist or Methodist church until they were able to dedicate their own church in 1891. As more people settled in the area, various other religious denominations found a home in McHenry.

Education was important to the early residents of the area. The first brick school in McHenry was built in 1859 at a cost of $6,000. It was used as a public school until the building of Landmark School in 1894. The brick school was then sold to St. Mary's Parish for use as a parochial school. It continued to be used until 1936 when it burned. The high school formed a separate district in 1919 and built McHenry High School in 1924.

Interest in sports was not limited to school teams, but continued into adulthood. Adult teams competed against neighboring towns as rivalries grew.

Dr. Lee Gladstone early recognized the need for McHenry to have a hospital. In 1956 his dream was realized with the opening of a 22-bed hospital in the McHenry Medical Group building. It was a small hospital but continued to grow as McHenry grew.

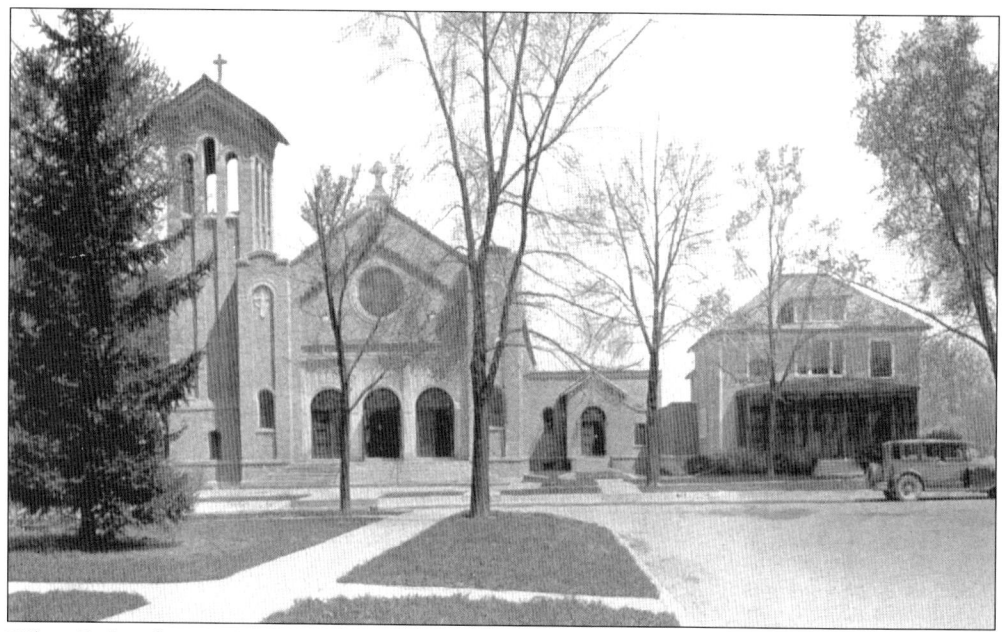

When Father de St. Palais was sent to McHenry as a missionary in 1840, he found the area settled by German and Irish immigrants. To minister to the residents he provided mass in various settlers' homes. Michael Sutton, George Frisby, or the Wall family's homes were often used. Notice of the priest's arrival was announced by the ringing of a bell, originally by Michael Sutton. The bell was necessary because the German settlers and the Irish settlers each spoke their own language. The first St. Patrick's church was completed in 1853 at a cost of $3,000. By 1922, Rev. Martin McEvoy, the pastor, saw the need for a new church. The new St. Patrick's church was dedicated on March 17, 1923, and is still in use today. (Courtesy of Patricia Schafer.)

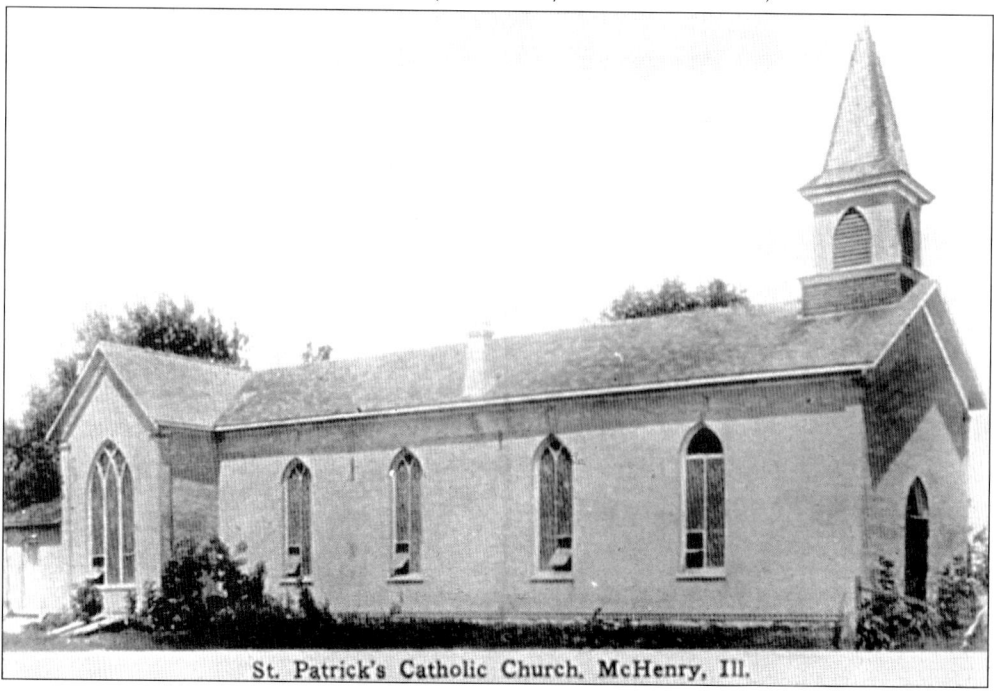

St. Patrick's Catholic Church, McHenry, Ill.

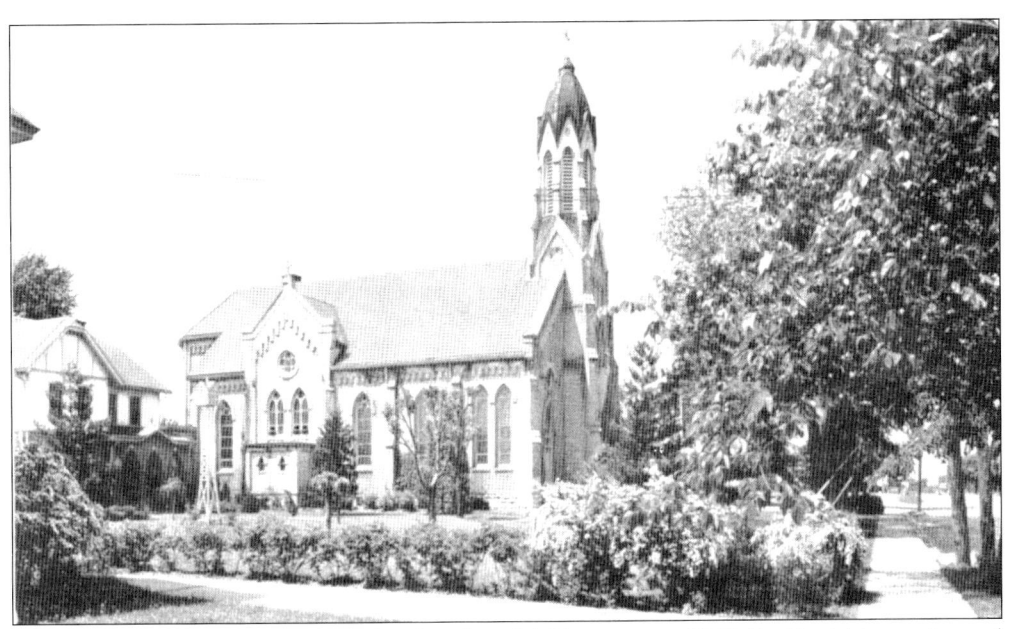

Although there had been a Catholic church in McHenry since 1840, St. Patrick's was focused on the Irish population. Often the German-speaking residents went to Johnsburg for services in their language. In 1894, Fr. F. J. Kirsch, a German speaking priest, was appointed pastor. Kirsch built St. Mary's church in 1894 for $16,750. In 1918, fire struck the church twice, destroying the rectory and severely damaging the church. (Above, courtesy of Michael Clark; below, Courtesy of Marya Dixon.)

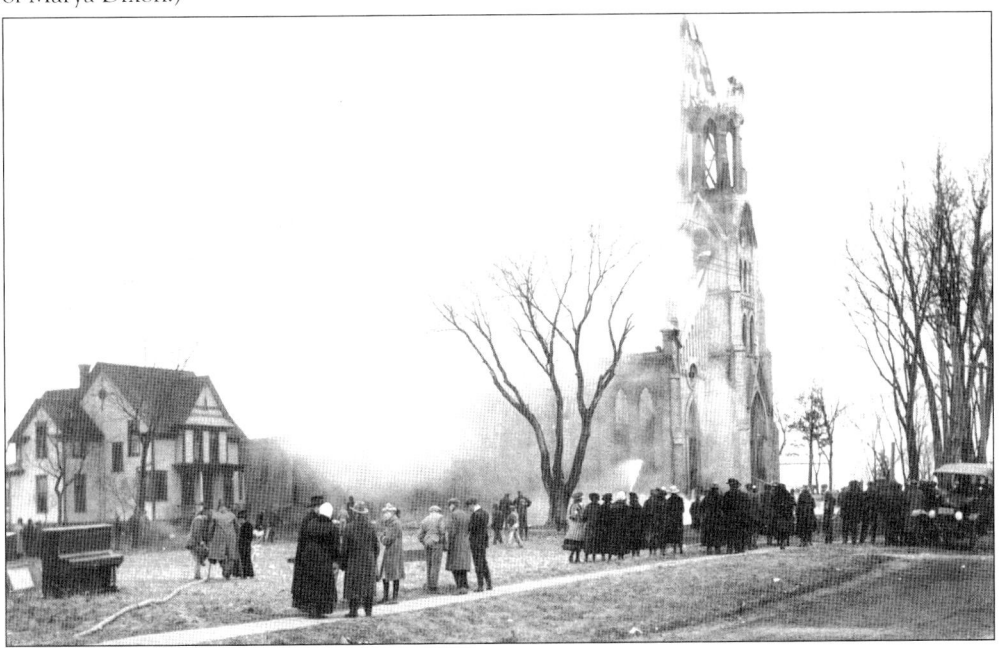

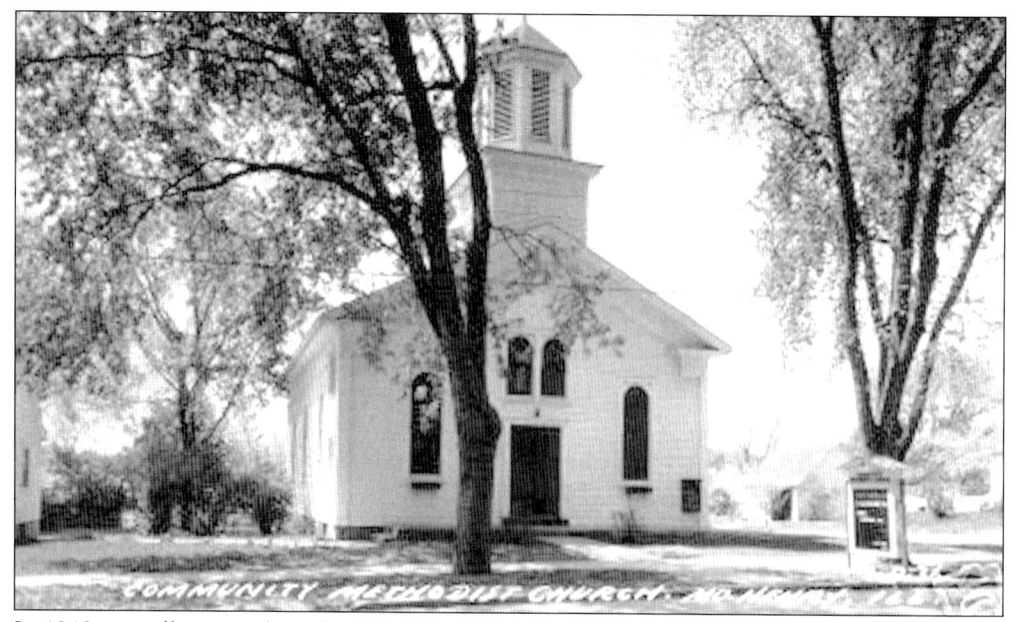

In 1840, a small group of people gathered together at the home of Ira and Mary Colby to form a prayer group. This group became the founding members of the Methodist church in McHenry. By 1859, on land donated by George and Martha Gage, the first Methodist church was built at a cost of $400. (Courtesy of Michael Clark.)

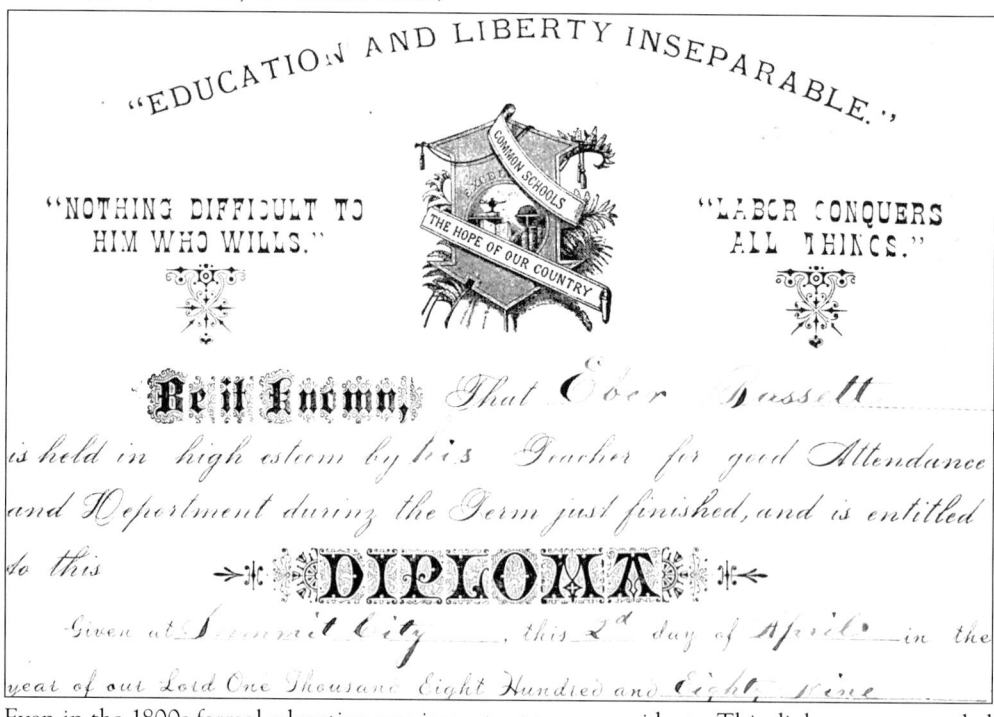

Even in the 1800s formal education was important to area residents. This diploma was awarded to Eber Bassett in April 1889 for good attendance and deportment during the school term. Note the diploma is dated early April, allowing students to be available for spring planting. (Courtesy of Ilene Wiedemann.)

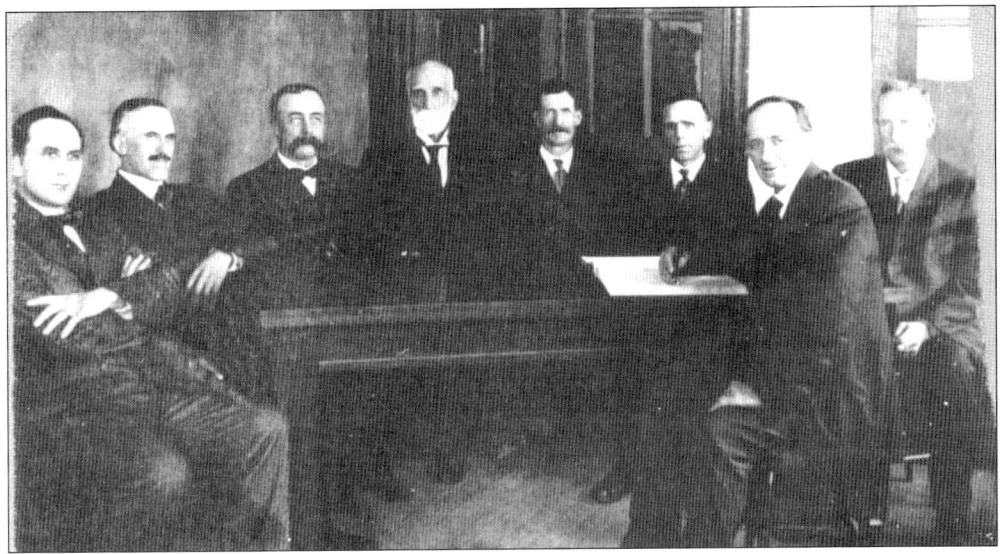

The 1916 school board included many prominent businessmen, who gave their time to promote education. Shown from left to right are A. E. Nye, William Bonslett, N. R. Justen, James Perry, William Welch, Stephen Freund, Charles L. Page, and John Clayton. (Courtesy of the McHenry Public Library.)

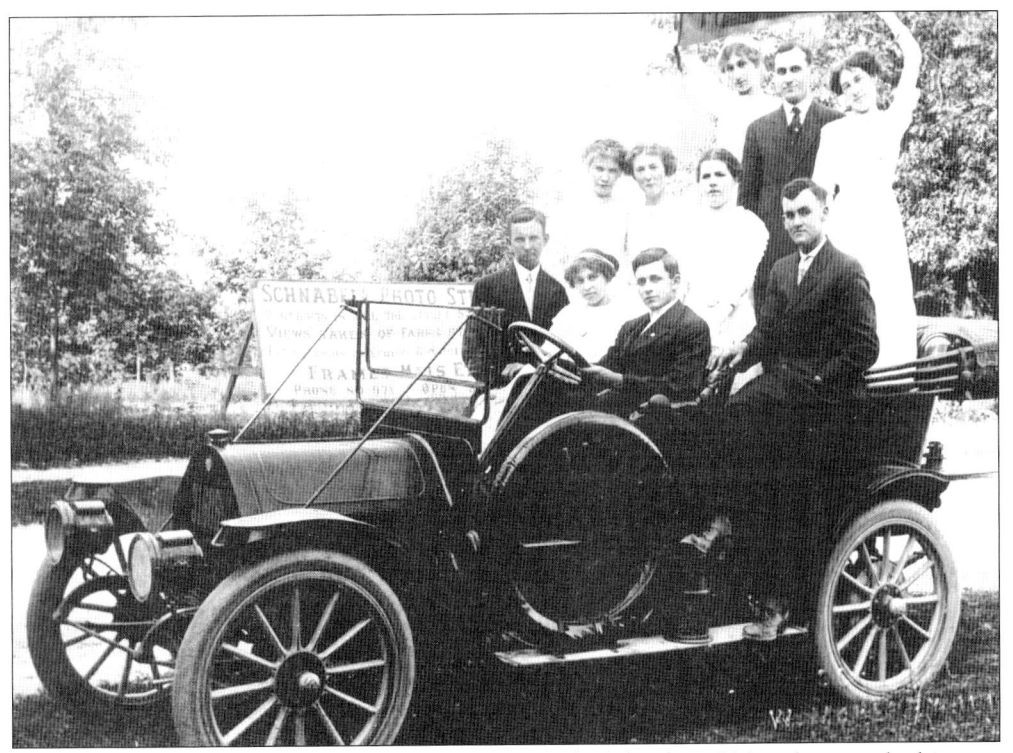

In 1912, the entire graduating class of McHenry High School could be photographed in one automobile. Sitting in the driver's seat is John Bolger with Ella Mollohan next to him. Standing in the middle rear is Prof. A. E. Nye with Margaret Buss on his right. (Courtesy of the McHenry Public Library.)

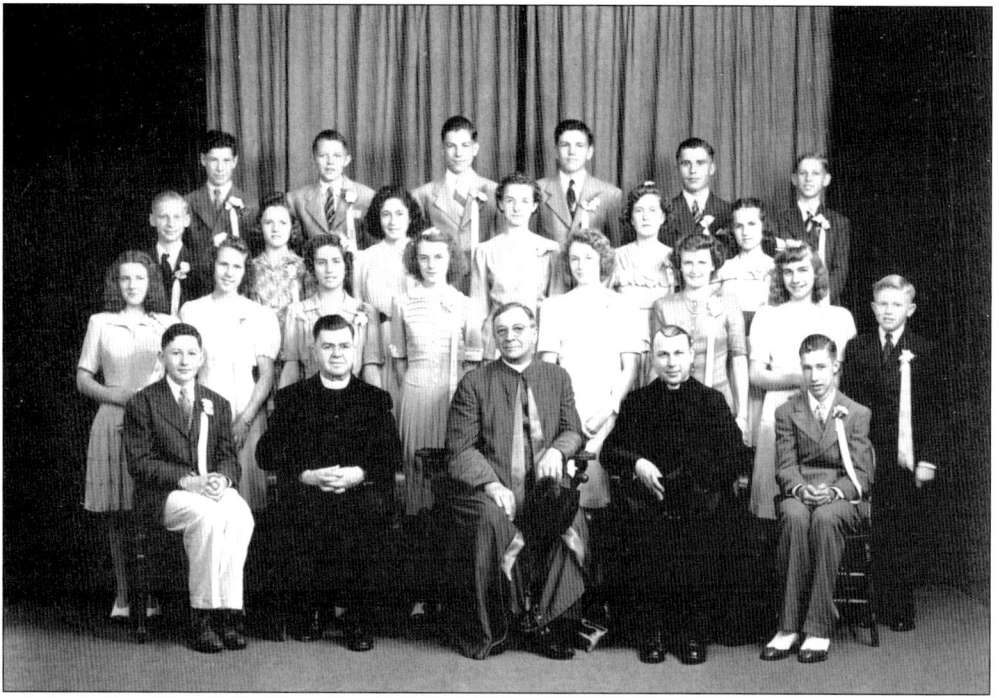

St. Mary's Catholic School proudly presented the graduating class of 1942 in this photograph. The school offered McHenry's first Catholic education in 1896 and continued in operation until 1937. Pictured standing in the fourth row, second from left is James Althoff. In the third row, on the far right is Rosalie Williams Doherty. (Courtesy of James Althoff.)

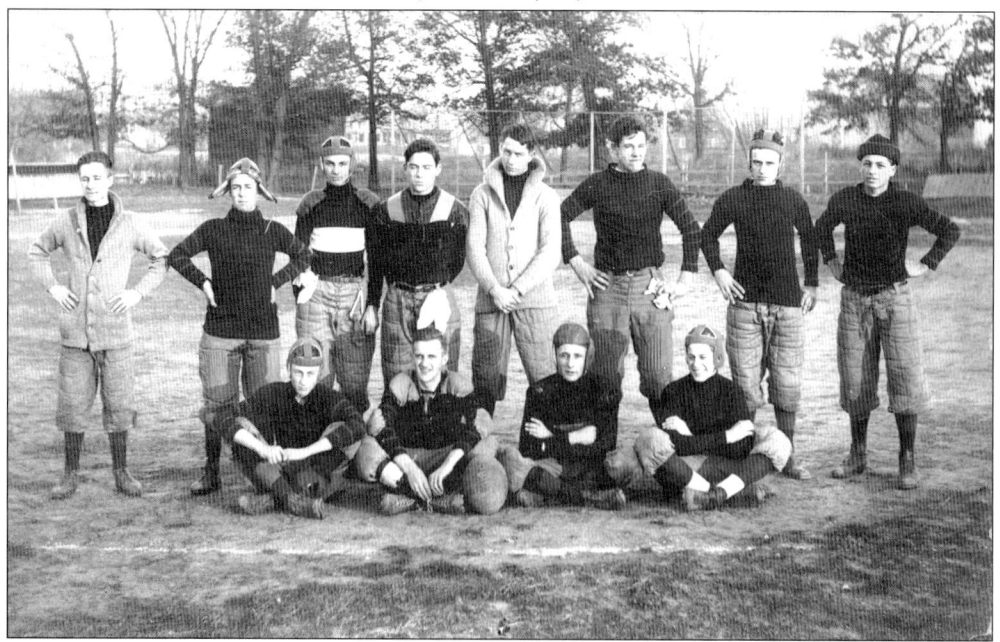

In the early 1900s, football was popular among high school students. The uniforms had a far different look than they do today. Wearing protective gear was not a priority. Henry John Miller is pictured fifth from the left in the second row. (Courtesy of John Henry Miller.)

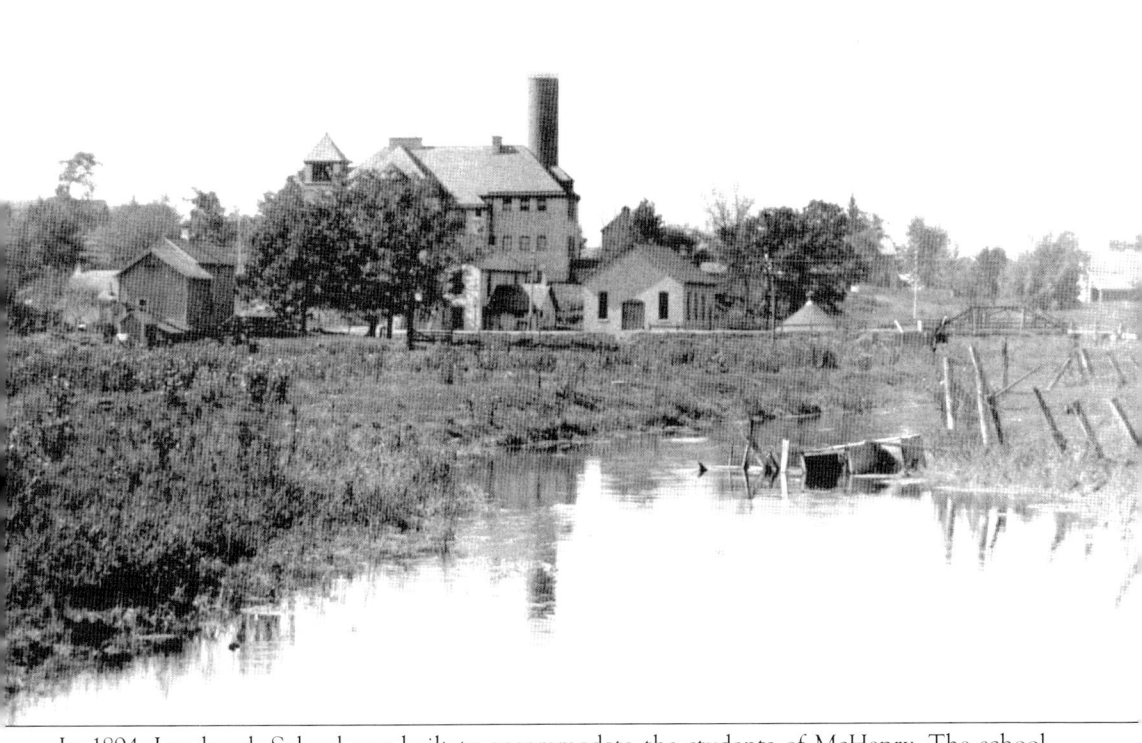

In 1894, Landmark School was built to accommodate the students of McHenry. The school was used as both an elementary and a high school at the same time. Originally the high school curriculum was a two year course. The first principal of Landmark, W. H. Strayer, taught the entire high school program. Agnes Perry succeeded him as the high school teacher when the curriculum was increased to three years. Superintendent E. C. Fisher introduced basketball in 1903 and added music to the program in 1905. By his final year, in 1906, Fisher had increased the high school curriculum to four years, which was accredited by the University of Illinois. Citizens of McHenry rose to protest when the school board planned to demolish the school in 1967. Over 1,000 people signed petitions to save the school causing the school board to reconsider. Today Landmark School is still in operation as a year-round school. The school's unique feature is a bell tower, which is still in working order. (Courtesy of the McHenry Public Library.)

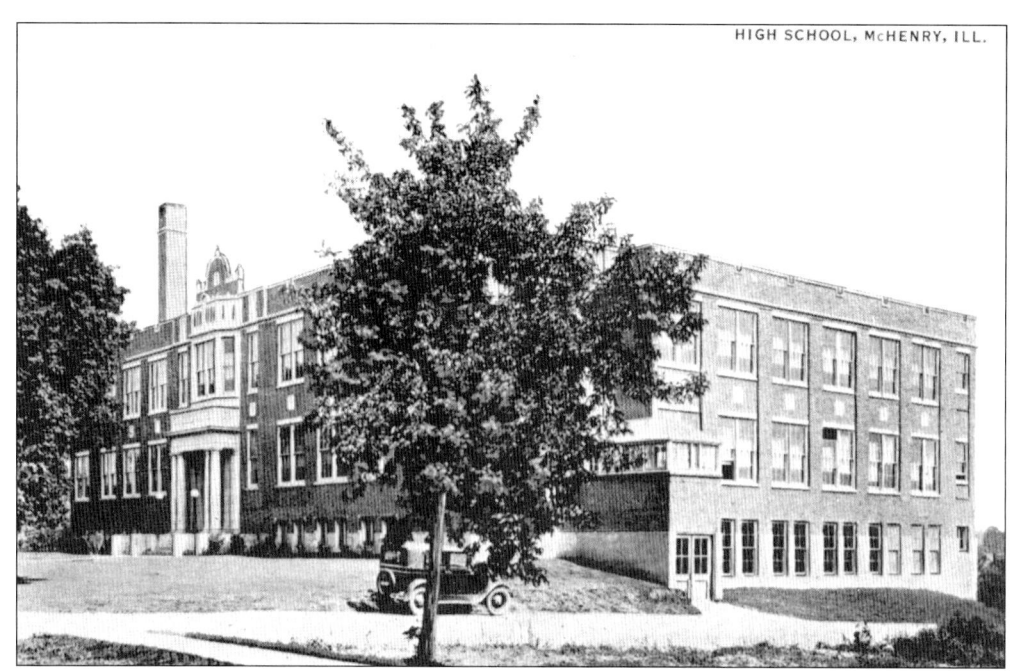

In 1924, the high school students moved out of Landmark School into their own building. The new campus was located at 1012 North Green Street. Addition of a gymnasium in 1947 and building expansion in 1957 were needed because of the ever expanding population. In 1968, an additional high school, the West Campus, was built and the old campus became known as the East Campus. (Courtesy of Patricia Schafer.)

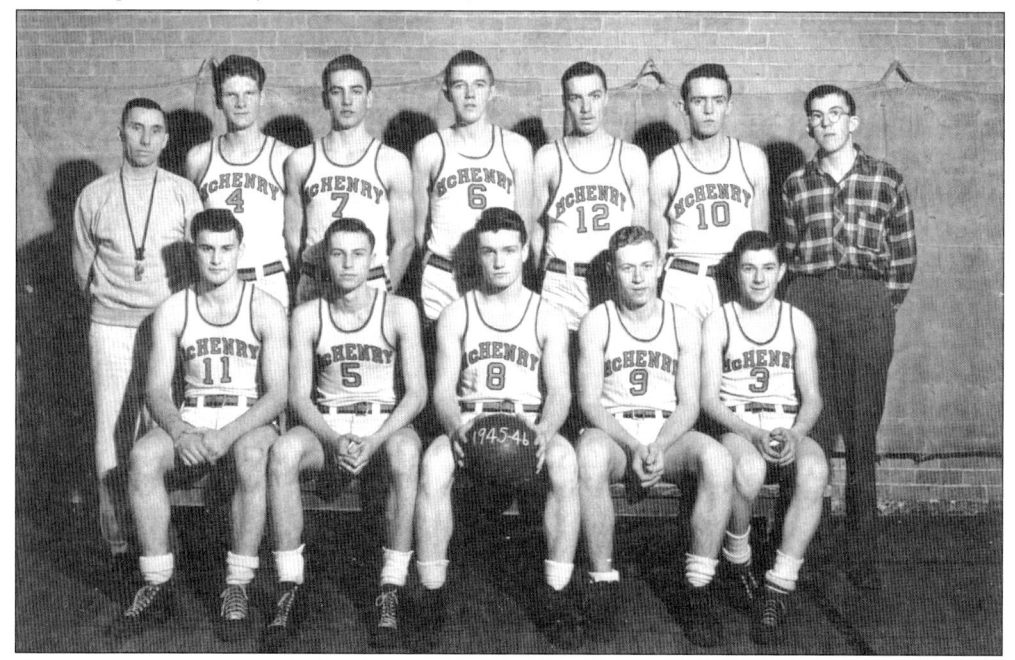

Sports were important to high school students. This photograph of the 1945–1946 basketball team, shows them posing with their coach proudly displaying their McHenry uniforms. (Courtesy of James Althoff.)

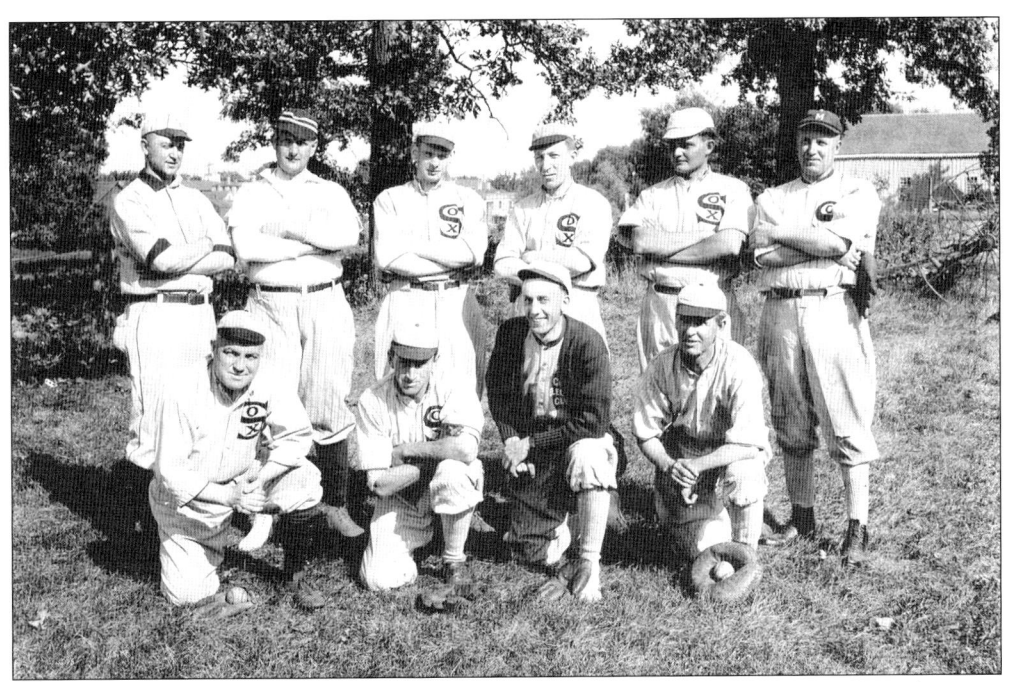

Local baseball teams were found all over McHenry County. Competition was fierce between the many towns and teams. This photograph is of the team known as the White Sox, not the Chicago variety but the McHenry team. (Courtesy of Patricia Schafer.)

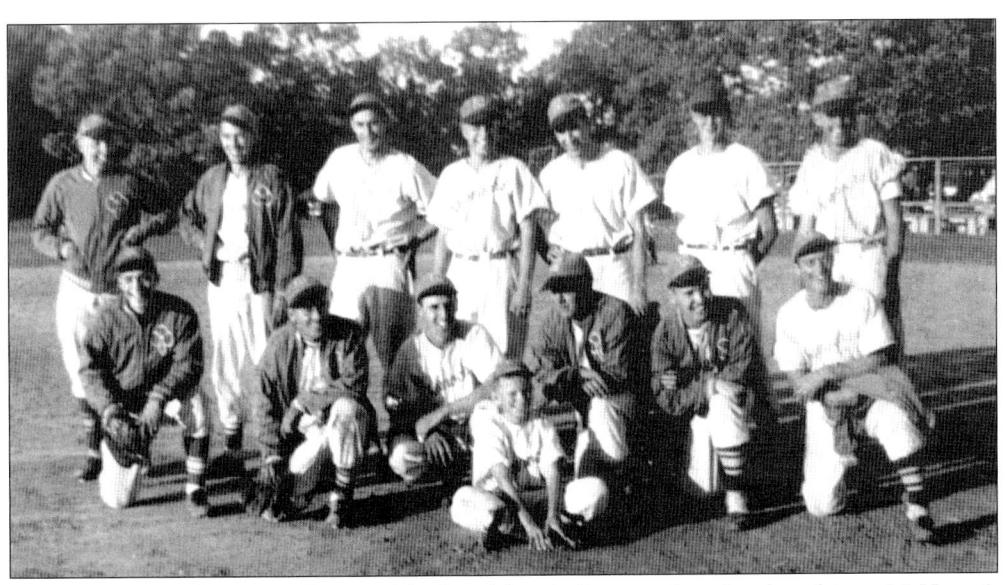

In 1938, Tom Bolger started a neighborhood baseball team that developed into McHenry's premier sports team. From 1942 to 1954, Tom's brother Bill managed the team. The Shamrocks had just defeated rival Johnsburg for the championship when this picture was taken. Identified here are John J. Bolger, Mike Santoro, Dean McCracken, manager Bill Bolger, Larry Stilling, Tom Bolger, Harry Stilling, Willard McCulla, Dick Conway, Gerald Larkin, Nick Freund, Paul Freund, and Sonny Miller. (Courtesy of William Bolger.)

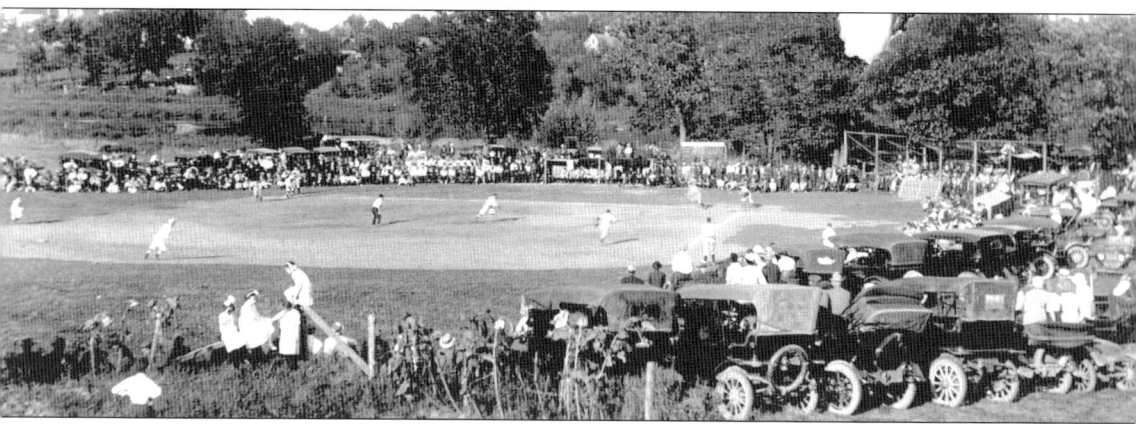

Summertime found McHenry residents outdoors playing or watching their favorite sport: baseball. But no game caused more excitement than the one played on Wednesday, September 9, 1914. For on that day the major league Chicago White Sox came to town to play against the local McHenry White Sox. Legend has it that the Chicago White Sox arrived in the morning by train and were housed at the Riverside House. In the afternoon, they were treated to a ride up to Pistakee Bay on the *Gladene*. That evening they faced the local competition with "Big Ed" Walsh on the mound. In spite of McHenry's best efforts, the Chicago White Sox won by a score of 13 to 1. (Courtesy of the McHenry County Historical Society.)

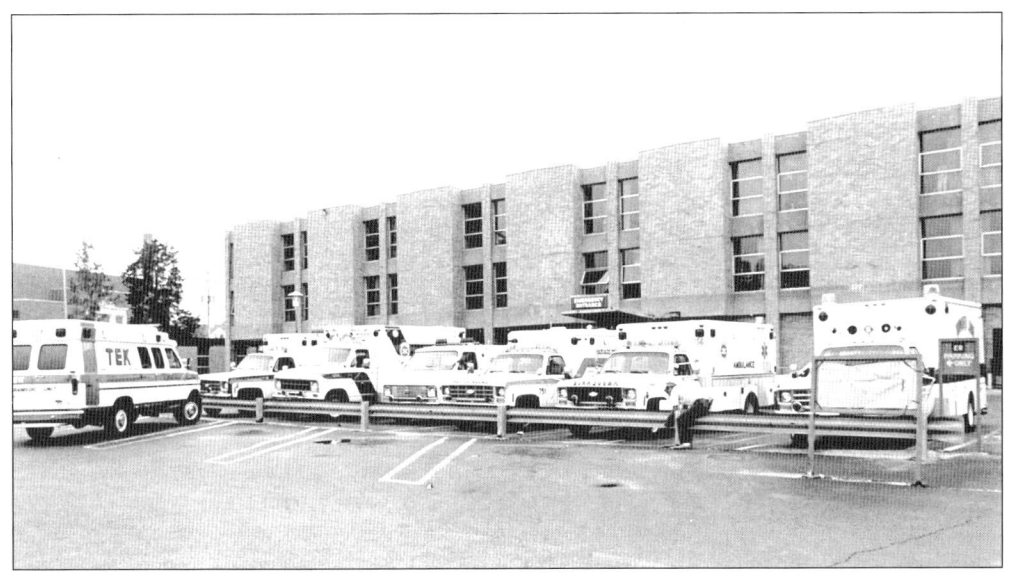

McHenry Hospital first opened its doors on September 4, 1956. The 22-bed acute care hospital was located on the lower level of the McHenry Medical Group building on Green Street. The hospital was a true community endeavor with community members donating much of the equipment needed. Dr. Lee Gladstone and Dr. George Alvary signed personal notes to guarantee the mortgage. A new three-story building was built in 1966 as the area's population grew and health-care needs increased. (Courtesy of Northern Illinois Medical Center.)

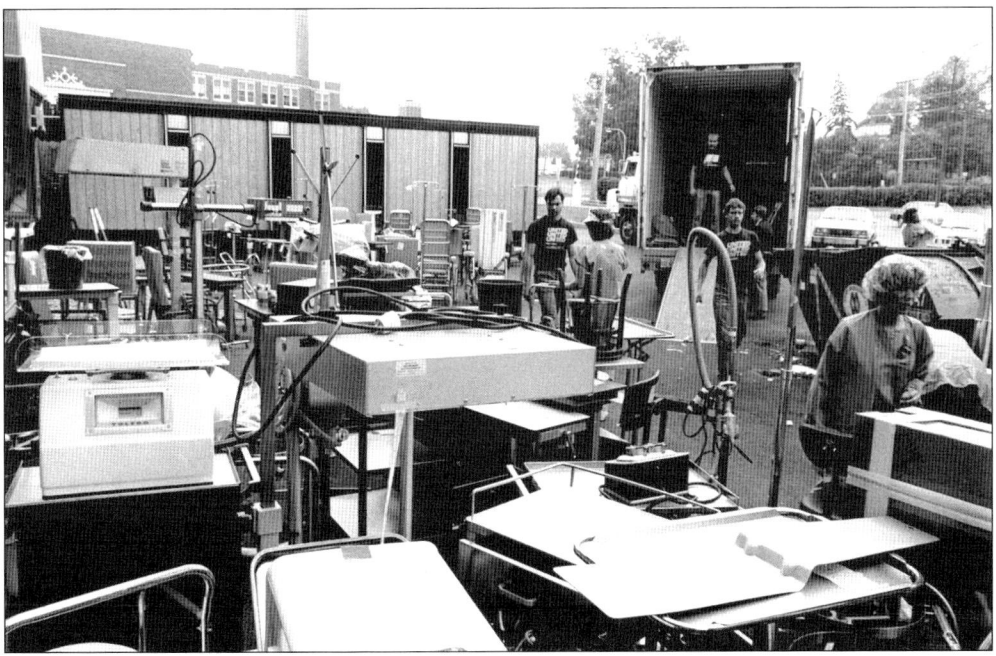

By the 1970s it was obvious that the hospital was not able to keep up with the needs of the growing population. Forty acres of land were donated by Clara Stilling from her farm on Bull Valley Road. Plans were made for a new regional medical center. In June 1984, the new hospital was completed. On moving day, shown here, hospital patients and equipment were moved using school buses, rescue squad ambulances, and trucks. (Courtesy of Northern Illinois Medical Center.)

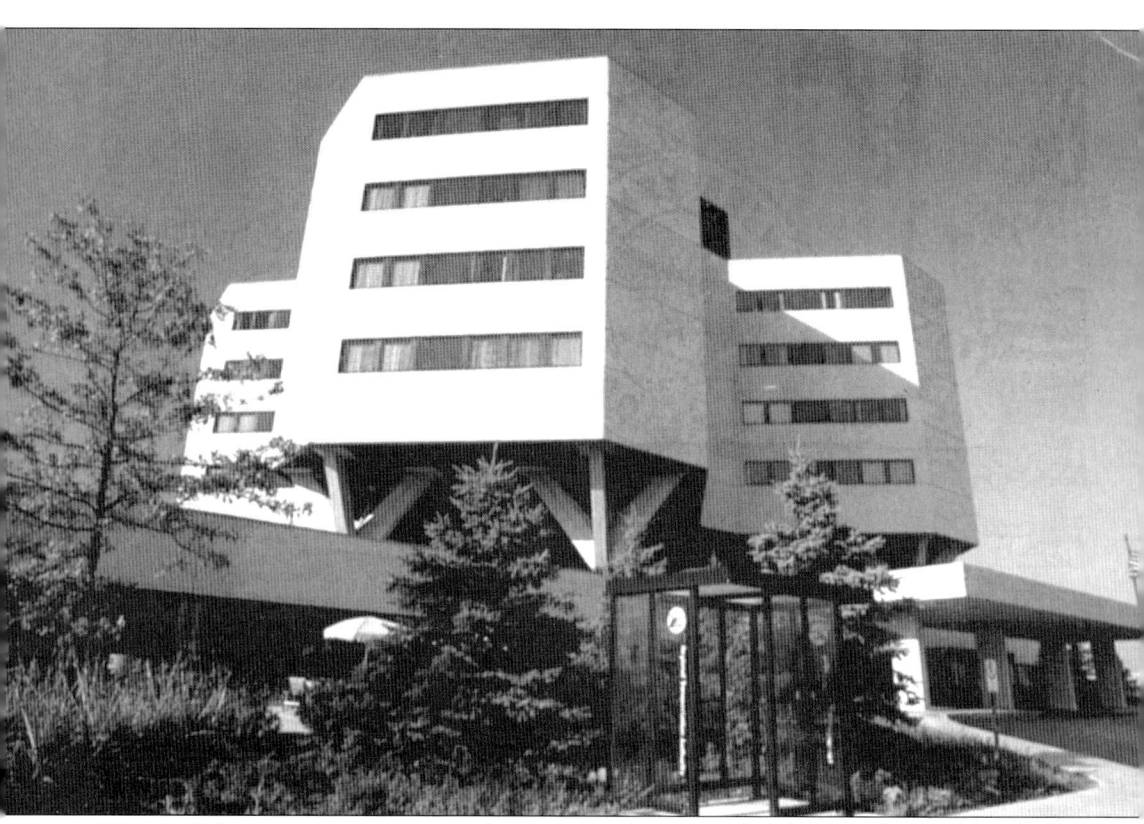

When all the moving was completed, the hospital patients found themselves in this modern four-story building built to accommodate 195 patient beds. The hospital name was changed to Northern Illinois Medical Center. The new hospital is located off of Bull Valley Road and Route 31. (Courtesy of Michael Clark.)

Seven
LIFE AT McCULLOM LAKE

West of the Fox River on the northwest side of the city of McHenry lies a small lake. This lake covers 245 acres, has a shore line of 2.9 miles, and an average depth of only four feet. Its water is supplied primarily by springs and groundwater runoff. In spite of this small size, it is a lake with an interesting history.

On July 14, 1837, William McCullom, along with his brothers David and John, pitched a tent on the western shore of the lake and became its first settlers. While David and John later moved on to other parts of the country, William remained in McHenry.

By the 1900s, McCullom Lake became a vacation destination. Small fishing shacks and weekend homes began to appear on its shores. For the children of the families who spent summers on the lake it was a place of unique memories and friendships.

In 1940, a private individual dredged the north end of the lake to a depth of 8 to 10 feet. Due to a decline in fishing in the 1950s, the Illinois Department of Conservation became involved and recommended a complete rehabilitation of the fish population. In 1959, the homeowners collected enough funds to treat the lake. In the 1970s, and again in the 1990s, a concerned group of people worked with the state biologist to solve lake problems.

Ownership of the lake itself has also been challenged. The Breyer family, considered to be the second family to settle McCullom Lake's shores, was sued by their neighbors when fences were placed into the lake in front of the Breyer property preventing access to the lake's waters. The majority of the lake bottom is now owned by the City of McHenry.

Today these early cottages have been transformed into year-round homes. Because it is a shallow lake, use of highly powered boats is prohibited. It is a serene lake where in the summer rowboats, canoes, kayaks, small sailboats, and an occasional pontoon meander along its surface. The several beaches attract swimmers and the festivals held at Petersen Park provide a partylike atmosphere.

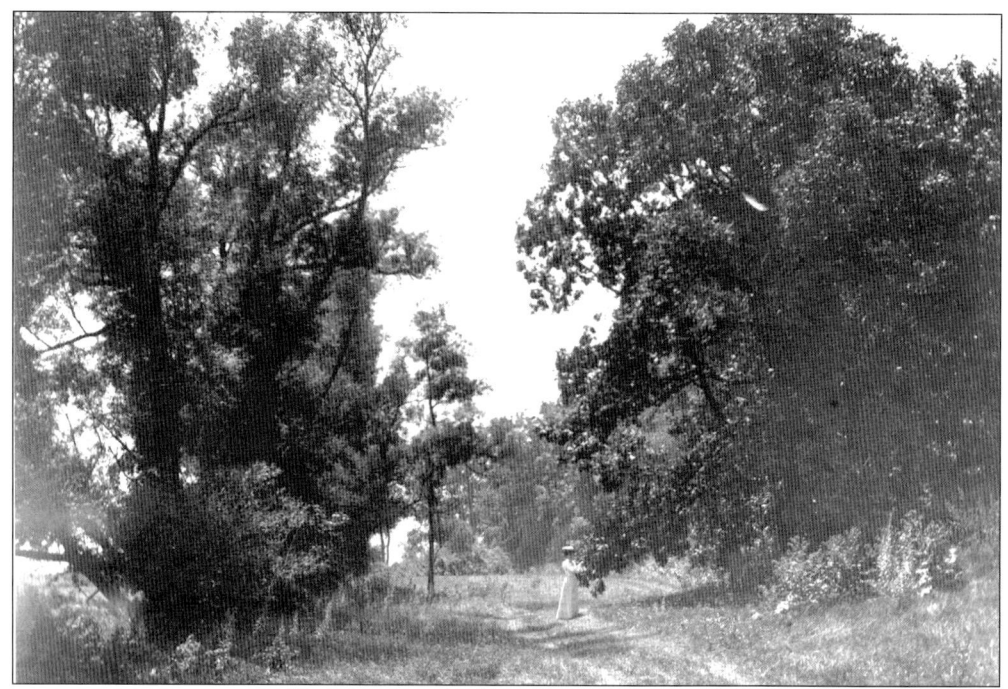

In the 1800s, the entrance to McCullom Lake was surrounded by large oak trees. This photograph is of a woman only identified as Alma as she walks down to the lake. (Courtesy of the McHenry Public Library.)

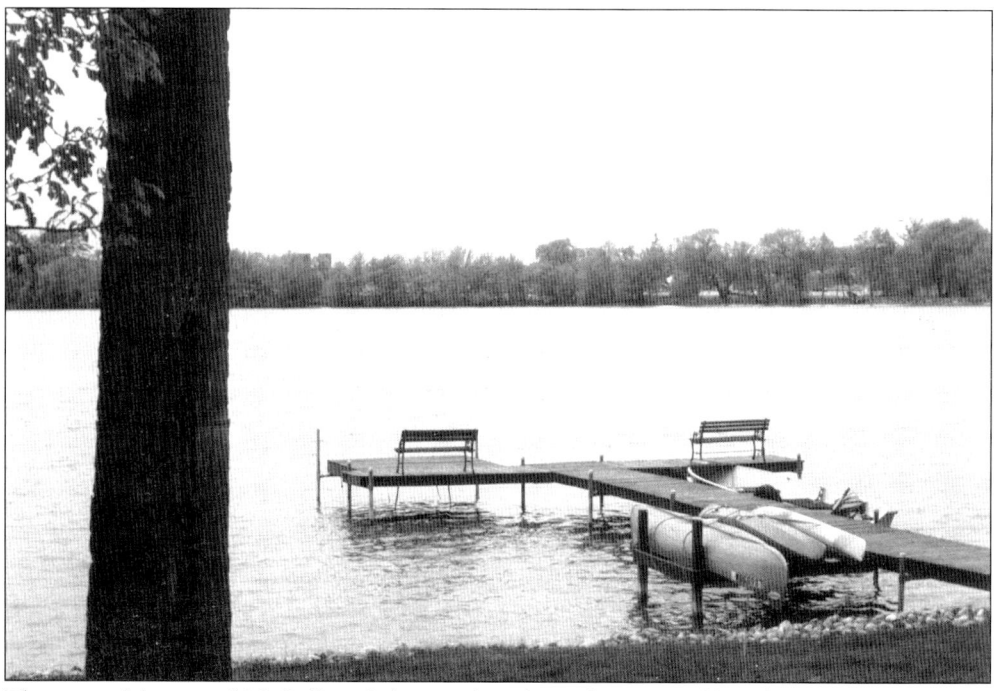

This peaceful view of McCullom Lake is taken from the Moerschbaecher family's pier. The benches are a place to sit and watch the evening sunset. Across the lake, the silos of the Mass Farm can be seen. (Courtesy of William and Amy Moerschbaecher.)

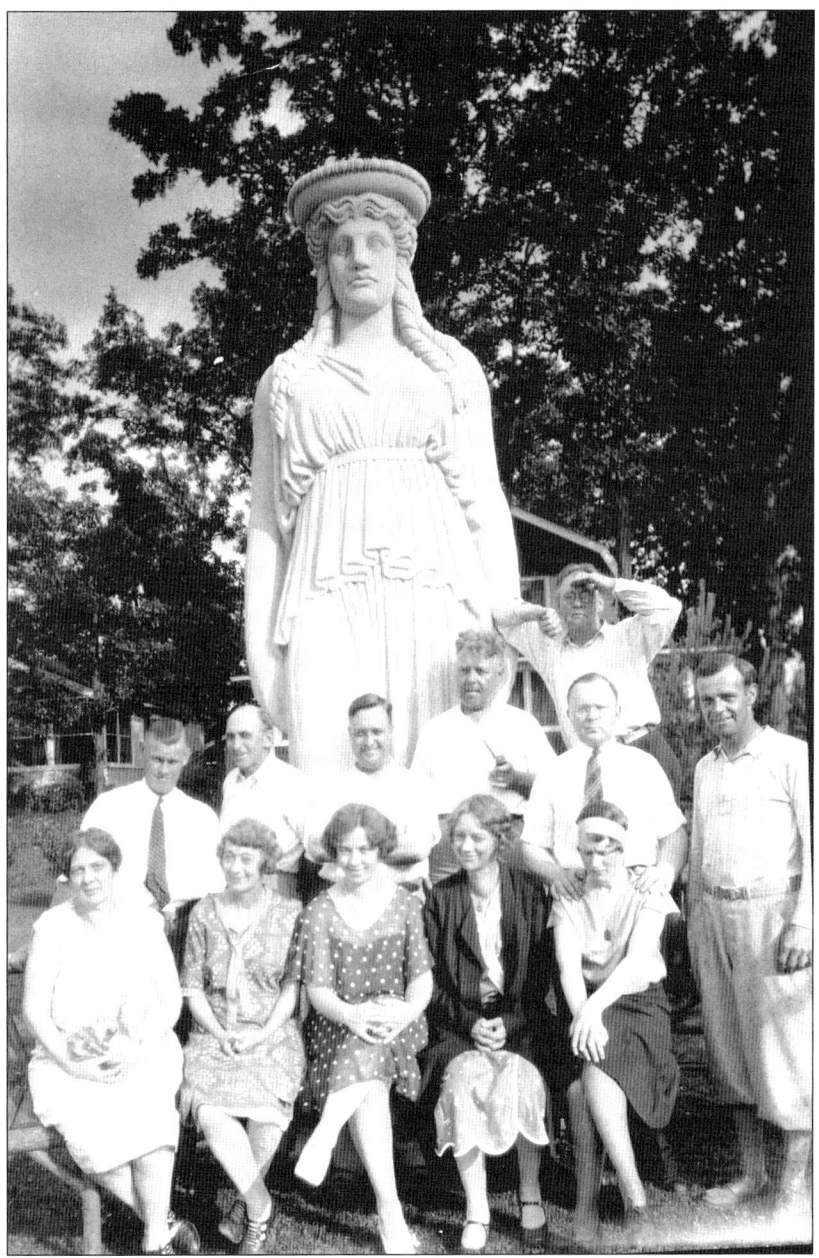

From 1925 to 1956, this statue graced the shore of McCullom Lake. Edward Simonson was working on construction at the Museum of Science and Industry, when the statue arrived with a broken toe. The statue was to be used as a pillar on the front of the museum. It was considered defective and therefore unusable to the museum. Simonson had the statue transported by flatbed truck to his home on Lakewood Road. The ride was a long and arduous one as many of the roads were unpaved. He then erected it in his yard facing the lake. For many years the statue was known as "Lady of the Lake." Pictured here from left to right are (first row) Hannah Johnson Simonson, Della Johnson, Sylvia Simonson Nelson, Olga Johnson Lakeburg, and Jessie Reiner; (second row) Zigi ?, August Lakeburg, Sanger Nelson, Edward Simonson, Bill Reiner, and Roy Simonson; (third row) Charlie Johnson (leaning on statue). (Courtesy Susan Rutherford.)

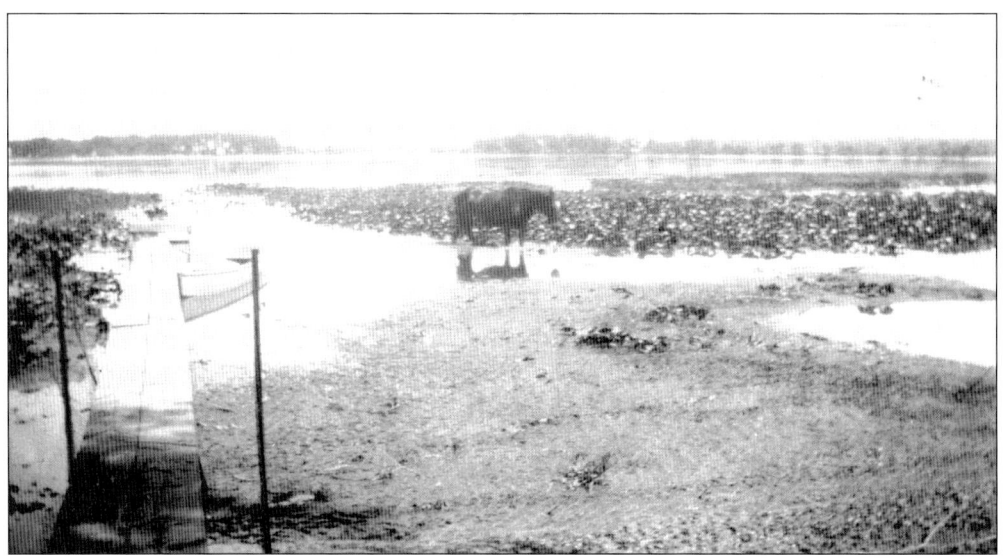

The year 1933 was not a year that residents along McCullom Lake could enjoy their usual water-based activities. The drought caused much of the lake to dry out. Piers and boats were now on dry land as the lake receded from the shore. Here a horse walks into the center of the lake for a drink of water. (Courtesy of the McHenry County Historical Society.)

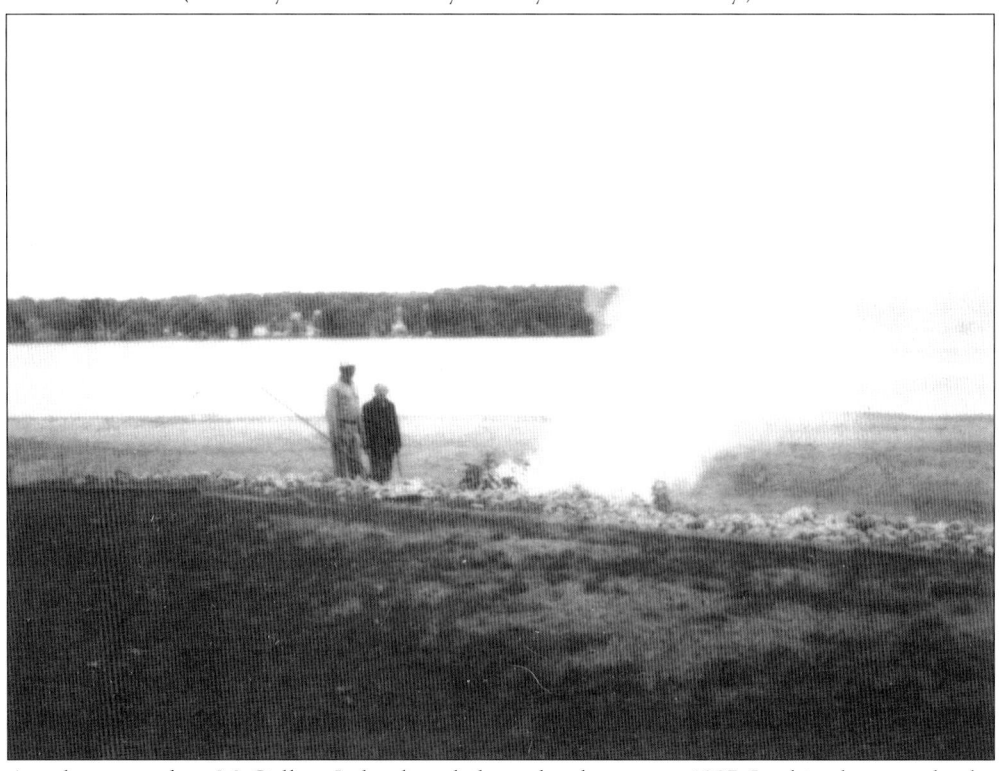

Another year when McCullom Lake shrunk from the shores was 1987. In this photograph, the Frisch family is sweeping debris from an area that is usually part of the lake bottom. Boats were beached. It was possible to walk across the lake without getting very wet. (Courtesy of the Frisch family.)

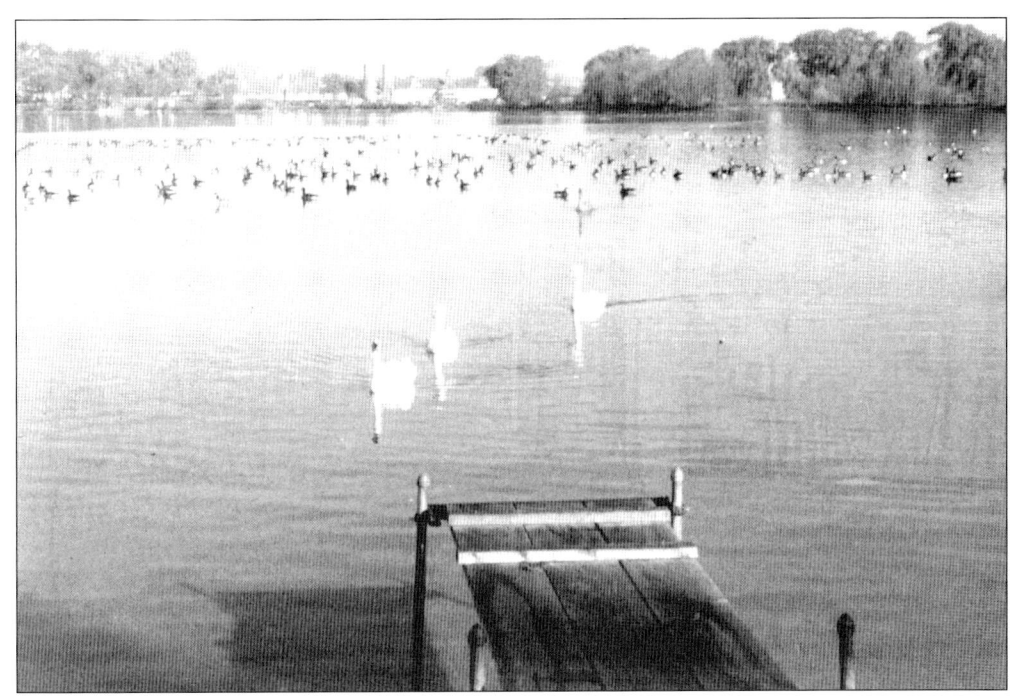

The lake is a haven for wildlife. Deer, coyotes, fox, and raccoons can be seen along the lake at various times of the year. The three swans in the foreground made themselves at home. The ducks and geese in the background are also enjoying the lake. The Mass barn can be seen across the lake. (Courtesy of John P. Haley.)

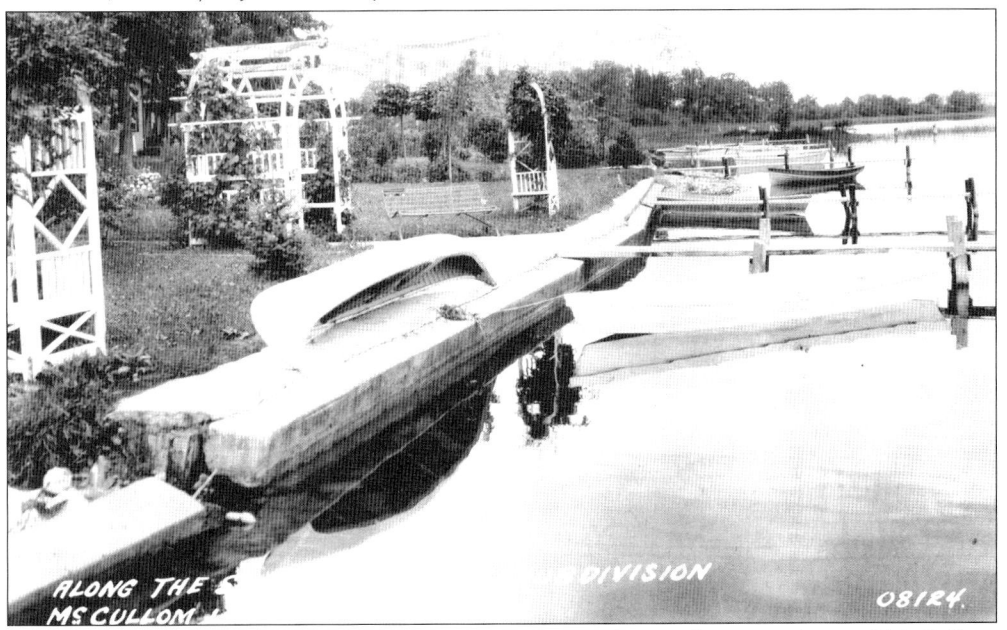

Along the shores of Colby's Lakewood subdivision, on the northeastern shore of McCullom Lake, the attractive white trellis along the waterfront presents a distinctive look. Rowboats, canoes, and kayaks are often present since high powered motorboats are not allowed. (Courtesy of William and Amy Moerschbaecher.)

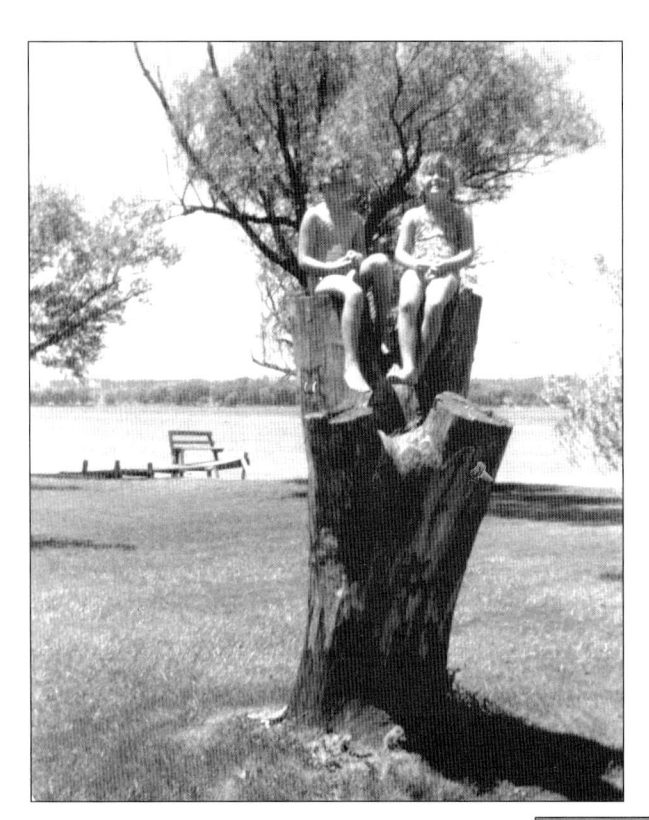

Always looking for new things to do at the lake, Marie Frisch (left) and Kim Williams find that climbing the stump of a recently cut tree provides a great view of the lake or just a place to sit and talk. (Courtesy of Nancy Williams.)

Summers on McCullom Lake were a time of swimming, fishing, boating, biking, and leisurely walks down Lakewood Road. But more memorable were the friendships that developed as families returned each year. Pictured are Dorothy Haley (left) and Charlene Toth who spent summers in cottages next door to each other. (Courtesy of John P. Haley.)

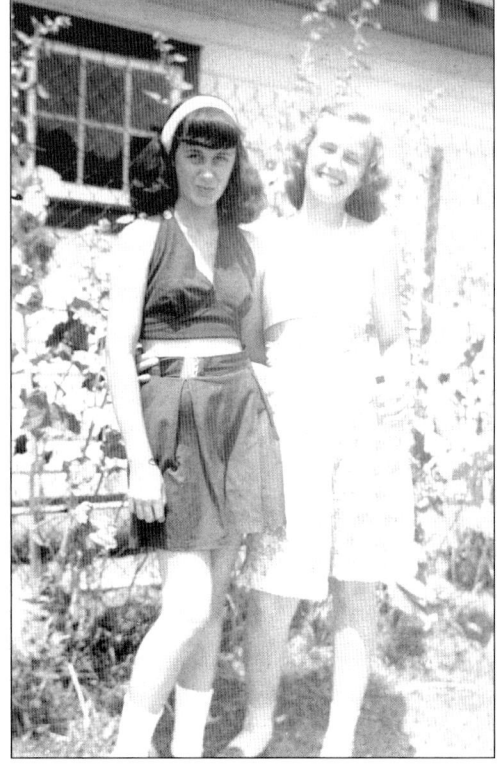

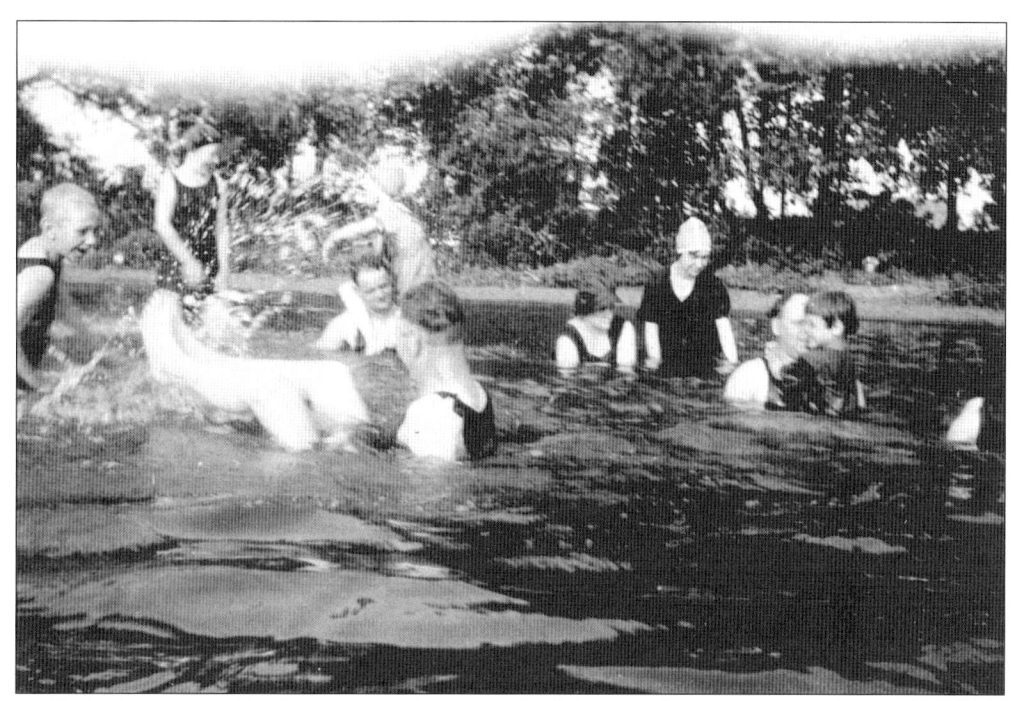

In 1916, this group of bathers enjoys playing in the lake. On the hot summer days, a dip in the lake was the quickest way to cool down. The man on the far right is holding his two-year-old daughter, identified as Dorothy. (Courtesy of John P. Haley.)

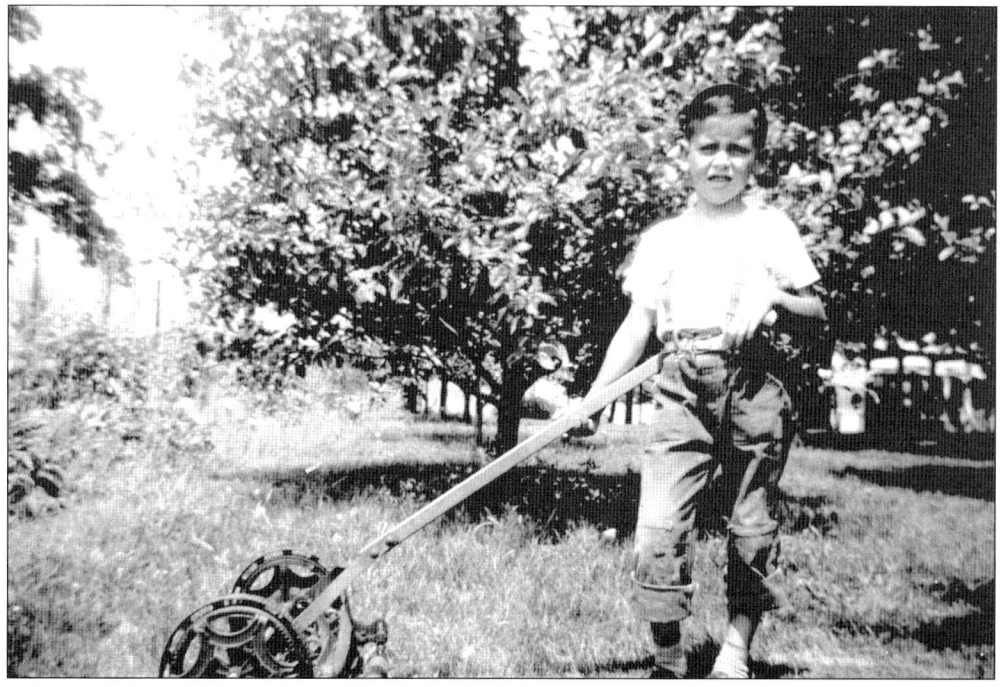

Life at the lake is not all fun as this young man has discovered. Chores still needed to be completed before it was time to play or swim. There was not an electric or gas mower, just push power. (Courtesy of John P. Haley.)

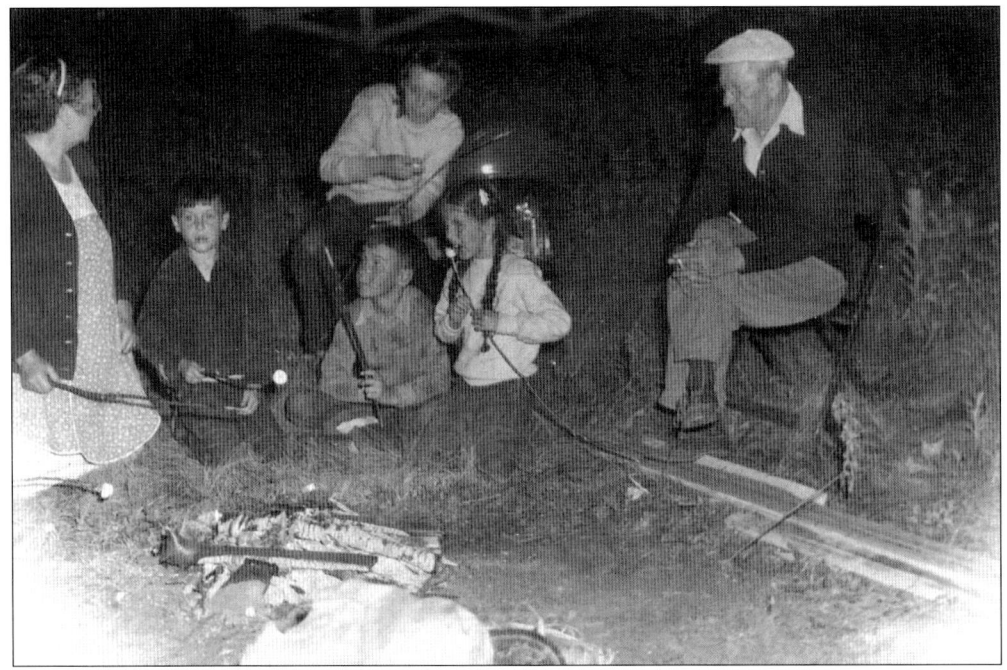

While days on McCullom Lake were filled with activities such as swimming or boating, evenings were a quiet time, sitting with neighbors around a campfire roasting marshmallows. Pictured around this 1948 campfire are members of the Krettler, Tabor, and Haley families. (Courtesy of John P. Haley.)

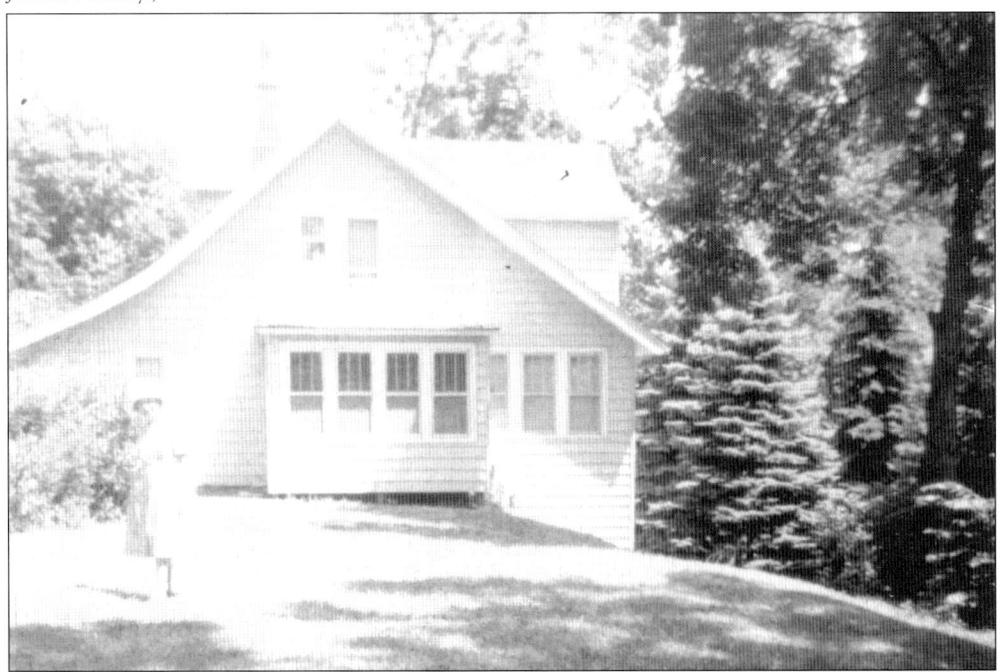

The Breyer family located along the western shores of McCullom Lake was considered to be one of the earliest to build on the shore. This home remained in the family until 1970 when it was sold to be used as a home for children. (Courtesy of the McHenry County Historical Society.)

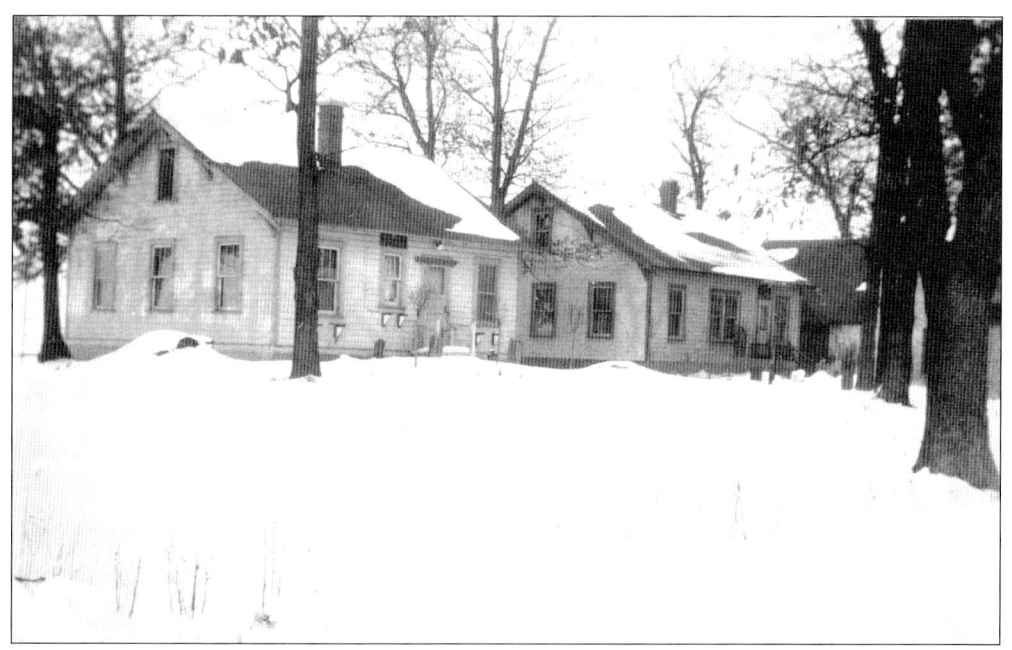

Many of the cottages along the shores of McCullom Lake were small, basic buildings meant for fishing or weekend visits. These two homes on Lakewood Road were built in the 1920s. They are identical and typical of many of the cottages of the time. (Courtesy of John P. Haley.)

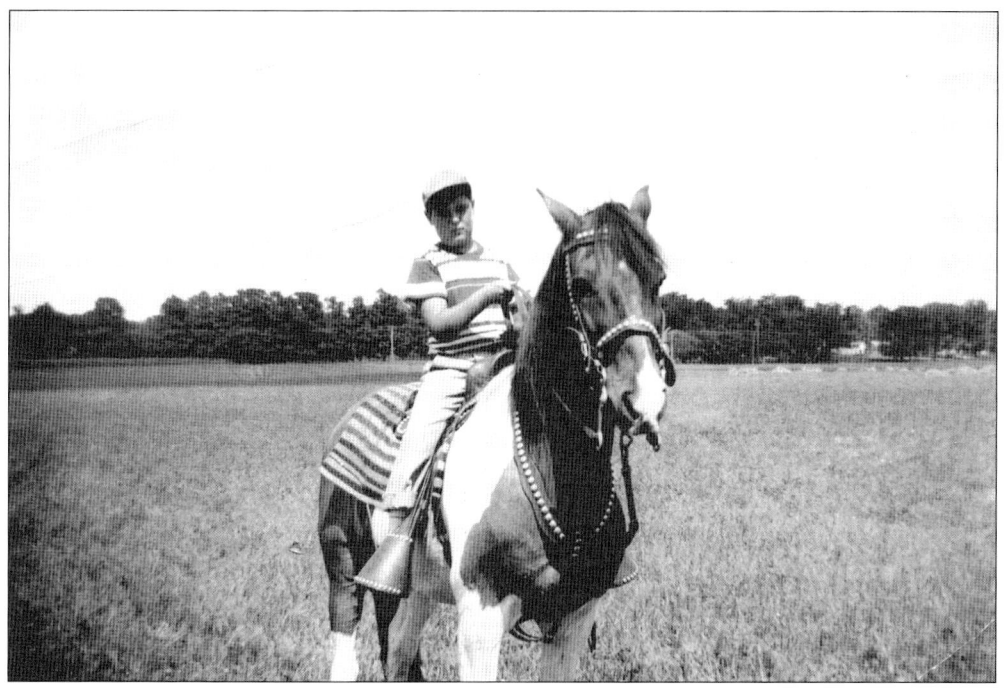

Time spent at the family home on McCullom Lake was not only about being on the water. Riding a horse across the fields of the Petersen Farm was another way to spend the day. Pictured is John Haley in 1952 riding the horse, Sam. (Courtesy of John P. Haley.)

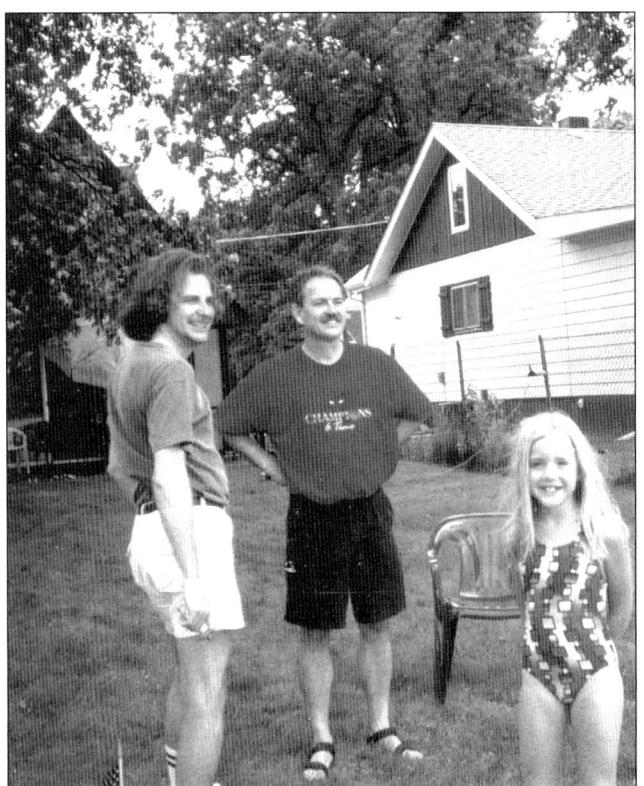

These 1998 visitors to McCullom Lake spend the afternoon enjoying a picnic while they wait for evening to fall. The fireworks at Petersen Beach for the July Fourth celebration are worth the trip. The display can be seen from the lakeshore or by rowing a boat out into the lake. (Courtesy of Priscilla Rutter.)

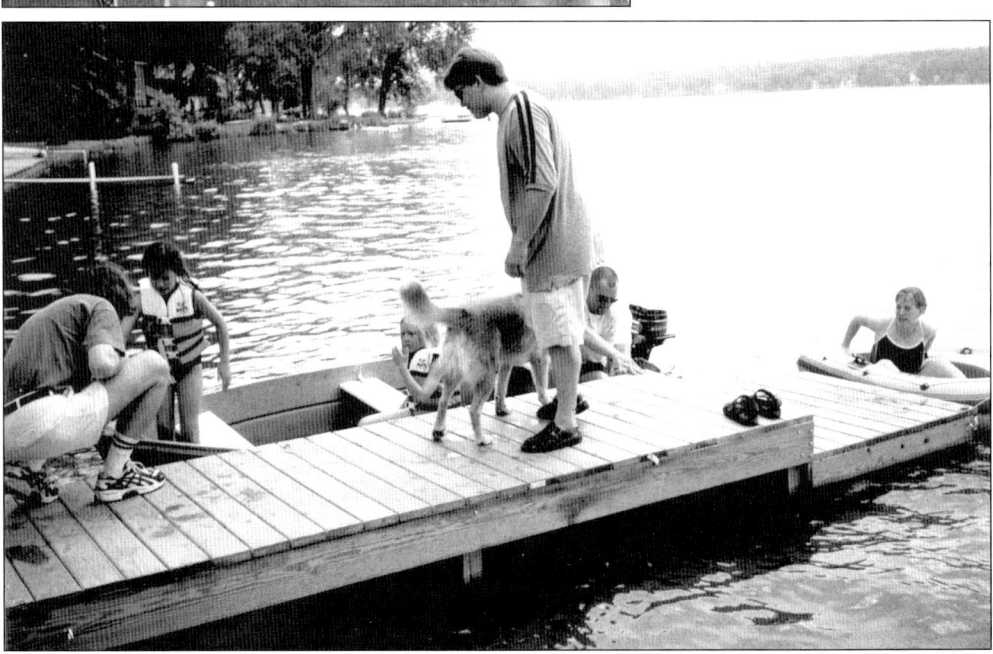

This group spends a Sunday afternoon enjoying the water at McCullom Lake. Even the dog gets into the act. The young girl steps out of the boat carefully, hoping to avoid a spill into the water as she steps up to the pier. While motor craft with high horsepower are prohibited, the small motors such as this one are allowed. (Courtesy of Priscilla Rutter.)

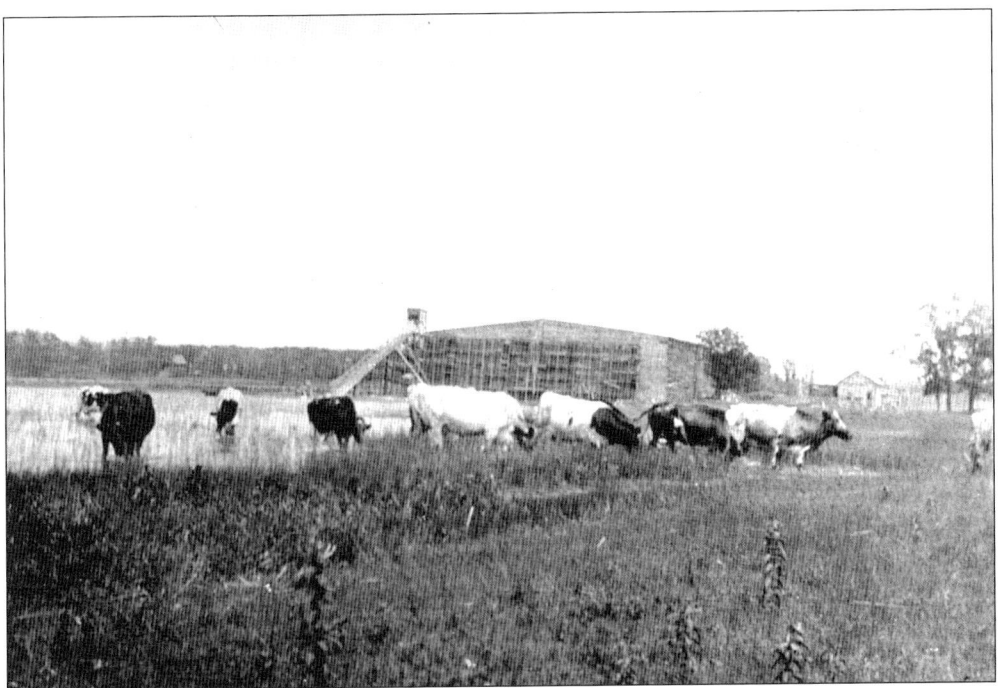

The Brand Ice Company was located on the northern shore of McCullom Lake. Ice was harvested throughout the winter out of the lake. The icehouse was struck by lightning in August 1922 and burned completely to the ground. (Courtesy of Pete Merkel.)

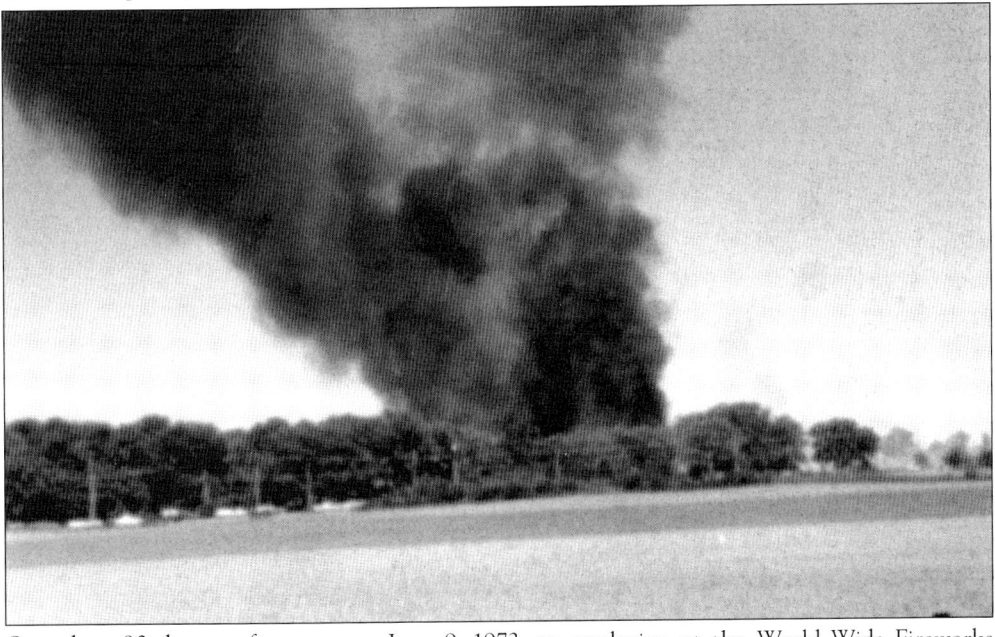

On a hot, 90 degree afternoon on June 9, 1973, an explosion at the World Wide Fireworks Company on McCullom Road was heard for several miles around McHenry. Residents around the lake remember plates falling from walls and breaking. The explosion and subsequent fire were believed to have been caused by spontaneous combustion. The smoke could be seen for miles. Damage was estimated at a half million dollars. (Courtesy of Nancy Williams.)

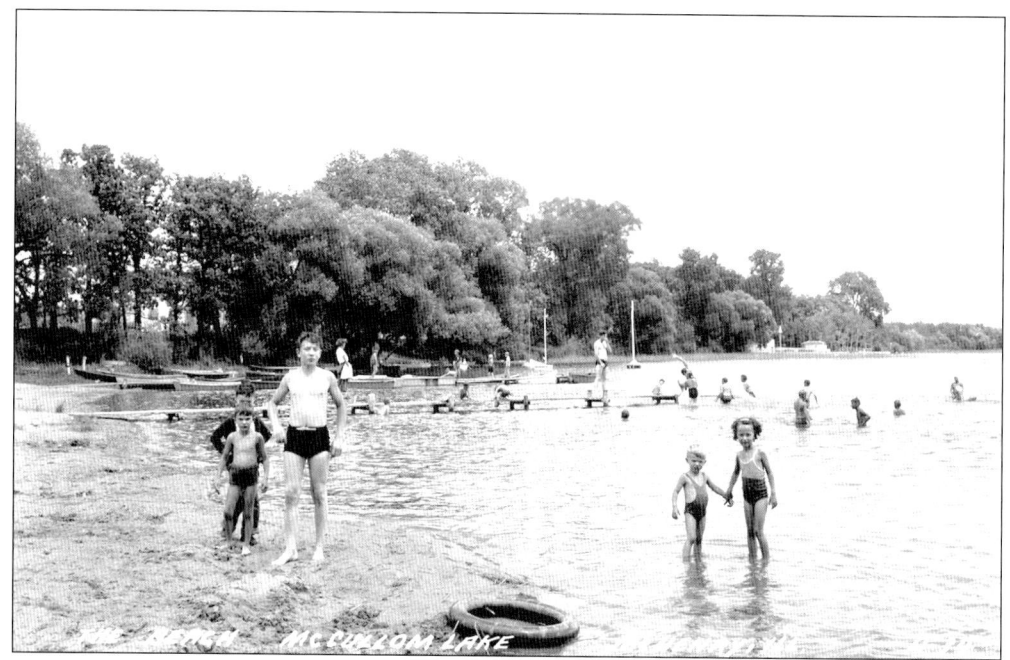

Swimming in McCullom Lake attracted many summer time visitors. Because the lake is shallow with a depth of only four feet in some areas, it is an ideal place for children to swim and frolic in the water. In the 1950s, clams were plentiful in the lake and swimmers would complain of cuts from stepping on the shells. (Courtesy of Michael Clark.)

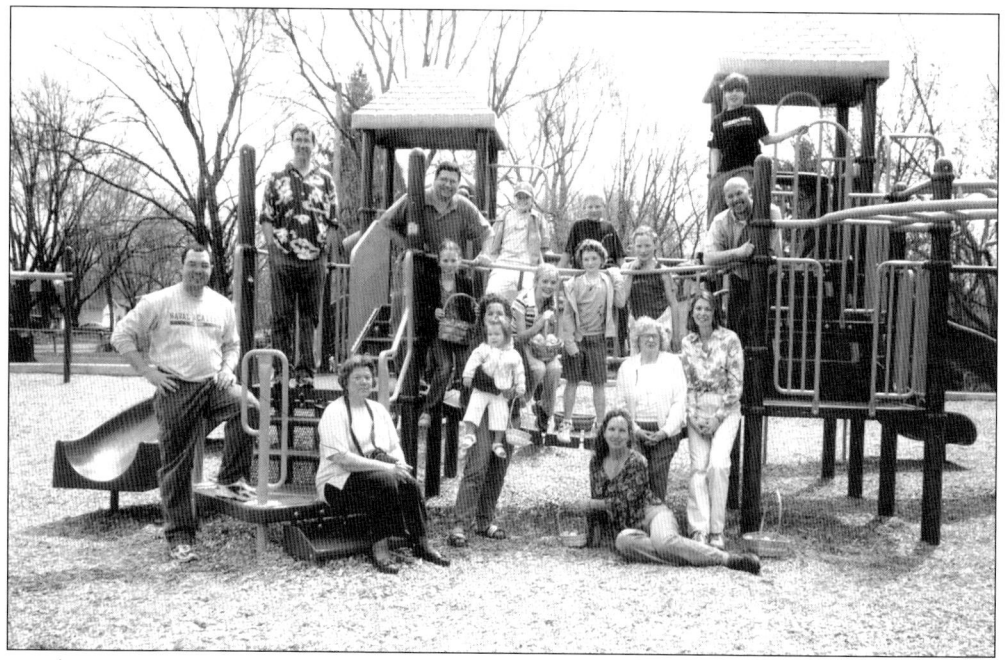

Residents and their extended families enjoy spending part of their holiday in the park. For this McCullom Lake family, it is an Easter tradition. Following an egg hunt in Peterson Park, they pose around the playground equipment for their family photograph. (Courtesy of Priscilla Rutter.)

Eight
A Small Village Grows

On the northwest shore of McCullom Lake, a small community evolved that was incorporated in 1955 as the village of McCullom Lake. Originally an enclave of summer cottages, it has become a community of moderate-income housing. It is a small community by most standards, with only 1,038 residents in 2005. The houses are not large or pretentious, many are the outgrowth of the original small summer cottages that have been updated to meet today's lifestyle.

The village has its own police department with two full-time officers and two part time. They are a part of the McHenry Fire Protection District and the children attend McHenry schools.

It is a community of little commercial business. In the early days there were two bars and a grocery store to service the community. While ownership of Whitey and Bernice's Tavern has changed, there is still a restaurant and bar at that location. Today it is known as the McCullom Knoll. The grocery stores of the 1950s and 1960s, Lottie and Gene's and later Jim and Jenny's, have closed.

Residents who lived in the village as children agree that it was the perfect place to grow up. Swimming, fishing, and boating and watching movies outdoors—which were projected against a two-story house—were some of the favorite summertime activities. Summer festivals, teen club, and dances were open to village teens from the 1950s to the 1970s.

Today the village has not had major changes. It is still a small friendly community where neighbors know each other. Village president Jeanne Hansen describes the village as laid back, where life is casual and people enjoy the simple pleasure of living near a lake.

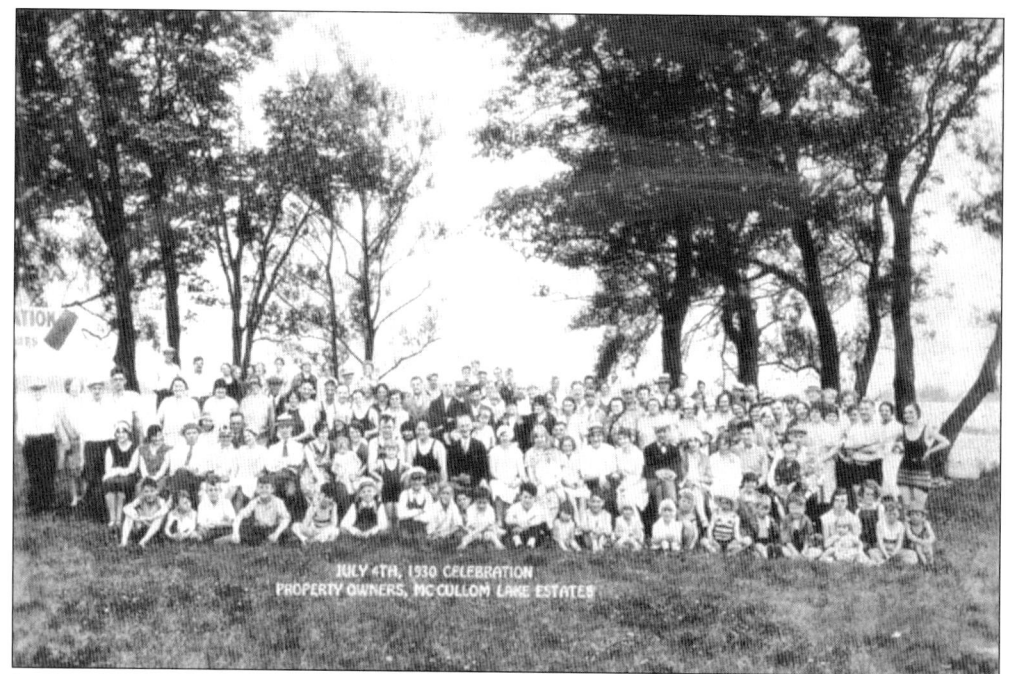

In 1930, long before McCullom Lake was incorporated as a village, the homeowners of McCullom Lakes Estates gathered together on July Fourth for this community photograph. Holidays were a time of celebration and a time to enjoy life at the lake. This subdivision is now the village of McCullom Lake. (Courtesy of Sandra Speciale.)

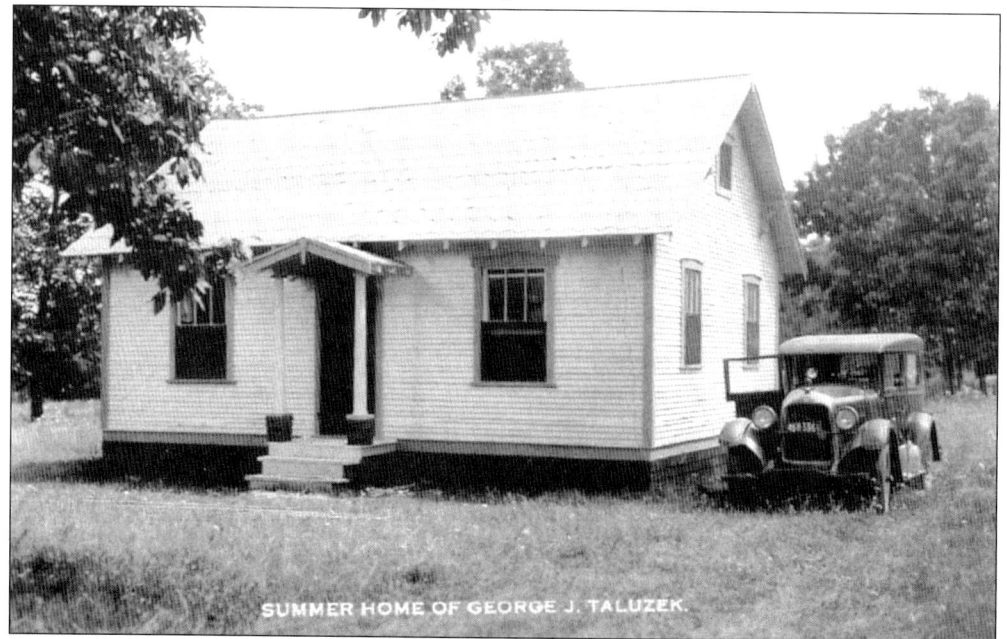

George J. Taluzek was the owner of this summer home on McCullom Lake. The cottage in the early 1900s was very basic. Landscaping was not considered a necessity as owners or renters were there to enjoy the lake. Note that the automobile is pulled up next to the house with no sign of a driveway. (Courtesy of Sandra Speciale.)

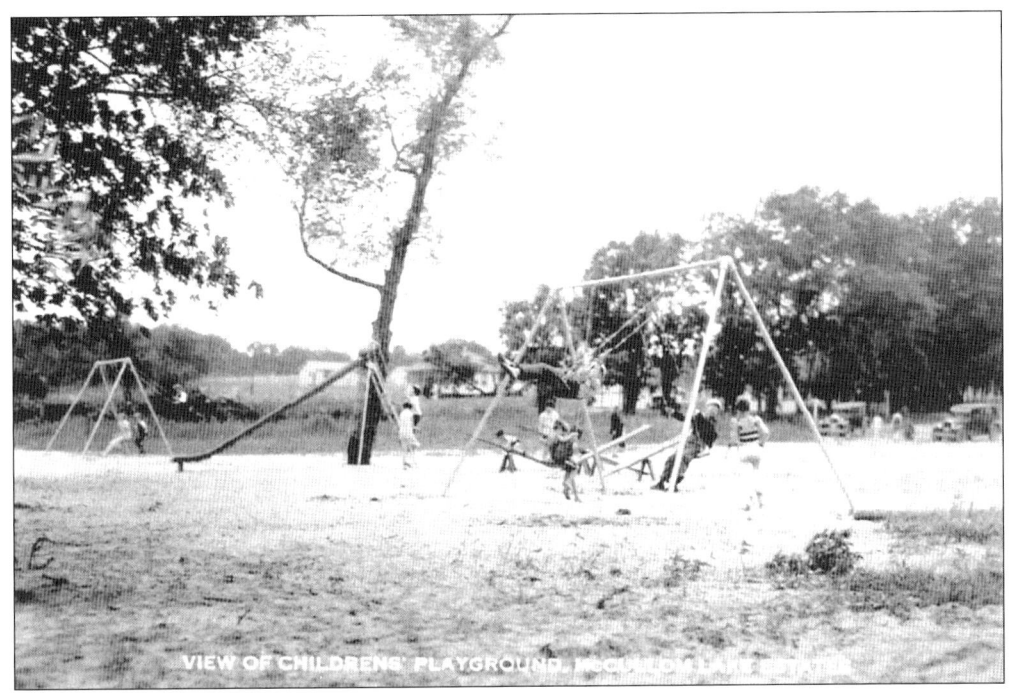

The children of the area enjoyed the playground along the beach. Swinging with friends and sliding down the slide kept them busy and active. When the sun became too warm, a dip in the lake was in order. (Courtesy of Sandra Speciale.)

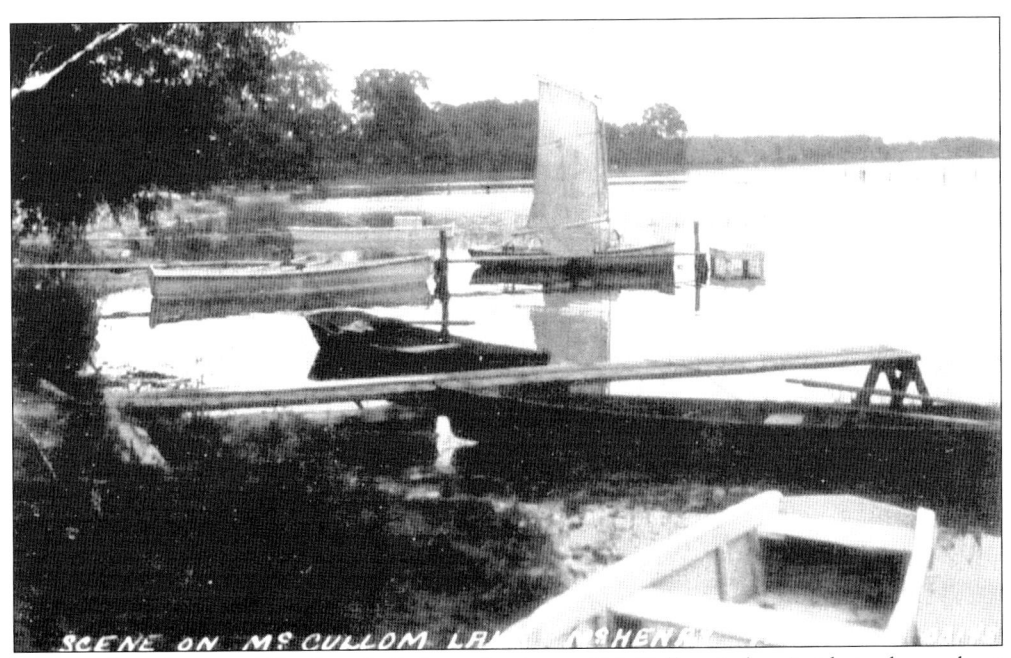

Boats such as these could be found all along the shore of McCullom Lake. A ride in the rowboat around the lake was a good way to burn off some excess energy. This small sailboat is waiting to catch a good wind. No need for high-powered motors. (Courtesy of Sandra Speciale.)

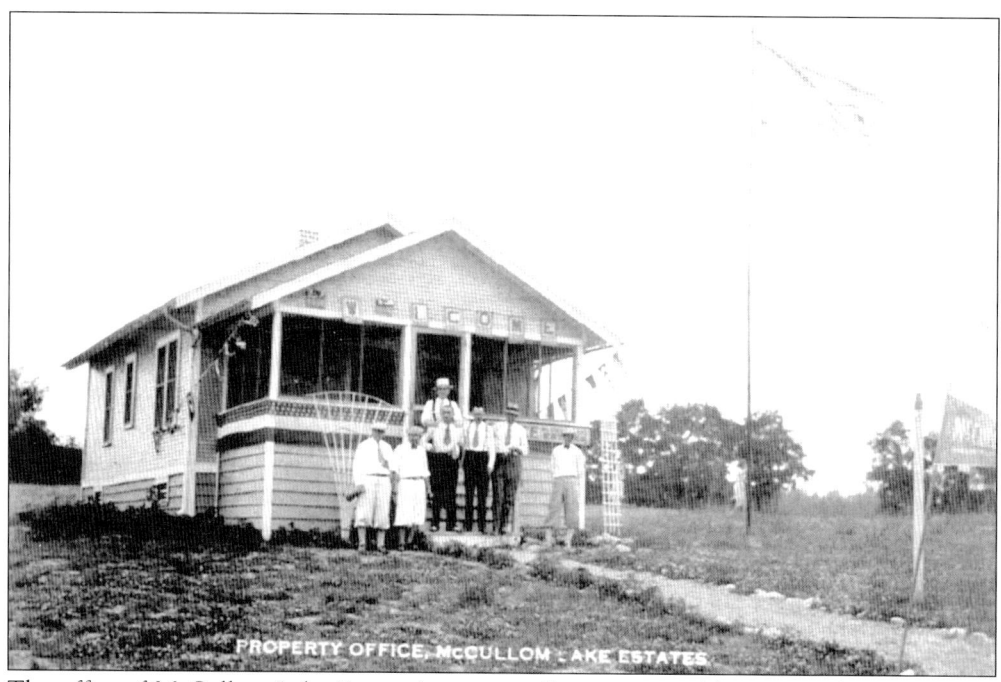

The office of McCullom Lake Estates began to sell property and houses in the 1900s. This building served as their office as the area was being developed for lake area homes. (Courtesy of Sandra Speciale.)

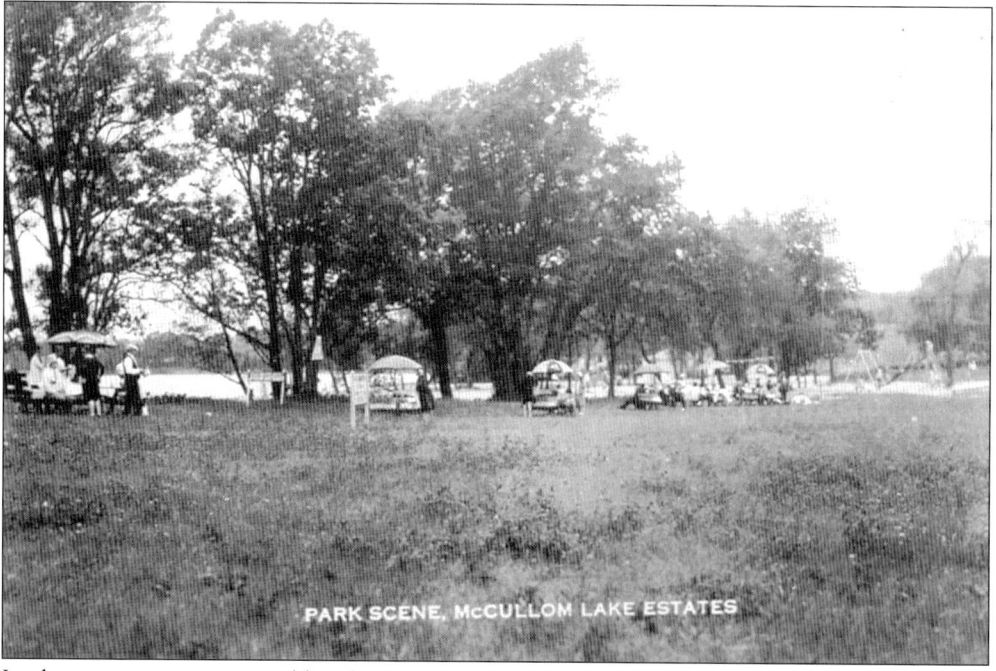

In the summer, visitors would make the trip, often from the city of Chicago, to spend the day in the country enjoying the waterfront. Families would come together and share picnic feasts at the lakefront. This beach was part of the McCullom Lake Estates subdivision. (Courtesy of Sandra Speciale.)

Agnes Sofranski pumps water at the Piotrowski home. The early cottages did not have indoor running water or sewers. Individual wells were drilled to a depth of 60 feet. Cliff Wirfs, a local resident, owned the well and pump business. (Courtesy of Sandra Speciale.)

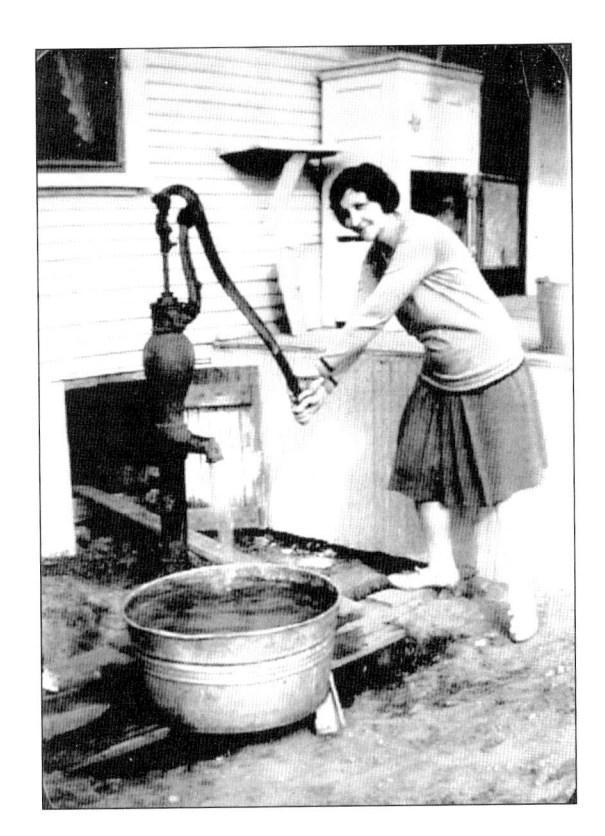

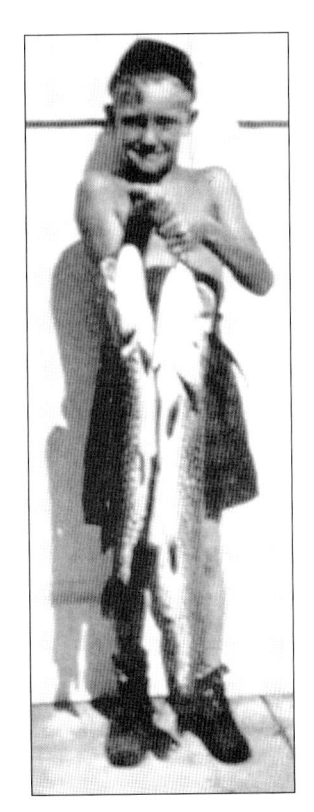

In 1942, these large northern pike were fished from the lake by Ron Piotrowski. Many game fish were found in the lake making it a popular fishing haven. These fish are pictured in front of the Kaiser Garage on Cloverhill and Parkview Streets. (Courtesy of Sandra Speciale.)

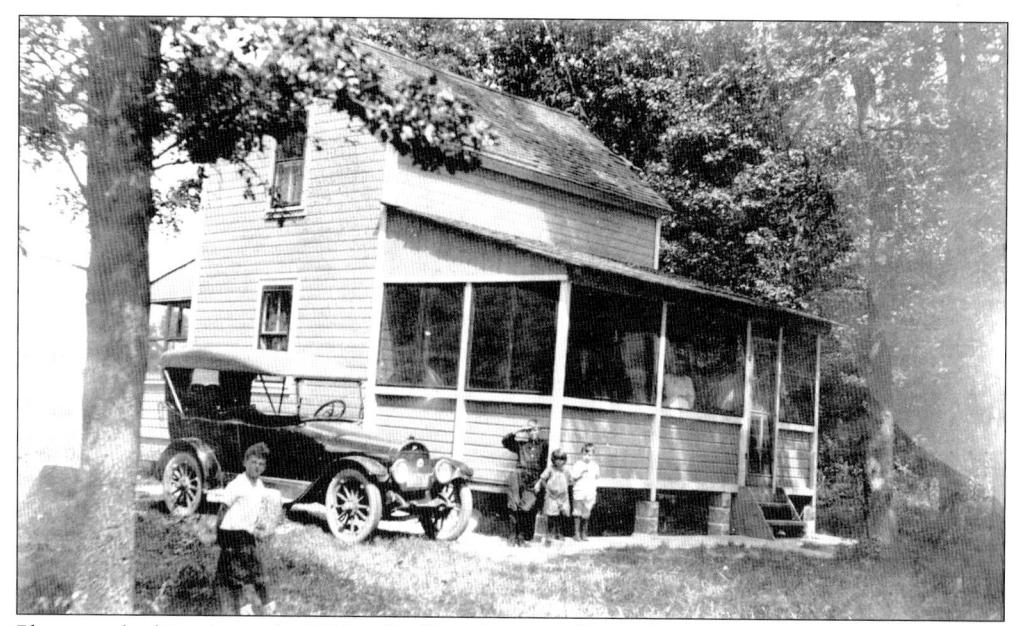

Photographed in the early 1900s, the Ryan house is located on the north side of McCullom Lake. In later years the Howard Estate was built on this site. The children in the photograph are unidentified. (Courtesy of William and Amy Moerschbaecher.)

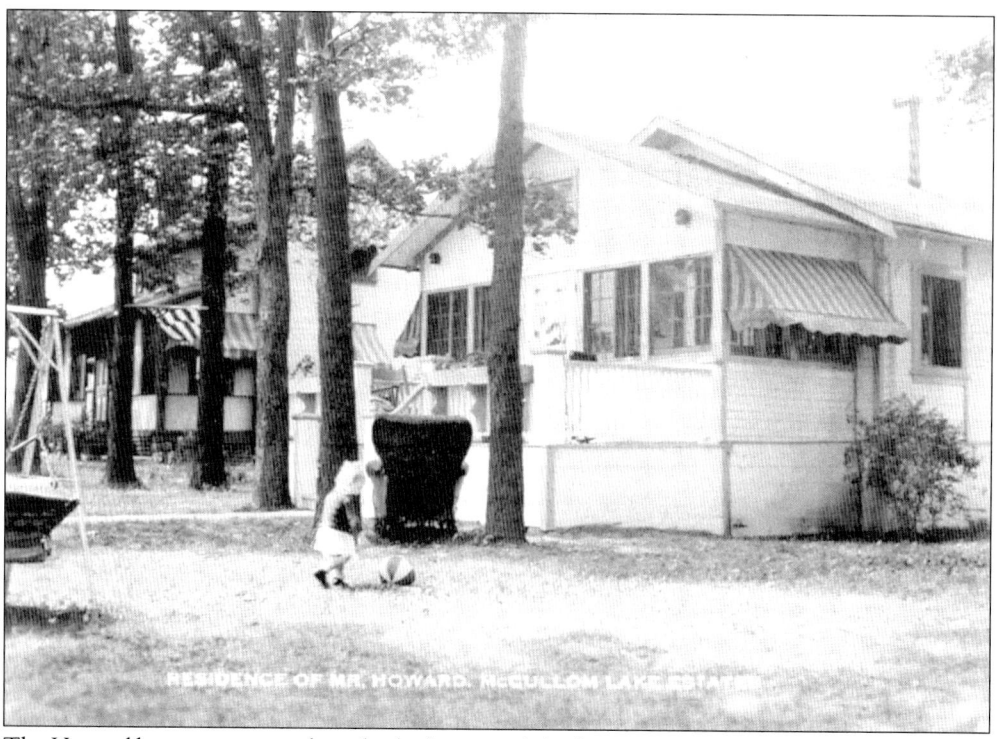

The Howard house appears to have had a front porch built onto it. Many of the cottages along the lake started out as very basic homes and had additions as the families grew or finances allowed. The small child enjoys playing with a ball on the lawn. (Courtesy of Sandra Speciale.)

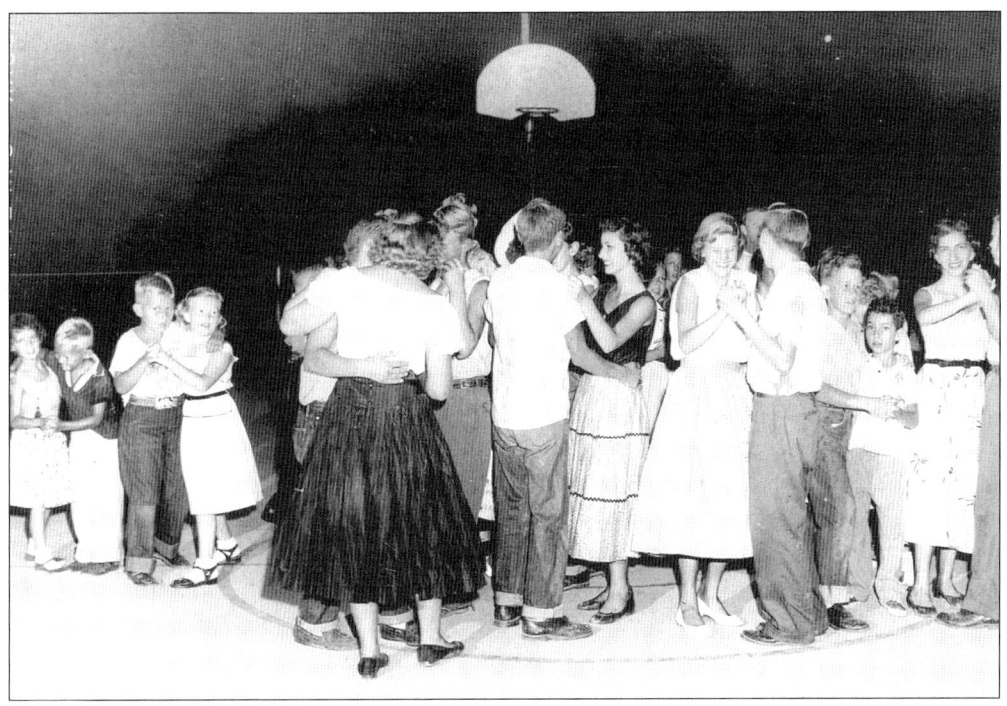

Those who grew up on the lake felt they were very fortunate for there were always things to do and a group of friends to share in the activities. The Teen Club was popular and sponsored dances such as this one. They were always well attended. (Courtesy of Sandra Speciale.)

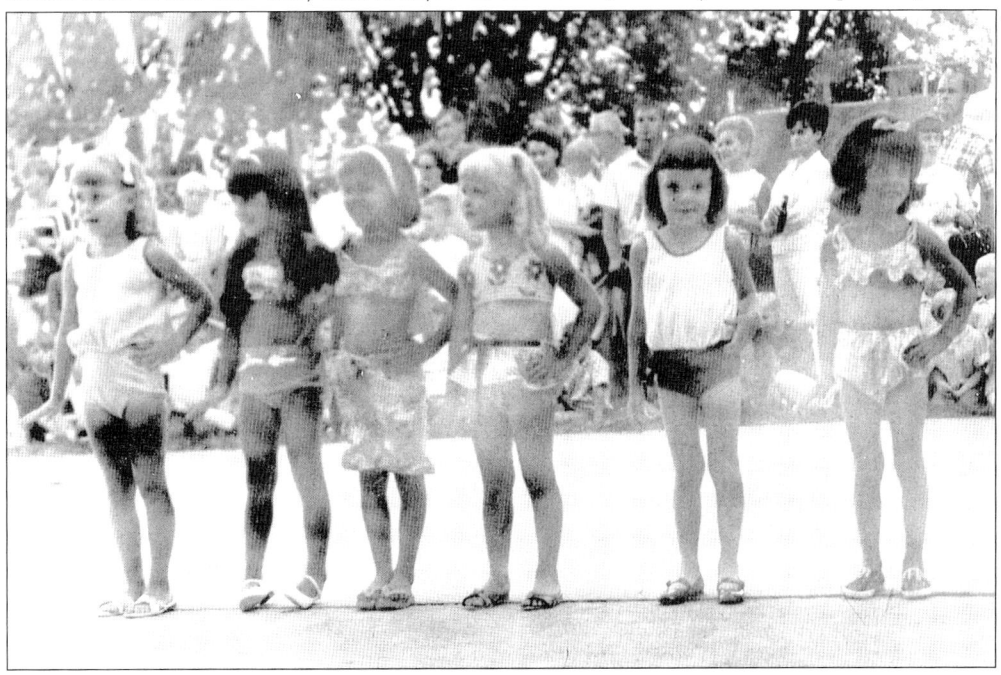

For many years, one of the highlights of the summer festivities was the crowning of Little Miss McCullom Lake. These bathing beauties are competing for the title. On the far left is Sandra Straumann in the 1967 competition. (Courtesy of Sandra Speciale.)

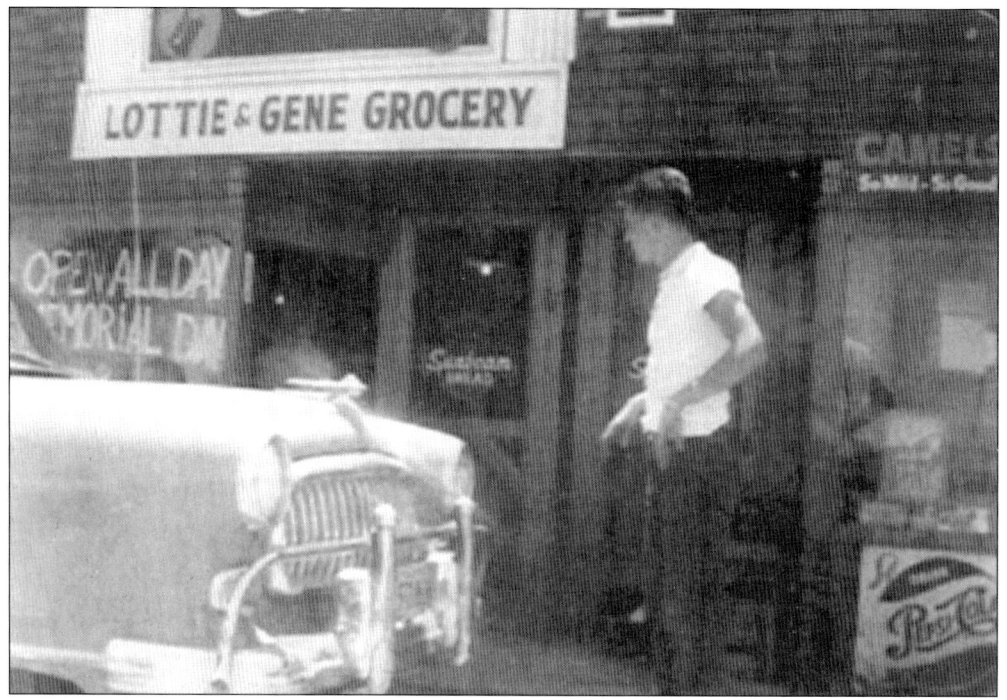

From the 1920s, when cottages were first being built around McCullom Lake, small grocery stores such as Lottie and Gene's Royal Blue Grocery supplied food for the summer visitors and year-round residents. Standing in front of the store is Ron Piotrowski admiring the automobile parked in front. (Courtesy of Sandra Speciale.)

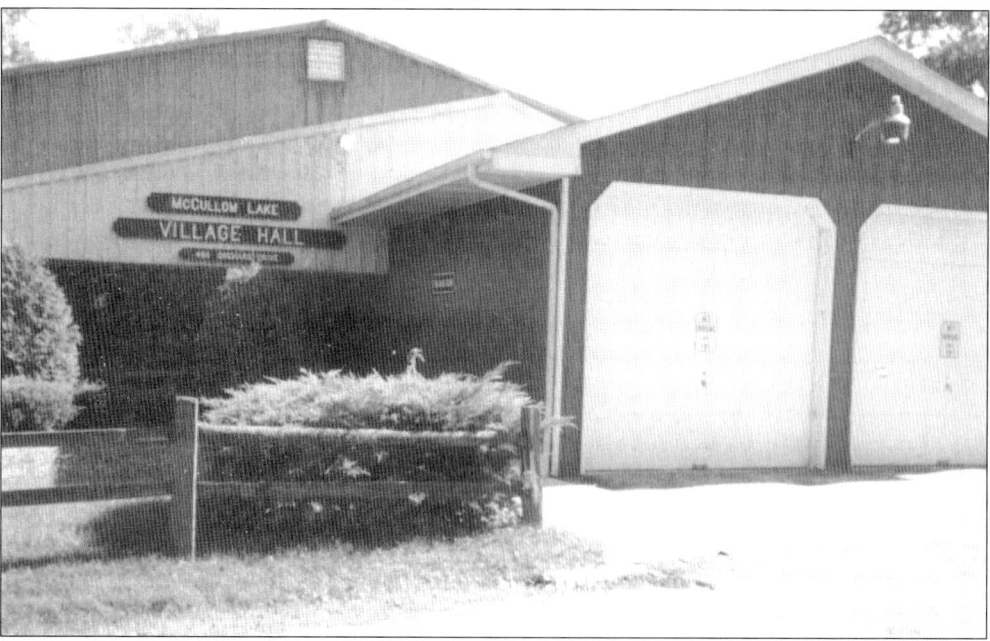

Village hall for the village of McCullom Lake is located on Orchard Drive directly on the lakefront. A large beach park surrounds the building. Housed here are the police department and the road services in addition to the office of the village president. (Courtesy of Sandra Speciale.)

Nine
McHenry Today and Tomorrow

As McHenry enters the 21st century, it is a far different city than it was when it entered the 20th century. Most of the farms that dotted the countryside have been replaced with housing developments or shopping centers. It is no longer one of the leading milk producers in the state. The boat builders along the Fox River are long gone. Harvesting ice from the river and the lake is obsolete. Boat service to Pistakee Bay no longer exists.

In spite of the growth of modern day suburbia around its perimeters, McHenry has maintained its spirit and continues to preserve the town centers: Riverside Drive, Green Street, and Main Street. Instead of the grocery stores, pharmacies, and hardware stores of the past, restaurants and antique shops now prevail.

Working together as a team, the school district, library, police, fire, park districts and the mayor's office are facing the problems of increased growth. As they address the needs of the city, they do so with an eye to retaining McHenry's hometown flavor.

McHenry's crown jewel, the Fox River, will play an important role in the future of the city. The riverwalk is a multi-million dollar undertaking, which will be completed over a period of years making optimal use of the waterfront, encouraging visitors as it did in the early part of the 20th century. The new riverwalk will be a blend of the old and new as a section of the original Pearl Street bridge will be placed over Boone Creek.

The park district continues to develop its many parks and beaches. There are plans to build a recreation center in the city complex. Festivals such as Fiesta Days and the Christmas Walk highlight McHenry's past and celebrate its future.

Local business demonstrates its faith in McHenry as evidenced by some very long-term family businesses that have prospered for over 100 years.

According to Mayor Susan Low, the future of McHenry is bright. McHenry will continue to develop its resources making the city a wonderful place to live and for those who can not live here, a great recreational destination.

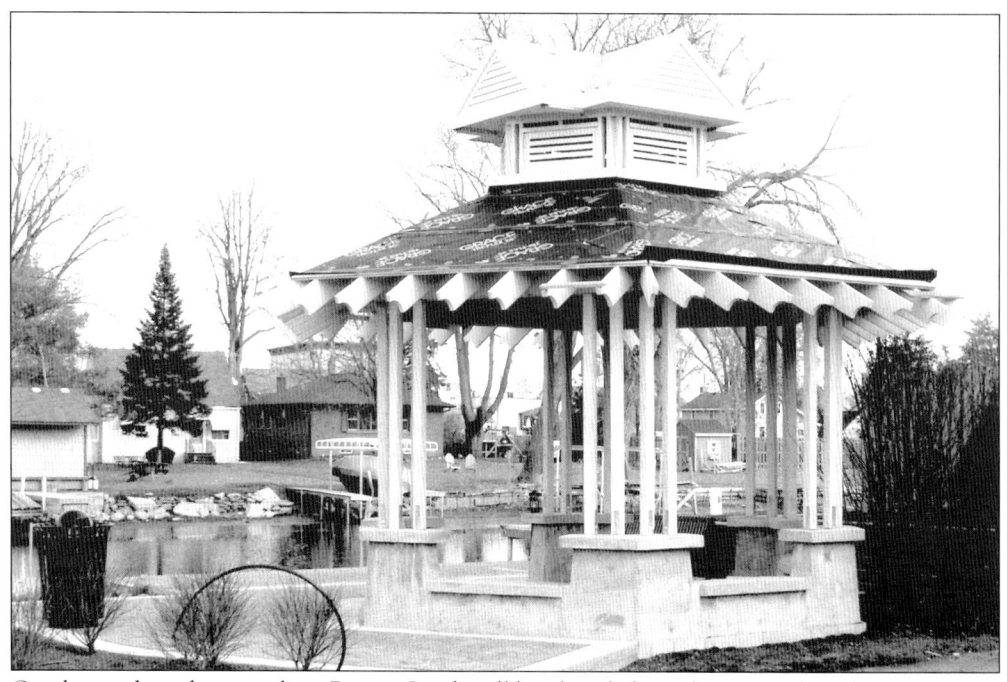

Gazebos such as this one along Boone Creek will be placed along the riverwalk, allowing visitors to sit and chat while enjoying the river and creek views. The river, which has always been a focal point of the city, will again be a recreation destination. (Courtesy of the City of McHenry.)

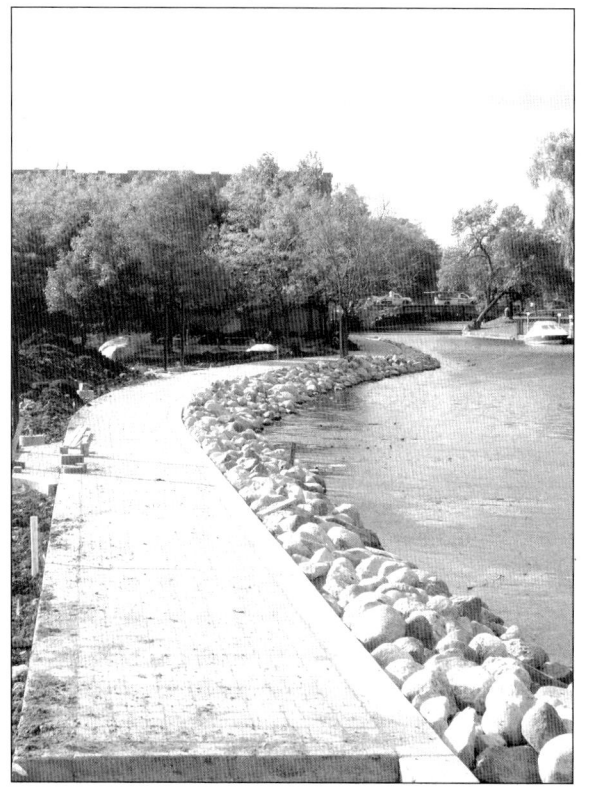

The first phase of the riverwalk was completed in 2006. This view of the walk from Green Street along the shore of Boone Creek leads to the pedestrian bridge. The riverwalk is expected to increase revenue to downtown business as more people come to spend time enjoying the riverfront. (Courtesy of the City of McHenry.)

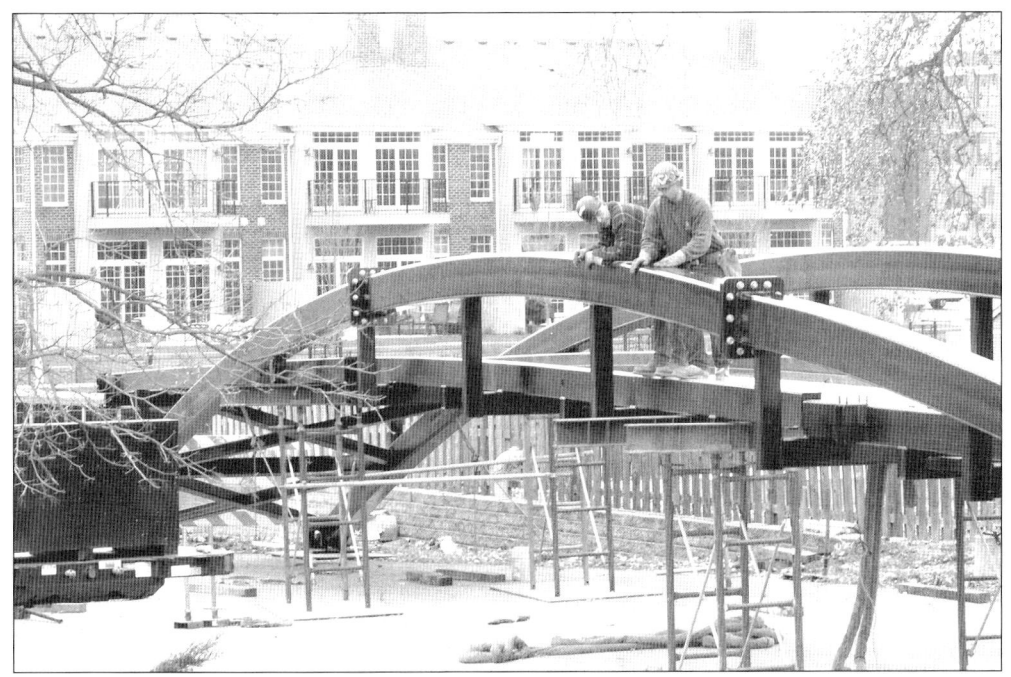

Two unidentified men are assembling the pedestrian bridge prior to its placement. The pedestrian bridge will link the first phase of the riverwalk with Riverside Drive across Boone Creek. (Courtesy of the City of McHenry.)

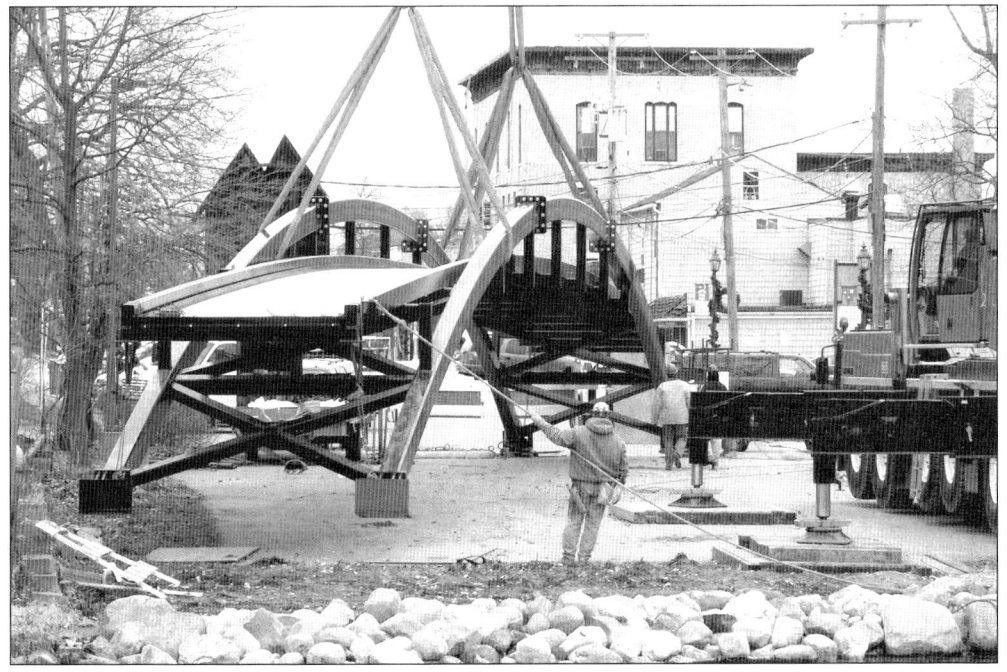

After moving the pedestrian bridge by truck through downtown McHenry, it is being guided into place across Boone Creek where it will connect downtown McHenry with the first completed phase of the riverwalk. The bridge was placed over the creek in the fall of 2006. (Courtesy of the City of McHenry.)

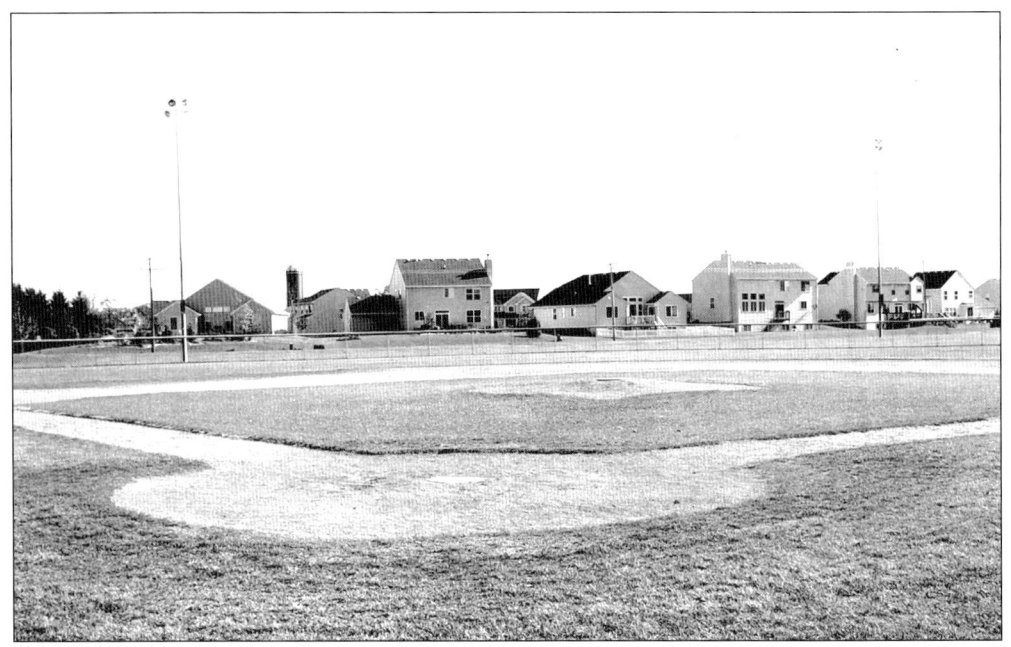

Baseball continues to be a favorite pastime of McHenry residents. This field in Petersen Park is one of many scattered throughout the city. In the background is one of the many housing developments that have appeared on the disappearing farmland of the area, bringing new families to McHenry. The silo from King Farm, one of the few remaining farms, can be seen in the distance. (Courtesy of the City of McHenry.)

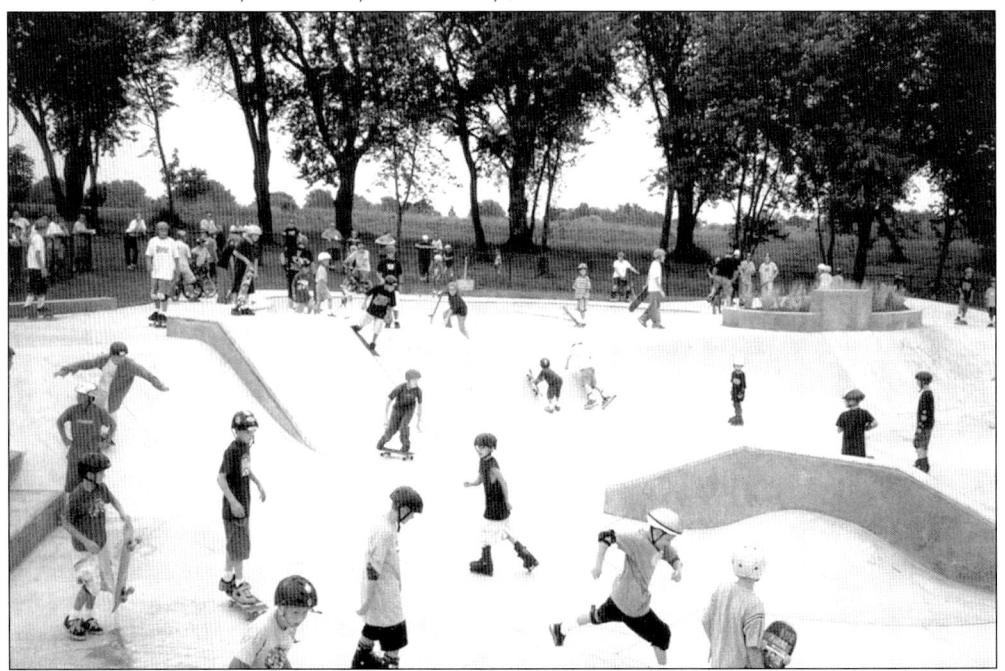

As McHenry's population has increased, the park district has continued to grow and provide new and different activities for the youth of McHenry. This skate park is a popular place for young people in the summer. (Courtesy of the City of McHenry.)

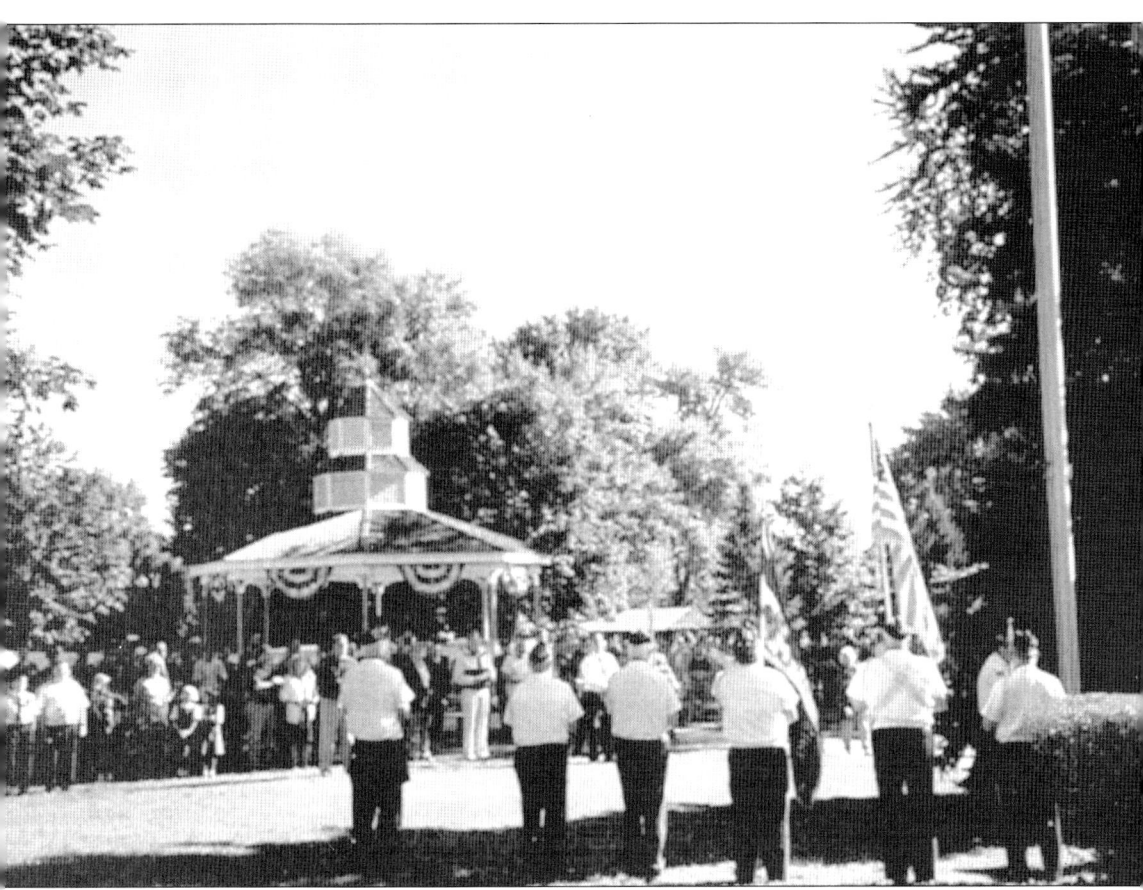

Concerts in the park have always been a part of the McHenry tradition. As McHenry moves ahead in the 21st century, the tradition of spending warm summer days sitting in Veteran's Memorial Park listening to musical concerts has not changed. Bands and flags are present as families and friends gather in Veteran's Memorial Park. While there are festive activities throughout the summer, today visitors take the time to remember and honor the many men and women who have served their country as members of the armed forces. Following speeches and color guard ceremonies, a parade moves to the Fox River to place a memorial wreath in the water. (Courtesy of the City of McHenry.)

Across America, People are Discovering Something Wonderful. *Their Heritage.*

Arcadia Publishing is the leading local history publisher in the United States. With more than 3,000 titles in print and hundreds of new titles released every year, Arcadia has extensive specialized experience chronicling the history of communities and celebrating America's hidden stories, bringing to life the people, places, and events from the past. To discover the history of other communities across the nation, please visit:

www.arcadiapublishing.com

Customized search tools allow you to find regional history books about the town where you grew up, the cities where your friends and family live, the town where your parents met, or even that retirement spot you've been dreaming about.

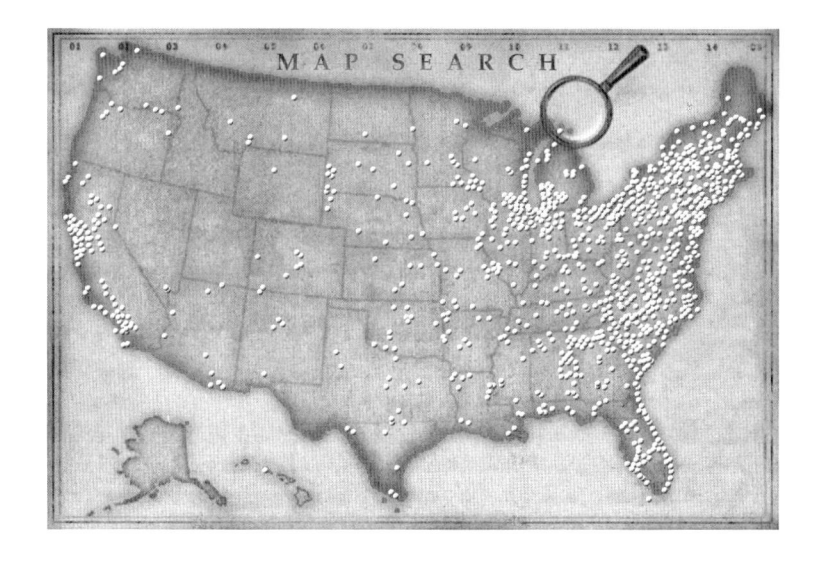